# Overcoming
## Conflicting Loyalties

# Overcoming
## Conflicting Loyalties

Intimate
Partner
Violence,
Community
Resources,
and Faith

THE UNIVERSITY
*of* ALBERTA PRESS

Irene Sevcik, Michael Rothery,
Nancy Nason-Clark, and Robert Pynn

Published by

The University of Alberta Press
Ring House 2
Edmonton, Alberta, Canada T6G 2E1
www.uap.ualberta.ca

**Library and Archives Canada Cataloguing
in Publication**

Sevcik, Irene, author
        Overcoming conflicting loyalties :
intimate partner violence, community
resources and faith / Irene Sevcik, Michael
Rothery, Nancy Nason-Clark, and
Robert Pynn.

Includes bibliographical references and index.
Issued in print and electronic formats.
ISBN 978-1-77212-050-9 (paperback).—
ISBN 978-1-77212-063-9 (epub).—
ISBN 978-1-77212-064-6 (kindle).—
ISBN 978-1-77212-065-3 (pdf)

        1. Family violence—Religious aspects.
2. Abused women—Services for. 3. Victims
of family violence—Services for. 4. Faith-
based human services. 5. Church work with
dysfunctional families. 6. Religion and culture.
I. Rothery, M. A., 1945-, author II.
Nason-Clark, Nancy, 1956-, author
III. Pynn, Robert, 1941-, author IV. Title.
Index available in print and PDF editions.

HV6626.S43 2015   362.82'92   C2015-902251-7
                                  C2015-902252-5

First edition, first printing, 2015.
Printed and bound in Canada by Houghton
Boston Printers, Saskatoon, Saskatchewan.
Copyediting by Kirsten Craven.
Proofreading by Joanne Muzak.
Indexing by Adrian Mather.

The University of Alberta Press is committed
to protecting our natural environment. As
part of our efforts, this book is printed on
Enviro Paper: it contains 100% post-consumer
recycled fibres and is acid- and chlorine-free.

The University of Alberta Press gratefully
acknowledges the support received for its
publishing program from The Canada Council
for the Arts. The University of Alberta Press
also gratefully acknowledges the financial
support of the Government of Canada
through the Canada Book Fund (CBF) and the
Government of Alberta through the Alberta
Media Fund (AMF) for its publishing activities.

The University of Alberta Press also thanks
The Calgary Foundation for funding provided
in support of this publication
(www.thecalgaryfoundation.org).

Canada  Canada Council   Conseil des Arts
for the Arts   du Canada

Alberta
Government

# Contents

VII  *Introduction*

1  Dissolving Solitudes

3  1 | Secular–Religious Conversations about Violence

25  Reflections

27  2 | Intimate Partner Violence
    *Definitions and Context*

57  Collaboration

59  3 | FaithLink
    *Building Connections between the Sacral and the Secular*

83  The Good Wife

85  4 | Finding Their Voices
    *Religious/Ethno-Cultural Women Speak*
    *about Intimate Partner Violence*

113 Mutations of the Heart

115 5 | Incorporating Spirituality into Practice
*How Service Providers Address the*
*Spiritual Needs of Clients*

143 Meditation

147 6 | Contemplative Meditation
*Its Efficacy with Service Providers*
*Working with a Victimized Clientele*

179 Faith and Belief

181 7 | Reflections on the Book
*A Panel Discussion, Part I*

199 The Road

201 8 | Reflections on the Book
*A Panel Discussion, Part II*

213 The Hours

215 9 | Conclusion


227 *Acknowledgements*
231 *Notes*
235 *References*
245 *Index*

# Introduction

## This book asks a fundamental question:

Does religion—and by extension religious communities—have a role to play in addressing social issues in a secular society? This theme is explored through the lens of intimate partner violence (IPV) within the framework of the FaithLink program—a grassroots practice and transdisciplinary model designed to create and foster collaboration and conversations between secular-based service providers and sacral communities and their leaders.

In its work, FaithLink encountered larger issues—of ideology, theology, and culture. These differing world views impact how IPV is defined, experienced by religious women, and responded to by sacral communities. They also impact how religious beliefs and practices are viewed and accommodated by secularly based service providers. It is at the intersection of these differing perspectives that the victims of IPV who espouse a religious perspective find themselves. What became evident through the work of the FaithLink program is that the divides that exist between the secular and the sacral can be bridged; that each has something to offer the other; and that when they work together, the victims of violence are better served.

This book explores these issues through a number of different avenues: philosophical, practical, research, and discussion. Chapter One explores the tensions between the religious and the secular in relation to violence. Chapter Two addresses intimate partner violence—its definition, its prevalence, barriers to leaving an abusive relationship, and the religious and cultural context within which some women live. The FaithLink program is presented in Chapter Three.

In Chapters Four through Six we present three unique qualitative research studies: how religious beliefs and cultural norms shape how victims of IPV define their experience and how their faith/ethno-cultural communities respond when incidents of IPV occur within their midst; how secularly based service providers address the issues of religious beliefs and spirituality when women of faith access their services; and the role a meditation practice can play in assisting those who work with victims of violence in managing work-related stress. Chapters Seven and Eight present a discussion among experts, representing secular service providers to IPV victims, academics, and theologians, of their reflections and implications, if any, of the work of the FaithLink program, the research findings, and the larger questions addressed by this book. The Conclusion (Chapter Nine) returns to the question of the role religion has in addressing social issues within a secular society.

Each of the co-authors of this book has been involved with the FaithLink program from its inception and has participated in various ways with its ongoing work. We represent different professions—sociology, theology, and social work— and differing perspectives. What we hold in common is our concern for those who experience and are impacted by family violence—victims, witnesses, and those who have acted abusively. Each has contributed from his/her area of expertise in the creation of this book. In keeping with the themes of collaboration and dialogue inherent within the FaithLink program, we sought to reflect this motif in how the book is formatted. Thus, you will hear each co-author's voice: Michael's and Irene's as chapter authors; and Robert's through the poetry that prefaces each chapter. Michael, Nancy, and Robert are heard as they comment on the content of various chapters.

We have also asked individuals from the broader community to respond to various chapters. These responders include service providers, a member of the Khmer Canadian community, religious leaders, and meditation practitioners.

A word about our approach to the research studies reported herein: a qualitative methodology was utilized for each. We were addressing issues that are experienced at a very personal level and in very individual ways—the experience of being victimized, religious beliefs and their application in daily living, the constraints imposed by ethno- and religious community cultures, and the effectiveness of a meditation practice in managing stress. These are issues that do not easily lend themselves to clearly defined variables. We were also aware that we were charting new waters in our attempt to understand the complexities of IPV within the context of faith and culture and the utilization of a meditation practice within the context of secularly based agencies. With a better under-standing of the complexities of each of these issues, our hope is that religious women and those of ethno-cultural communities can receive better, more effective, and efficient services from both the communities of which they are apart and from secular services they may choose to access. It is also our hope that by demonstrating the efficacy of a meditation practice in managing stress, we can offer a practical avenue through which the effects of vicarious trauma can be lessened by those responding to those affected by intimate partner violence.

With each research project we attempted to implement a systematic and disciplined inquiry. Our analysis sought to identify similarities and differences of experience, meaningful elements, and how these fit together into categories and themes. We recognize the uniqueness of each project and have no expectations that, if replicated, the same findings would result. This was not our goal—rather we sought to bring depth and texture to the complexities inherent within the context of religion and/or culture when IPV is an issue. The three studies reported herein are only a beginning of understanding—much more research is required.

A final clarification: Throughout this book the feminine pronoun is used to refer to victims of intimate partner violence. This is not to suggest that only women are victims of abuse and that only men engage in abusive behaviours. We recognize and acknowledge that anyone—whether male or female—can engage in aggressive and destructive actions against a partner. We also recognize the relatively recent developing body of writing and research about the abuse of men by women, along with beginning attempts to mount programs responsive to this phenomenon.

It is not possible, within the scope of one book, to include a discussion of all relevant aspects of intimate partner violence and faith communities. A fully inclusive book would have to address, in addition to men's issues, the problems of child maltreatment, elder abuse, and more—each of which has an often intricate relationship to families' religious beliefs and practices. Within the overarching objective of this book, our focus is on religious/ethno-cultural women who have been victims of abuse and how they and their communities have responded. We welcome further research that broadens our understanding of the complex and contentious issues that are inherent in the dynamics of intimate partner violence.

# Dissolving Solitudes

We fix a gulf between us,
see duality in what is one,
despair in the abyss
that would consume any movement across.

Why do we keep an account of ills,
pace the floor boards of accusation?

Who told us scarcity and conflict are our master story?
At odds we perpetuate its lie.

The great primeval tuning fork sounds the fundamental—
Love is the power of union, the energy of non-dual seeing.

Come surrender to its abundance and heal the inner allusion.
Walk across the abyss on solid ground.

—ROBERT PYNN

# 1

# Secular–Religious Conversations about Violence

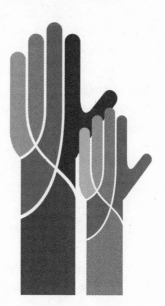

## This chapter explores reasons

why religious and secular helpers responding to intimate partner violence (IPV) tend not to trust one another, which results in women finding their already complex, painful circumstances made worse. Religious helpers may see themselves as defending the sanctity of marriage and the family by recommending that a woman forgive an abusive partner. Secular helpers may see that same woman's safety as paramount, and may accuse their religious counterparts of putting her (and her children) at risk by encouraging an ongoing commitment to a dangerous relationship. Thus, a woman who desperately needs effective support may find herself balancing conflicting loyalties. While seeking aid from secular helpers (and their programs) may be the only effective escape from ongoing physical, emotional, and spiritual abuse, it can also be seen as a betrayal of her religious community. Such binds can be extremely demoralizing, compounding the stress she faces at a time when the pressures on her are already daunting (Nason-Clark, 2004).

What makes this tension between paradigms especially unfortunate is that both parties, religious and secular helpers, have much to offer. Religious women using the services of a shelter or community agency do not set their spiritual beliefs and practices aside at the door; for many, the same religious community that may be making their problem solving more difficult is also their spiritual home, a source of strength and values that guides them. On the other hand, shelters and community agencies provide resources and a specialized expertise that religious communities normally cannot offer. Discouraging women from accessing those services may be counterproductive at best, or, at worst, dangerous.

Our particular focus is IPV, but the tensions we will discuss are prominent phenomena in our culture at large—they are a feature of modernity that can be seen wherever one looks (Taylor, 2007). Thus, the context for FaithLink's work (and for this book) is in part larger questions about religion and its legitimate role and relationship to the rest of society.

Of course, these larger questions have a history, being part of the story of how Western cultures have evolved since the Enlightenment—and one aspect of that history is a battle we still fight, between different beliefs about how to help others when our help is required.

## RELIGIOUS AND SECULAR HELPING: TENSIONS WITH A HISTORY

In 1775 two men found themselves in competition with one another. Johann Gassner was an unassuming Roman Catholic priest and a renowned exorcist. Franz Mesmer, by Ellenberger's (1970) account, had a monumental ego and a revolutionary healing method to promote, a method that could replace Gassner's with something more scientific. Initially, Mesmer's method was simply called magnetism, then animal magnetism, then mesmerism and, finally, hypnosis. The question of the relative merits of each man's approach was remarkably interesting to the public of the day, and formal investigations (process and outcome evaluations) were conducted (Benjamin Franklin served on one expert panel). Mesmer recognized Gassner's success as a healer but thought his positive practical results were rooted in faulty theory. The hypothesis that people in distress were possessed by demons logically supported an approach to healing utilizing rituals in which the demons were expelled and cast aside—but Mesmer was certain that this way of thinking was outmoded superstition. He claimed the same results could be obtained within a more scientific, secular explanatory frame, a very attractive suggestion at a time when the Enlightenment was a new, powerful social and intellectual force.

In the two centuries that followed Mesmer's life and work, agnostic or atheistic secular humanism came to prevail over faith-based understandings like

Gassner's (McGrath, 2004; Taylor, 2007). Today, in any modern Western country, it is easier to find a professionally certified clinical hypnotist than an exorcist,[1] and the influence of Mesmer's work on other current schools of counselling and psychotherapy has been considerable. Ellenberger (1970) sees a direct path from mesmerism to Freudian and other psychodynamic methods, while through the hugely influential efforts of Jay Haley (1977) and others, the work of the hypnotherapist Milton Erickson was incorporated into systemic family therapies. There are many other examples, including EMDR[2] (Shapiro, 2001, 2002, 2003), an influential therapy with similarities to hypnosis that is often offered to clients recovering from the effects of trauma, including IPV.

In an increasingly secular, scientific age, human services programs in universities and their graduates have become ever more strongly committed to the belief that counselling and psychotherapy should pursue secular, modernist priorities. One such priority that has been insistently stressed is that our work should be evidence-based (McLaughlin, Rothery, Babins-Wagner, & Schlieffer, 2010); it is argued that with advances in research methods and accumulating objective knowledge, our interventions in the lives of our clients can and should be guided by evidence about what works from the social sciences rather than taking guidance from less empirical disciplines like religion.

A strong, sometimes strident, version of the secularist humanist's position holds that religion is not merely an unreliable, inferior source of knowledge and values but a dangerous and morally corrupt one. Religious traditions stand accused of *causing* many of the problems that we are heir to, including violence in its various forms. For some, this train of thought leads quite logically to an ethical stand (Clifford, 1947), holding that the set of ideas we allow to guide our actions is a moral issue beyond simple efficacy (see Charles Taylor, 2002, for his discussion of W.K. Clifford's argument). Militant modern atheists (e.g., Dawkins, 2006; Hitchens, 2009) sometimes write as if an attraction to religious frames of reference is a kind of sin, an alliance with dark forces.

Yet, after more than 200 years of apparently inexorable progress, it seems a secular–humanist victory and the demise of religious helping are not at all assured. Indeed, it now seems there is real interest in taking a fresh look at the legitimate role religion can play in the helping enterprises. This openness to what religious traditions have to say has emerged unexpectedly, and it is grounds for optimism.

This reorientation is part of a much broader cultural shift toward a renewed respect for religion as a cultural force, which has taken many observers by surprise. Theologian Catherine Pickstock (as cited in Kennedy, 2007) reflects on the rapidity of this change:

> Ten years ago when I was studying, nobody really thought theology was an important subject. It seemed to be something one did if one was a rather marginal person. But *now* theology is a subject [that is] increasingly popular. You can scarcely open a newspaper without some reference to it. And it does seem to me that, quite suddenly, theology is becoming important in a way that it wasn't before.

Mesmer and Gassner were seen as adversaries, and a competitive, win-lose narrative has framed discussions of the relationship of science and religion to this day. This, too, is changing, as books recommending a different view appear more and more frequently in publishers' catalogues. Dozens of recent volumes on religion and science—especially physics, neurological and cognitive science, and evolutionary biology—argue that they can and should relate as complementary efforts to understand our world, rather than as antagonists.[3]

Theologians and scientists are now talking about a transdisciplinary agenda, aiming to find that common ground where useful conversations can occur when people committed to different disciplines want to discover what they have to learn from one another (Clayton, 2008; Van Huyssteen, 2006). FaithLink's work has been carried out in precisely that spirit, seeking to facilitate a transdisciplinary dialogue between secular human services workers and members of faith communities, hoping that the resulting conversations will generate more effective responses to religious women seeking help because of intimate partner violence.

We think the adversarial, competitive spirit that has shaped the discussion between religious and secular helpers to date will not move us forward in ways that benefit our clients. Therefore, we anticipate increased interest in discussions between our two traditions as we recognize that the needs of our clients require us to collaborate better. If, as this implies, our future will require a broader, deeper discourse between traditions that remain wary of one another, what might we talk about?

Indeed, there is much to discuss and real gains will result if we approach the task in good faith. The rest of this chapter is devoted to anticipating what we may find ourselves addressing as the conversations proceed. As we should expect, some tensions may prove relatively easy to resolve, while others look intractable—this is par for the course when transdisciplinary work is undertaken.

## ARE RELIGIONS TO BLAME FOR VIOLENCE?

Sixteen centuries ago St. Augustine (1961) related in his *Confessions* that his father was unfaithful and had "a hot temper" (p. 195) but his (Augustine's) profoundly Christian mother Monica practiced unwavering patience in relation to her husband. As a consequence, she was not beaten and this surprised her women friends (who were)—in their discussions about how best to deal with violent husbands, she counselled forbearance and friends who followed her rule bene-fitted from it: "Those who accepted it found it a good one: the others continued to suffer humiliation and cruelty" (Augustine, 1961, p. 195). Despite the passage of considerable time, present-day IPV researchers and projects like FaithLink continue to confront this powerful theme: Peace in the family is the woman's responsibility, and patient forbearance in the face of violence is one of the virtues women should exercise in their efforts to maintain that peace (Grodner & Sweifach, 2004; Nason-Clark, 1997). We can applaud the fact that Augustine saw the IPV that was common in his mother's circle as a problem, but his solution to that problem is concerning. It is still a powerful narrative in religious communities today.

In any forthright discussion of religion in the lives of their clients, reasonable secular helpers from the IPV community may well cite cases where religious traditions and doctrines regarding women, marriage, and the family have been used by religious men to support and justify abuse. Certainly, the women FaithLink talked to indicated that seeking help around IPV can be in part a struggle with questions of religious doctrine and traditions regarding the family. They identified many ways in which their search for a safer life was impeded, as well as supported, by the beliefs that have come to them through their churches, synagogues, and temples.

Thus, as secular and religious helpers discuss their roles respecting IPV, they will address questions about faith and violence that are at once current and centuries old—there is a long record of observers being troubled when ideologies that idealize peace and compassion seem easily bent to violent causes. Religion has been implicated in causing or failing to prevent everyday localized (therefore less visible) violence like IPV, but also often large-scale violence: crusades, wars, cultural imperialism, and genocides. No religion is innocent respecting the difficulties we are discussing (Armstrong, 2006; Jerryson & Jurgensmeyer, 2010; Strozier, Terman, Jones, & Boyd, 2010; Marty & Appleby, 1991b, 1993).

People on the secular side of the discourse may press and expand the point that not only has religion frequently supported violence, it has more often at least failed to *prevent* it. If religions exist in part to make us compassionate, they have arguably failed.

With this record on the table, secularists (especially those who have been attracted to the work of the "new atheists") might propose that despite ostensibly peaceful goals, it seems it may simply be natural for religions to set people and communities against one another—that religious doctrines necessarily promote contexts in which violence is protected and encouraged, and that they are therefore dangerous (Dawkins, 2006; Hitchens, 2009; for a more balanced analysis, see Marty, 2005).

But is all this evidence that religions are inherently dangerous and that we should therefore applaud their continued demise? A religious person responding to these challenges may well recognize the seriousness of the issues raised but suggest that when religious doctrines are used to protect those who perpetrate abuse and disempower women it is not those doctrines per se we are dealing with so much as faulty interpretations regarding what those doctrines mean or intend. This is a useful point, since we know that because religious beliefs are filtered through cultural, familial, and individual lenses, they can easily be distorted in the service of nonreligious priorities, even priorities that are diametrically opposed to the religious values that were originally being expressed.[4]

Continuing, religious discussants will propose that attacks on religion per se are misguided in a more basic sense and that we should not be too hasty in diagnosing the problem (religion) and prescribing a cure (secular humanism). A more nuanced understanding of the problem we face requires us to address the observation that as religion has given way to secular–humanist world views, communal and familial violence have not declined but have persisted unabated:

When we examine more closely some of what we might call the religious uses of violence...we find that all this can easily survive the rejection of religion, and recurs in ideological-political forms which are resolutely lay, even atheist. Moreover, it recurs in them with a kind of false good conscience, an unawareness of repeating an old execrable pattern, just because of the easy assumption that all that belonged to the old days of religion and therefore can't be happening in our Enlightened age. (Taylor, 2007, p. 688)[5]

With others, Taylor raises a critical point, that in our time, when the influence of religion has been in steep decline, we see no concomitant cessation of dismaying brutality; the past century is surely the worst on record in this regard, thanks to the depredations perpetrated under nonreligious (even avowedly atheist) creeds: Nazism, Marxism (Stalinist and Maoist), Fascism, and more (see Gray, 2007).[6] Indeed, nonreligious ideological goals—intense nationalisms for example—can mobilize powerful group allegiances and can justify extreme cruelty toward people seen as enemies to the cause. Defence of the fatherland can unleash what is worst in us as easily as a zealous adherence to the perceived word of God.

Thus, a way forward in the discussion seems to open up for us: While religious people should never be sanguine about how easily their ideologies can be pressed to serve violent ends, secular parties to the discussion need to be equally concerned. The problem, it seems, is that ideologies, be they religious or secular, can breed violence. A shared concern will surely be to understand how this comes to pass.

In our exploration of this common concern, it will be necessary to recognize the final point that neither religious nor secular ideological movements are *necessarily* violent—they simply have that potential. In fact, when progress in human political and social affairs is made, it is normally a consequence of ideologies that have worked well. Democracy is as much an ideology as fascism, for example, and recent improvements in the rights and protections due to women worldwide would not have happened without strong feminist ideologues leading the struggle.

Thus, the way forward is not to imagine we can or should stand against ideologies in general or religions in particular. Faced with socio-political realities that are both good news and bad, we might recognize instead that the only responsible course open to us is to consider which of our goals, beliefs, and practices can be made to serve destructive purposes (and how that outcome can be avoided).

## DO RELIGIONS SUPPORT VIOLENCE BY PROMOTING PATRIARCHY?

Gender is a constant in our personal and social lives, an issue that touches almost everything we do. Ideologies that shape our values, goals, and practices cannot therefore ignore gender, though some address it with more directness and detail than others. The importance of gender in our cultures is amplified by religions, which see the family and family relationships as a special, critically important, moral space:

> Religions worldwide invest the family with sacred significance, and this extends to gender, and interpersonal relations. The family...embodies primary relationships in which religious values are expressed, and in this sense it is frequently taken as a microcosm of a universal moral order. Its relationships (parent/child, husband/wife) are frequently used as models of the relations ideally pertaining between divinity and humanity. (Hardacre, 1993, p. 129)

Clearly, a meaningful dialogue between secular and religious helpers will devote time to issues concerning patriarchy—ideological treatments of gender relations that value male privilege.[7] This is an area that has attracted much scholarship in recent decades, and it is not possible (nor necessary) to do it justice at this juncture—it will be visited often in chapters to come. For our present purposes we must simply recognize the power of patriarchy as a destructive ideological given in most cultures, and in all of the main religions (Hardacre, 1993; UNFPA, 2005).

As transdisciplinary discussions tackle the patriarchy question, it will be noted that it is not at all an exclusively religious problem. Secular ideological movements are commonly destructively patriarchal as well—the cult of masculinity associated with Nazism and its stunning conflation of misogyny with racism is a stark example (Nussbaum, 2001). Less dramatic but equally dangerous examples of patriarchal beliefs are present in a large majority of IPV situations (including nonreligious families); they are something that professionals working in the field are well attuned to, since they encounter them all the time.

Voices on the religious side of the discussion may point out that at least some of the world's major religions began with inclinations toward gender equality, including Buddhism (Muesse, 2007, Lecture #15), Islam (Armstrong, 1993), and Christianity, with women recognized as crucial witnesses to the crucifixion and resurrection, and also heading a number of the first Christian communities founded by St. Paul (Cook, 2007, Lecture #2). Whatever egalitarian intentions were there did not last, however. Accommodations to the patriarchal ideologies prevalent in the mainstream cultures were fast and thorough, and in our present day, discrimination against women by established religions is entrenched. Women are very influential in many religious communities, but their access to positions of formal leadership is unusual in most and unheard of in some, discriminatory practices that are sometimes defended as compliance with essential traditional values.

There is potentially significant common ground where an openness to change exists on either side of the table. Feminist theologians and those respectful of their thinking, for example, will have no difficulty talking to secular colleagues about patriarchy and the risks it represents. Still, these are deep ideological currents and when religious helpers defend patriarchy as being an essential part of their faith traditions, it is easy to see how this could trouble a secular helper committed to gender equity—and a difference that can appear to be irreconcilable may be encountered.

## ARE ACCEPTANCE AND TRANSCENDENCE OF FAMILY PAIN A VALID GOAL?

Fifty thousand years ago (give or take a few millennia) our species was born, gifted with a remarkable brain, powerful symbolic language capabilities, a capacity for compassion, and a restless, questing spirit.

Great works of art were left on the walls of caves, some of them accessed through tight tunnels as much as a kilometre long. The paintings depict what would have been mundane daily realities like the hunt for game juxtaposed with something different, the world of the shaman in which a human form may have a bird's head, or abstract geometric shapes signalling the transition to a para-normal consciousness. Carefully placed hands press against the walls as if in an effort to push through to whatever lies behind. Van Huyssteen (2006) argues that we see our own restlessness in this work, with rudimentary science, art, and religion all expressing the surprising need to expand our understanding of our world and what it means.

Most religions hold that our everyday material reality exists in relation to something else—that there are ways of being that are available to us beyond our ordinary lives in our mundane world. This is a powerful belief for most religious people that very many secular humanists do not share. The truth of beliefs in transcendence in their simple and most declarative form may be an irreconcilable difference.

There is, however, a broader sense in which the idea of transcendence affects us, and conversations that set the narrow definition aside may prove useful.[8] The discussion might well start with the recognition that transcendence is a basic human need, even for people convinced that the material world is everything. We can likely agree easily enough that it is human nature to be dissatisfied, and we can all recognize the need to get behind the wall of the cave, to discover possibilities beyond the world we know. When people talk or write about the thrill of scientific breakthroughs or the sublimity of some perfect piece of music, they describe a general sort of transcendence much like the joy of religious insight— a sense of leaving the ordinary for a time and experiencing something more.

Powerful needs are usually good and bad news, and the bad news side to the need for transcendence is that it can be expressed destructively, through misusing drugs and alcohol, through pointless risk taking, and through violence. An excited crowd exiting a sporting event (or rock concert) can occasionally turn ugly, and the same energy that began as the exuberant joy of shared release results in vandalism or worse.

Conversations respecting transcendence and violence would benefit from some sober reflection on *why* violence both repels and attracts us. Again, St. Augustine (1961, pp. 121–123) shows us that these issues are not new when he writes about a friend who became literally addicted to the extreme violence that passed for entertainment at the Roman Colosseum. Violence has an allure, and as Chris Hedges (2002) shows in one compelling example after another, it is so attractive to us for precisely this reason: It takes us out of the mundane and into something powerful and strangely meaningful.

A yearning for the transcendent is, then, an appropriate and powerful aspect of many peoples' lives that can be easily enough misdirected by nonreligious and religious people alike. In our transdisciplinary explorations of IPV, we can recognize how the drive to move beyond our accustomed boundaries, expanding experience so that it encompasses more than an impoverished self, offers both creative and destructive possibilities in intimate relationships. The *feeling* of transcendence is a powerful reward, whether it is achieved through spiritual practices or explosive violence. Marjorie Suchocki (1999), a theologian, applies this insight to the puzzling fact that intimacy and violence are so often entwined:

> [Understanding] transcendence allows us to…account for the vulnerability that allows us both richness and destructiveness of being. It brings [our] interdependence and therefore [our] obligation into view. (p. 43)

Compare Suchocki's theologian's analysis with what one finds in the secular professional literature on IPV regarding fear of intimacy and violence—the opportunities for a useful conversation are impressive (for an especially apt example, see Goldner, Penn, Sheinberg, & Walker, 1990). What these writers tell us is that intimacy is by nature transcendent—this is partly why it is such an unshakeable preoccupation. When things go well, tremendous growth results; when the news is bad, the consequences can be destructive.

A final issue concerning transcendence that merits discussion has to do with how we respond to painful realities—if women are advised to meditate or pray for the strength to endure rather than taking practical steps to keep safe, for example, there is a sense in which they are being asked to respond to their problems by transcending them. This, of course, can be dangerous advice; however, it is interesting to note the emergence in the secular helping world (influenced by Buddhism) of ACT—acceptance and commitment therapy—a move away from the mainstream secular insistence on seeing all pain as problems to be solved.

## DO RELIGIOUS UTOPIANISM AND APOCALYPTICISM PROMOTE ACCEPTANCE OF ABUSE?

Utopianism is a very close ideological cousin to transcendence; indeed, a utopia may be the hoped-for outcome of successful efforts to transcend our flawed mundane condition. Apocalypticism is the view that a destruction of the present order is a necessary prelude to the emergence of a new and utopian world; therefore, violent means are the only final path to utopian ends (see Gray, 2007). Karl Popper (1971a, 1971b, 1986) turned his attention to the question of ideologically driven violence toward the end of the Second World War. He had fled Nazism as it overran Europe and in his analysis of that paradigmatically evil ideology he concluded that utopianism was a foundational element. In making his argument, Popper looked back to Plato (an important philosopher in the intellectual development of Christianity, Islam, and Judaism), who, in *The Republic* (1993) created a blueprint for a utopia that recommended horrifying dehumanization of citizens whose basic rights were sacrificed on the altar of an imagined perfect state.

Popper concluded that utopianism not only breeds violence but that violence is a *necessary* consequence of utopian strivings. The goals of liberal democracies, he thought, could not be sustained if utopian programs were pursued—utopianism was inherently dangerous and should be rejected in all its manifestations.

This is, of course, a serious challenge to religions—religious parties to our discussion will likely recognize they are in varying degrees explicitly utopian, promising a perfect world or cessation of suffering to the faithful at some future date. In fairness, they may also insist that there are also problematic secular utopian fantasies such as the Nazis' Thousand Year Reich or the Marxist dictatorship of the proletariat.

Concerns about utopianism are sharpened when we include apocalypticism (both secular and religious) in the discussion (see Gray, 2007)—apocalypticism holds that violence is the only way to achieve utopian goals. "Think of apocalyptic violence as a form of ultimate idealism, a quest for spiritual utopia," writes Robert J. Lifton (1993, p. 13).

This is a serious turn, since violence is now seen to have redemptive power. It is welcomed as part of a transcendent plan, as part of a solution to be embraced rather than a problem to be solved. As with Noah's flood, the hope is that when wholesale destruction has wiped the slate clean, it is finally possible for something infinitely better to emerge.[9]

Are these abstract considerations relevant to the very practical purposes of this book? We do not have to look far for evidence that in fact they are— again, religious women seeking help because of IPV are affected by ideological narratives that have very concrete consequences. They may, for example, be discouraged from doing what they must if they desire a safe life free of unnecessary pain, when utopian (especially patriarchally utopian) family values are given more weight than any one individual woman's rights.

Still, in response to Popper, some scholars have argued that for all the risks it carries, utopianism (at least the nonapocalyptic variants) is also entirely necessary to religious purposes: "Religion is...humanity groping towards its vocation. That vocation always lies in a utopian direction, a direction that until the end always transcends the present" (Porpora, 2004, p. 166; see also Paden, 2000). The ability to envision an idealized good is essential not only to religious ideologies but to modern secular movements as well (e.g., feminism, democratic reforms, civil liberties, and so forth)—utopian ideals can be an essential compass and motivational support.

## WHAT MAKES IDEOLOGIES DESTRUCTIVE?
## THE ISSUE OF FUNDAMENTALISM

A theme developing in the previous sections is that ideologies are necessary and often are both good news and bad. It is not always issues like transcendental strivings or utopianism per se that are problematic. Rather, the potential for violence is increased when such priorities are advanced in a particular way, when the stance of the seeker is fundamentalist. We are concerned here not so much with the substance of belief as with the cognitive style in which it is wrapped. Even patriarchal arrangements, which are inherently nonegalitarian, can be more or less pernicious depending on how fundamentalist they are in their operationalization:

> Fundamentalism is not...synonymous with orthodox belief and
> practice, or any particular beliefs or practices, but is rather a
> particular way of holding and believing the tenets of any particular
> religion, philosophy, or political theory. (Jones, 2010, p. 216)

Drawing on Marty and Appleby (1991a, pp. ix–x), we suggest that fundamentalism is by definition a broad concept that describes ideological movements with these properties:

- they are militant;
- they see themselves defending important beliefs and practices against outsiders;
- they themselves enjoy certitude about these beliefs and tend to see doubt as weakness;
- they are thereby protecting an ideal (often a past or future utopia);
- they believe their struggle has a transcendent aspect in that it is supported by and serves something larger than the self or community.

The "something larger" in the last bullet can refer to divine purposes in the case of religious fundamentalisms or to all-important social, cultural, or political purposes (e.g., nationalisms) in the case of secular ideologies.

Much work has been reported regarding fundamentalism in recent years, largely as a result of religiously motivated terrorist attacks on secular states (Armstrong, 2006; Marty & Appleby, 1991a, 1993; Strozier et al., 2010). Fundamentalism can be considered at different levels: as an individual issue associated with particular personality traits, as recognizable group dynamics characterizing families and small groups, and as a cultural phenomenon that shapes the thinking and behaviours prevalent in still larger social units.

The fundamentalist style is puritanical. It favours clear positions over nuanced analyses, idealized (and simple) images of self and others over a recognition of complexity in subjective experience and relationships, a good versus bad orientation to moral and ethical issues, and a strongly categorical approach to roles and responsibilities. As such, fundamentalism has deep effects on family life with constriction of women's and children's opportunities to flourish being common (Hardacre, 1993).

A suggestion emerging in previous sections is that religious and secular ideologies require of us a balanced response—recognizing that they can be very good, as well as very bad, news. Such a balance may be elusive at times, but it does seem that ideas about fundamentalism help—instead of insisting that beliefs we do not share are problematic, we focus instead on the style with which those beliefs are maintained.[10]

Robert J. Lifton (1989, 1993) devoted much of his life to understanding our capacity to be cruel to one another and drew conclusions that tell us much about what an *antifundamentalist style* looks like:

> For many years, I have been exploring the dark side of human behavior—Chinese thought reform (or "brainwashing"), the Vietnam War, Hiroshima, and, darkest of all, Nazi doctors. I have done so in the hope that, by probing the psychology of evil and destructiveness, we would be better able to combat this behavior and seek alternatives....The protean self [identity maintained in a spirit of openness and creativity] represents an alternative to violence. Violence always has an absolute quality: behavior is reduced to a single, narrow focus; and in that sense, violence is a dead end. Proteanism, in contrast, provides a capacity to avoid dead ends. (1993, p. 11)

For Lifton, a core issue for violence prevention, relevant for individuals as much as for whole cultures, is a capacity for doubt. Fundamentalist ideologues do not value doubt and may see it as weakness, or as a lack of real faith. Within many, if not most, ideologies, however, there is room for alternatives that undermine fundamentalism—stylistic options such as curiosity, a dislike of dictators, a rejection of spiritual pride, a mature ability to live with doubt and openness,[11] and a predisposition toward humility.

## IDEOLOGICAL GIFTS: COMPASSION VERSUS VIOLENCE

Our discussion so far has given weight to the risks of religion and other ideologies for the part they can play in promoting and supporting violence. Religious women that FaithLink worked with, however, suggest that there is another more positive story to be told—about the importance of spiritual supports for resisting violence and creating a life in which they can flourish. Apologists for religion in our transdisciplinary discourse have good grounds to argue that it has been a force behind many creditable things our cultures have done. They might quote retired Princeton physicist Freeman Dyson (2002), who expresses this view succinctly:

I am myself a Christian, a member of a community that preserves
an ancient heritage of great literature and great music, provides
help and counsel to young and old when they are in trouble,
educates children in moral responsibility, and worships God in
its own fashion. (p. 21)

They are seldom mainstream, but there are (and always have been) voices
raised promoting nonviolence, alternatives to war, and safety for vulnerable
people—and these are very often the voices of religious people who draw courage
and moral clarity from their different faiths. The abolition of slavery, apartheid,
and segregationist policies has all come about with and through the involvement
of religious people and organizations. Antipoverty movements and programs to
combat HIV have likewise benefitted from the help of religious organizations—
indeed, the roots of professional social work are in religious soil (Majonis, 2004).
Modern heroes who have been self-sacrificing advocates of nonviolent means
for attaining social justice—very prominent examples include Aung San Suu Kyi,
Ghandi, the Dalai Lama, Mother Teresa, and Martin Luther King—have seen their
accomplishments as an expression their religious faith.

Prominent among contemporary thinkers who see religion as an
ideological force promoting nonviolence is René Girard (2001, 2004); violence,
he argues, is a result of "mimetic" processes, whereby we determine what
we value by taking our cues from one another. Our finely tuned sensitivity to
other peoples' needs and desires (empathy) is a large part of what makes us so
thoroughly social, but it can also fuel competitions with violent conclusions.
Tensions arise and in the interests of regaining communal equilibrium a scapegoat is chosen—a member of the community is assigned responsibility for the
building tensions and is removed (banished, punished, or even killed). Parallels
between this scapegoat dynamic and the well-documented cycle of violence that
so often culminates in IPV will be immediately apparent to many readers.

In Girard's view, the religious antidote to scapegoating and violence is to
recognize the innocence of the victim. He credits Christianity, with its central
focus on Christ's execution, with this critical insight, but his focus at that point
in his argument has become unnecessarily narrow. Both religious and secular
parties to a transdisciplinary exploration may favour a more credible and inclusive analysis. Starting by recognizing that all religions consider compassion a

core value (Armstrong, 1993; see also http://charterforcompassion.org/), they may note further that compassion requires not just the perception of innocence but recognition of the full humanity of people at risk. We cannot, everyone agrees, scapegoat our neighbours if we allow ourselves to see their complexity and richness.

With others, Charles Taylor (1989) maintains that all cultures extend basic ("strongly evaluated") rights and protections to their members; freedom from unnecessary pain and dignity are examples. There is, however, a circle we draw, a boundary defining who is eligible for these provisions and who is not. This is a "circle of compassion," and since there are people who have the misfortune to be marginalized, who are defined as outside the circle (they may be gay, or poor, or mentally ill, or female, for example), it is of enormous practical importance. Exclusion is a licence to withhold compassion, with a consequent justification to deny help or inflict other cruelties.

Compassion is understood by most to be a feeling of concern for others, and as such, it is easily endorsed by people, both secular and religious, who work in the social services. The ability to respond compassionately to someone fleeing IPV is so obviously a positive (even necessary) response that we salute it and move on to the practicalities of implementing it in everyday life.

But compassion is more than an emotional response (or at least a far from simple one). As Nussbaum (2001), citing Aristotle, argues, it is a feeling for others that occurs in a cognitive framework:

> Compassion…has three cognitive elements: the judgment of size (a serious bad event has befallen someone); the judgment of *nondesert* (this person did not bring the suffering on himself or herself); and the *eudaimonistic judgment* (this person, or creature, is a significant element in my scheme of goals and projects, an end whose good is to be promoted). (p. 321)

Compassion can therefore be seen as a value that informs ideology— especially when it is championed, as it commonly is, by religions that embrace it as something that sits at the core of what they stand for. It is a set of beliefs incorporating social goals that are worth fighting for—and fight we must, since there is an anticompassion ideological thread that has been very influential from at least the stoics of ancient Greece, continuing through Nietzsche's denunciations of religion as weakness (and declarations about the death of God) to our present culture, in which it remains quite powerful. The arguments against compassion generally equate it with a cultural drift toward weakness (a concern for fundamentalists of all stripes) and a drain on social and economic resources that would be better used to promote strength and reward achievement.

When compassion becomes part of our transdisciplinary conversation, we should find ourselves on common ground, talking about the promotion of compassion as a powerful shared goal—and an enterprise with which religious people and their organizations have many centuries of experience.

## A CONCLUDING NOTE: VIOLENCE AND THE DENIAL OF RICHNESS AND MEANING

Thoughtful observers rooted in religious traditions have a deep concern about nihilism, a belief that the material world we see through the deterministic, reductionistic lens of science is all there is—that there is no meaning, value, or underlying purpose as part of the mix. Nihilism is a logical extension of much modernist (and postmodernist) thinking, and the consequences can be thoroughly dehumanizing.

When women from relationships involving IPV decide to seek a safer life for themselves, the process almost always involves, to a large degree, thinking through and clarifying values (Rothery, Tutty, & Weaver, 1999)—examples being values about one's rights to safety and freedom from pain, or one's obligations to shield children from the effects of violence, or about a husband's duty and responsibility in relation to his family. Good answers to such questions about values (and the difficult accommodation of ideals with what is possible in reality) can be critical, even life saving. Religious thinkers are helpful when they highlight such tensions. Spiritual traditions are powerful sources of value, sometimes values that are explicitly perfectionistic; at the same time, religious moral teachings have always (at their best) recognized that the pursuit of ideal values in a very imperfect world requires a flexible weighing of one "good" against another (e.g., commitment to a marriage versus commitment to providing a safe and loving family for oneself and one's children).

Of course, secular humanist helpers are unequivocal in their nonviolence values, but it is nevertheless also true that the modernist and postmodernist traditions in which they are usually situated have generated philosophies that diminish the importance of individual selves and that regard such values as those abused women struggle to clarify as being social constructions. They are seen as mere products of consensus; therefore, they are always open to negotiation.[12] Because religions have consistently challenged these lines of thought, religious helpers have something vital to offer in discussions that focus on such matters.

We cannot be compassionate and violent at the same time—these ways of being in relation to one another are antithetical. And, as we have argued, when we affirm human importance and richness, and when we advocate keeping the circle of compassion open to everyone, we are promoting values that support compassion and therefore will prevent violence. On these points conversations between secular and religious helpers will easily and emphatically agree— compassion is a foundation for collaboration that is strong and will surely endure.

Kurt Lewin (1951) among others is credited with the observation, "There is nothing more practical than good theory" (p. 169). We have (hopefully) been making the case that broad and abstract knowledge about religion and violence has concrete relevance to the very practical work of the FaithLink project. This is as we asserted earlier a book about practice, and it is on practicalities that we will focus from this point forward. Still, in reading the chapters that follow, it will be evident that the daily problems and choices with which the FaithLink staff and their clients wrestled are not just issues of local, limited importance— having roots in matters with a deep and abiding cultural relevance, the narratives provided by the women we served have a truly universal significance.

· ·

## CO-AUTHORS' COMMENTS
### From the Desk of Nancy Nason-Clark

I was invited to give a public address in a series entitled *Ideas That Matter*, an initiative of the Faculty of Arts at the University of New Brunswick to bring together people from the community to hear about some of the research initiatives of faculty on our Fredericton campus. The lectures have been well attended and the series has been considered a success.

The subtitle of my talk—"Religion as Part of the Solution to Domestic Violence, Not Just Part of the Problem"—was meant to engage sectors of the community in dialogue about domestic violence. Its purpose was to initiate a conversation between secular and religious voices concerning abuse in the family context. I asked two community activists—one a Baptist minister in a downtown historic church; the other the executive director of a local agency—to respond to my research results and the implications I draw from them.

The feedback one receives from such events is always very interesting. One colleague from campus mentioned in passing that she was not coming because she could not bring herself to attend anything that was held in a church. Another was surprised that any faith groups would be willing to collaborate with community-based workers in response to violence against women. Others noted that it was a daring move to suggest that faith communities and secular agencies involve themselves in collaborative ventures to respond to families impacted by abuse.

As always, I am surprised by the persistence and level of suspicion on both sides. And yet, over the years, I have witnessed and participated in many collaborative ventures between secular and sacred perspectives aimed at reducing violence and responding with compassion to its devastating impact. FaithLink, the Calgary-based initiative that is highlighted in our book, drew its inspiration from both secular and religious conversations—about violence, about compassion, about best practices, and about what it means to meet the deep emotional and practical needs of another human being. These are grounded in philosophical positions explored within the pages of this chapter.

Vulnerability and resiliency are two key concepts—intertwined in the experiences of us all. We need the secular conversations about domestic violence to highlight the primacy of safety concerns and the practical and emotional resources that are needed when the emotional and physical well-being of a woman and her children cannot be assured. For women of faith, the healing journey often involves the language of the spirit as well—the traditions, prayers, sacred messages, and rituals that bring solace to the soul. Yet, regardless of our philosophical positions, healing and wholeness of the body and the spirit often require both the secular and the sacred.

The narratives of the women told throughout this book and the stories of those who walk alongside them as agency workers or religious leaders compel us to never forget that violence has no place in homes across our nation. All of us can play a part in raising our voices for change.

## From the Desk of Robert Pynn

I would like to draw attention to the emergence of a contemporary search for grounded spiritual insight. For some the deep pain of abuse has ignited this search for a deeper knowledge. Alas, the traditional carriers of spirituality, namely established religious institutions, have often forgotten how to steward such sacred mystery. Certainly, it seems that much of North American society is emotively predisposed to see religion as a dry well, or a well of tainted water that should be avoided.

In reality there still remains a deep underground stream flowing beneath the world religions waiting to be drawn upon. We call this flowing river of life, *Wisdom*. Dr. Cynthia Bourgeault (2003) defines this Wisdom as "a precise and comprehensive science of spiritual transformation that has existed at the headwaters of the great religions and is in fact their common ground" (p. xvi). Ancient sapiential sciences united theory and practice long before the modern concepts of social praxis were promulgated. The theory part consists of a bold and spacious vision of humanity's purpose and destiny. The practice aspect and disciplines of Wisdom's Way of inner transformation are directed toward our growth into that purpose.

Wisdom teaching contains some important missing pieces that have fallen out of human civilization's cultural world view. As one grapples with the questions of peace, meaning, and dignity in our fragile and overstressed world, there are pieces that can bridge the gulf between religion and science, reunite psychological health and more integrity, and provide a pathway for transformative justice (for the abused and those who choose to abuse). The practice part of the Wisdom tradition resides at the base of all the great world religions and its fundamentals are easily received into each, although the ascribed meaning may vary.

You can see how I was drawn to "Wisdom's way of knowing" as a foundation for FaithLink's approach to uniting secular service providers and religious communities in the common goal of preventing and transforming abusive attitudes and behaviours. The key ingredient is Wisdom's upgrade of our mental operating system. The conflicts of religion and modern secular thinking are really based on the same epistemological platform. Both have bought into the dualisms of binary analysis that tend to see truth as a unity of meaning on one level. Such an approach assumes that our intellectual centre is the sole vehicle for establishing and defending this univocal version of truth. Logicians would call this a category mistake that believes our intellectual faculty to be the essential centre of the self. But this isolated faculty is not capable of dealing with our total existence. We cannot think our way into an encounter with our true self and the very ground of our being. It is this ultimate mysterious centre that gives us a place to stand that is beyond the control of negative forces that confound our reason.

Transformational justice and its contemplative disciplines can help to reintegrate our binary mental operation system into a larger frame of perception. It is a *unitive* perspective that connects with, and draws upon, deep wells of wisdom and creativity within the heart.

# Reflections

Where do I go
when trust is fractured
and my daily bread
is betrayal and fear?

How can we talk when words
become knives and
conversation is crushed into
an iron fist?

I was talking on the phone
when his look cut through me.
He ripped the receiver from my hand,
completing my sentence with a curse.

Now, I cower on the floor
in this corner,
bleeding,
ribs beating pain on my temple;
looking at my image
reflected in the tears,
draining
from my children's eyes.

—ROBERT PYNN

# 2
# Intimate Partner Violence

## Definitions and Context

**INTRODUCTION**

The abuse of women by their intimate partners knows no geographic, economic, cultural, or religious boundary. Its dynamics are complex; its effects significant. Through a substantial body of research and clinical knowledge, our understanding of the factors inherent within this phenomenon has increased. Much of this understanding is grounded within a secular, humanistic perspective. The concern of the FaithLink program was that of women victims whose identities and social connections were grounded within a religious/ethno-cultural perspective. As becomes evident in the research reported herein, religious beliefs and practices, community and cultural norms become defining factors for these women. But before we venture into these areas it is first necessary to understand the issue—intimate partner violence (IPV).

This chapter offers an overview of how IPV is defined, its prevalence within our society, and some of the barriers women face in leaving abusive relationships. Given the theme of this book, we are particularly concerned to understand how beliefs, culture, and community influence how IPV is defined by religious women and how they and their communities respond to it. We do so by addressing the religious/ethno-cultural context for women within Christian, Jewish, and Khmer Canadian communities.

## UNDERSTANDING THE ISSUE: DEFINITION AND PREVALENCE

The questions of definition and prevalence are interrelated. Depending on how IPV is defined, the rate of occurrence will vary. Additionally, the concept of IPV is not monolithic: Behaviours that, within a North American context, would be labelled as psychological abuse may not be classified as such within another cultural context (Yick & Berthold, 2005). Conversely, behaviours within some ethno-cultural communities may be considered abusive but not included in generally accepted definitions framed within the mainstream cultural context (e.g., gambling, extramarital affairs as a humiliation tactic, hindering the development of skills needed to increase independence, and harassment of extended family members) (Bhuyan, Mell, Senturia, Sulivan, & Shiv-Thoraton, 2005). Within the context of this work, intimate partner violence is defined as

> The attempt, act or intent of someone within a relationship, where the relationship is characterized by intimacy, dependency or trust, to intimidate either by threat or by the use of physical force on another person or property. The purpose of the abuse is to control and/or exploit through neglect, intimidation, inducement of fear or by inflicting pain. Abusive behaviour can take many forms including: verbal, physical, sexual, psychological, emotional, spiritual, economic and the violation of rights.[1]

It is recognized that either partner of an intimate relationship can act abusively to the other. As noted in the Introduction, the subject of this book is the experience of women victims of IPV. How IPV is defined, its prevalence, the reality women face in leaving abusive relationships, and the religious/ethno-cultural contexts in which they live reflect this focus.

Violence within intimate relationships is a phenomenon found within all population groups. This truth is borne out by research, clinical experience, and the testimony of victims. From their review of studies conducted in 24 countries between 1993 and 1998, Kroeger and Nason-Clark (2010) succinctly sum up its prevalence:

> Violence against women exists in every country of the globe, among all people groups. Abuse occurs within every faith

community. And it knows no socioeconomic boundaries....all
women are potential targets of violence, and all women are at
some degree of risk. (p. 17)

Nor are Canadian women exempt. A large, random survey (Statistics Canada, 1993) revealed that three in 10 Canadian women had experienced at least one incident of physical or sexual violence by a current or previous partner. Although more recent data (Statistics Canada, 2008) suggest a decrease in the number of Canadian women experiencing abuse, IPV still accounts for 15% of all violent incidents reported to the police across the country. Females continue to be the most likely victims of police-reported spousal abuse, accounting for 83% of all victims. Spousal homicides represent 17% of all solved homicides in Canada, with female homicides outnumbering males by between three and five times.

Research over the past two decades has confirmed that women of religious communities are at equal risk of being abused by an intimate partner as their more secular sisters. Utilizing a sample of 343 evangelical Christian pastors from the Atlantic Canadian provinces, Nason-Clark (1997) concludes that

The most common counselling scenario for conservative pastors
is a woman who has an abusive partner. Eight out of every ten
pastors (81%) have counselled this type of situation...57% of
evangelical ministers have counselled a man who is abusive toward
his children, and 70% have worked with a man who abuses his
wife. (pp. 68–70)

Kroeger and Nason-Clark (2010) conclude that violence "is all too common an experience in the life of women believers within ordinary evangelical and mainstream churches" (p. 47). Similarly, Miles (2008), noting that 25% of American women report being raped and/or physically assaulted by a current or former intimate partner, takes the position that Christian women and men are as likely as all other couples in the United States to face situations of abuse.

In her review of the research data regarding the prevalence of IPV within the Jewish population, Altfeld (2005) concludes that the results of numerous, localized studies cannot be generalized to the larger whole. She thus suggests that actual rates have not yet been established. Grodner and Sweifach (2004) agree, noting that the focus of discussion has been primarily on the stigma associated with IPV rather than on the issue itself. Acknowledging that violence occurs within Jewish homes, they suggest it "challenges the emotional and religious fiber of the community" (p. 306). In their review of relevant research, DeVoe, Borges, and Conroy (2001) also speak to communal denial and the difficulty encountered by researchers due to low participation rates. These researchers conclude, however, that "available evidence suggests the incidence and prevalence of domestic violence in the Jewish community are similar to rates in other communities" (p. 23). Altfeld's (2005) survey results of rabbis, community members, and women's leadership representatives in the Chicago area indicate an acknowledgement that Jewish women are abused at a rate that is similar to that of the general population. Speaking from his clinical perspective, Kivel (2002) addresses the tendency of the Jewish community, particularly men, to deny or minimize the occurrence of violence within the family, to collude with men who have acted abusively, as well as to withhold supports and resources from victimized women.

Although there is extensive literature addressing IPV, including prevalence rates, within the general population, there has been limited equivalent focus on immigrant women and/or ethno-cultural communities. Menjivar and Salcido (2002), citing studies by Easteal (1994) and Goldman (1999), note that "statistical evidence pertaining to the number of immigrant women who experience domestic violence in receiving countries, like the United States and Australia, is unavailable" (p. 899). Speaking of South Asian women living in the United States, Raj and Silverman (2007) cite three studies that indicate a prevalence rate of 20% to 40% but suggest that these percentages may be low considering that many South Asian women may not be disclosing the abuse they suffer. From their secondary analysis of a large Canadian cross-sectional survey of victimization conducted by Statistics Canada, Hyman, Forte, DuMont, Romans, and Cohen (2006) found that recent immigrant women (i.e., five or less years of residency) reported significantly lower rates of IPV than did nonrecent immigrant women (i.e., more than five years of residency). These researchers interpret this difference as reflecting the

> changing perceptions and interpretations of IPV as newcomers
> learn what acts constitute abuse in the context of the adopted

country and develop the language skills necessary for identifying and speaking about their experiences. If so, then previous cultural norms of what is considered abusive behavior change over time to accommodate new constructs, which result in higher reported rates of IPV. (p. 657)

Khmer American women interviewed by Bhuyan et al. (2005) report that IPV is regarded as a common issue within families, although it is not considered acceptable behaviour. Menjivar and Salcido (2002) note that a

review of the scholarship shows that the incidence of domestic violence is not higher than it is in the [host country] population, but rather that the experiences of immigrant women in domestic violence situations are often exacerbated by their special position as immigrants. (p. 901)

Christian, Jewish, and Khmer Canadian women with whom FaithLink worked and who participated in research projects certainly confirm the presence of IPV within their congregations and communities. They did not question whether abuse was present but rather spoke of it not being acknowledged: "It [IPV] happens...[and] it's hidden." "It's very hidden." "It's been hidden for so long." "I'm sure there's so many women out there [in congregations] that are going through this and they don't even know what it's called." "It's a silent crisis."

Some spoke of the endemic nature of IPV within the cultures from which their parents emigrated: "When we look at the generation of our parents, at that time it was not accepted to get divorced. I am from the background of Russia... people used to live everyday with abuse and it was okay. You were lucky you could hide that from your kids, but I know so many people from my own experience. I knew that my Mom would be beaten up every day...every night...and it was part of the daily routine. Everyone in the neighbourhood was experience[ing] the same thing. There was no way you could get out of it."

## FACING THE REALITY OF IPV

### Effects of Abuse on Direct Victims

The effects of IPV on its victims have been compared to those experienced by victims of other forms of trauma: criminal victimization, natural disasters, accidents, combat, kidnapping, being held hostage—when one's assumptions about oneself and the world are suddenly shattered, the sense of having control of one's life is lost, when safety and security is replaced by vulnerability. Life no longer holds the same meaning and is experienced as being unfair and unjust. These impacts reverberate through every aspect of one's being: feelings, thoughts, relationships, behaviours, attitudes, dreams, and hopes. Women describe being fearful of continued abuse; retaliation and the loss of children; anxiety in anticipation of further abuse; experiencing insomnia, panic attacks, loss of hope, a desire to die; being physically injured; being broken-hearted and depressed. The longer victimization is experienced, in whatever form, and the more severe the abusive incidents, the greater the likelihood the victim will experience post-traumatic stress disorder (PTSD) (Bhuyan et al., 2005; Tutty, 2006; Williams & Poijula, 2002).

### Barriers to Disclosing and Leaving

Women in abusive relationships have described to clinicians and researchers the factors that kept them from disclosing and leaving their situations. Although every woman's situation is unique, they identify common, but not mutually exclusive, barriers. The first impediment is coming to terms with the realization that they are, in fact, being abused by their partner. Nonphysical forms of abuse may be denied; physical assaults may be minimized. Acknowledgement may only come when physical injuries are obvious and can no longer be hidden. Victims also speak of the immobilizing effects of pervasive fear: fear for their own, and their children's, safety; fear that threats made by their abuser will be fulfilled; fear that their disclosure will place other family members in danger; and, if an immigrant, fear that police involvement will complicate immigration-related issues. Fear also blinds victims from realizing the choices available to them. Other victims identify a strong need to protect the integrity of the family unit. For these women, it is more important to keep the family together than for any member, including themselves, to be safe and free of violence. Victims may place the needs of others, particularly those of their partner, over their own needs and accept responsibility for keeping the family together and happy. It is not uncommon for victims to speak of their sense of powerlessness, self-blame, hopelessness, shame, and embarrassment (Beaulaurier, Seff, Newman, & Dunlop, 2005; Davies, Lyon, & Monti-Catania, 1998; Hathaway, Willis, & Zimmer, 2006; Kroeger & Nason-Clark, 2010; Rothery et al., 1999). A Jewish woman expressed the emotional struggle this way: "It's shame, but it's also a feeling of failure to keep the family together and the home together. And so that is part of that whole feeling of failure. You know, what could I have done differently?...because...my home's falling apart."

Many victims cling to the hope that their partners will change and the abuse will end. This is particularly true for women of faith. For example, Christian women may hold strong conviction about the primacy of marriage, a commitment to their wedding vows, and a belief in the need for perpetual forgiveness. The anticipated nonsupport of extended family members, spiritual leaders, and congregations and/or communities acts as a strong barrier to ending an abusive relationship (Kroeger & Nason-Clark, 2001).

When religious beliefs and ethno-cultural norms are closely entwined, the combined forces can pose strong disincentives for disclosing abuse and leaving a violent relationship. Jewish tradition, cultural norms, and religious beliefs place high value on the centrality of the family; the wife's responsibility for ensuring domestic tranquility (*Shalom Bayit* [peace in the home]); and strong sanctions against women who separate and seek divorce. Even for women who are not observant in their religious practices, the influence of cultural values and background can be significant. For those who are religiously observant and within an Orthodox tradition, the prohibitions to ending an abusive marriage can be formidable: the shame and self-blame of not achieving the ideals to which Jewish marriage is held; the embarrassment of seeking help from within their community; concerns that seeking help from resources outside the community will bring shame upon all Jewish people; and a deep sense of failure on both the emotional and cultural levels. Within the family unit, certain religious roles and rituals are performed by the husband—the passing on of traditions and practices from father to son. If a wife were to leave the marital relationship, important observances (e.g., Sabbath, festivals, life-cycle events) would become difficult to uphold and her sons would lose their father's mentorship. Obtaining a religious divorce poses another significant barrier (DeVoe et al., 2001; Grodner & Sweifach, 2004).

Jewish women speaking to FaithLink workers and researchers describe the barriers victims within their community face in leaving an abusive relationship:

> I think a lot of those problems [disclosing abuse, seeking assistance, and leaving an abusive relationship] stem from some of the other traditions that we have, and rituals and laws that we have with the divorce system. [Obtaining] a gett [a religious divorce] is very, very difficult because it is a very humiliating and very demeaning experience....[I]t is not [an] easily accessible answer to getting out of a bad situation...[I]t's not just that you are in an abusive...situation, it's all the circumstances that filter into that. The jeopardy for children... It's...about knowing what is accessible and if you have the means, how you take advantage of [what's available]...you can try to secure all sorts of things but to secure...independence is a bigger factor than anything. Trying to secure independence would be huge.

Women of colour and those who hold immigrant status face even more daunting barriers. They may face punishment from their families and communities, including being abandoned, ostracized, and deported. If police are involved, these women fear their husbands will be mistreated. Speaking of Cambodian immigrants to the United States who are victims of family violence, Bhuyan et al. (2005) identify their concern for community disapproval if they involve the police or separate from or divorce their husbands. These women also did not want to separate their children from their fathers.

Other barriers that hinder or delay a decision to seek safety from an abusive partner include extreme poverty and lack of access to dignified jobs; uncertain legal status; limited host-language skills; and isolation within their ethno-cultural communities and from the external mainstream society. Without ready access to individuals and/or resources within their communities that can provide assistance and support, not being aware of the resources that are available within the broader community, their options are indeed very limited. In the face of their abuse and the potential consequences of seeking relief, women "may become depressed or take their lives rather than lose the support of their cultural community or family, here in Canada or back home" (Javed, 2006, p. 43; Beaulaurier et al., 2005; Menjivar & Salcido, 2002).

All religious women, regardless of religious affiliation and/or cultural context, who do seek help from within their community may receive counsel that reinforces the requirement to maintain the marital relationship, to uphold cultural norms, and/or not be referred to appropriate IPV services.

## The Decision to Leave

Notwithstanding the significant challenges all abused women encounter, victims do disclose their situations and seek help. They describe reaching a point of readiness. This turning point often comes at a point of crisis—most often an escalation in the abuse or the realization of how the violence is affecting their children. Victims reach a point of feeling they can no longer endure the abusive situation. The fear they feel for their own safety, and for that of their children, becomes greater than the fear of disclosing and leaving the relationship (Hathaway et al., 2006).

Disclosing and leaving is, however, a complex process. As Rothery et al. (1999) note, "Change is seldom tidy and linear; more often it is character-ized by uncertain progress and frequent re-acquaintance with old problems before a clear sense of direction is acquired and new options firmly established" (p. 13). The decision to disclose the abuse may be followed by careful planning to leave the relationship, or the disclosure and the leaving may occur together at a moment of crisis. It may involve repeated acts of separation and reconcili-ation before a permanent separation is achieved, a process that is infused with emotional, cultural, and religious considerations, and the responses of those to whom the victim has turned for support (Anderson & Saunders, 2003). As one of the participants commented, "So, in a way, as many institutions as a community builds or...as many open arms as we can offer and love and care—unfortunately the person is being abused and that person is also the only one in the end who could bring themselves out and that's probably the biggest challenge."

Regardless of when and how her leave-taking transpires, there are significant practical factors that she must address: housing, finances, and employment; child care; safety and legal issues, e.g., child custody; education; the loss of social support. As such, the abuse victim faces a dramatic change in her circumstances. She may suddenly find herself single, living alone; a single parent, without a permanent home or the financial means to maintain herself and her children. In light of her circumstances, if she is a woman of faith, it may be her spirituality that gives her the courage and strength to face the risks, make the necessary decisions, and implement her plans (Davies et al., 1998; Javed, 2006; Kirkwood, 1993; Kroeger & Nason-Clark, 2010; Rothery et al., 1999).

## UNDERSTANDING THE CONTEXT

This brief review of some of the dynamics involved for the victims of intimate partner violence helps us to understand its impact and the struggles they often face in seeking safety for themselves and their children. But, when we move the discussion to that of offering help, we must also be aware of context—those aspects of culture, beliefs, values, and community that provide a frame of reference for our lives and relationships, and infuse meaning into our lives. Without an understanding of the victim's context, our offers of help may be misguided, limited, and/or ineffective.

A few definitions will sketch this landscape.

- *Culture*: "The shared, more or less integrated way of thinking, understanding, evaluating and communicating that make up a people's way of life"; "the learned norms, values, knowledge, artifacts, language and symbols that are constantly communicated among people who share a common way of life" (Calhoun, Light, & Keller, 1997, pp. 28, 116).
- *Religion*: "A set of beliefs and practices pertaining to sacred things that unite people into moral communities" (Calhoun et al., 1997, p. 377); "time-tested traditions filled with proven pointers on how to proceed through life" (H. Smith as cited in O'Hanlon, 2006, p. 91). Organized religion is defined as "a context for learning and transmitting religious and often secular beliefs, values and practices" (Nason-Clark, 1997, p. 13).
- *Community*: "A population knit together by common values and interests, relatively dense and enduring ties, frequent face-to-face interactions and a sense of being close to one another" (Calhoun et al., 1997, p. 563). Jenkins (2002), quoting historian Peter Brown, gives an ancient example of the inclusiveness of community that is still applicable today: "The appeal of Christianity still lay in its radical sense of community: it absorbed people because the individual could drop from a wide impersonal world into a miniature community, whose demands and relations were explicit" (p. 76).

These three factors—culture, religion, and community—are closely intertwined and influence our day-to-day lives and decisions. This is true, to varying degrees, for secular and sacral communities and social groups. For those whose identities are rooted within sacral–communal structures—whether a Christian congregation or an ethnically based people group—the interconnection of culture, religion, and community has significant implications when intimate partner violence is present—both for the individuals directly involved and for the community's response to it. The ties that provide meaning, support, and connection can also be ties that bind. Some of the factors that "bind" victims within abusive relationships are evident within Christian, Jewish, and Khmer Canadian communities—the three religious/ethno-cultural groupings with which FaithLink worked.

## Christian Context

The Christian tradition includes several divisions and branches: Roman and Orthodox Catholic; mainstream Protestant denominations (e.g., Anglican, United, and Presbyterian); and a variety of evangelical denominations (e.g., Baptist, Christian Missionary, Alliance, Nazarene). Although basic tenets of the faith are held by all, there are differing doctrinal emphases and applications. Organizational structures also vary.

Religious beliefs do not cause violence, but they matter. Hegen (1993) notes, "Certain beliefs seem to interact with other factors to provide an environment where abuse can occur. In such an environment, would-be abusers find it possible to justify their behavior through distortion or extension of religious teachings" (p. 83).

Tenets that affirm male dominance, female submission, and the primacy of marriage are viewed within many Christian denominations as the model for human relationships. Although Miles (2008) would argue that the strictness with which these historical positions are held is a matter of scriptural interpretation and translation, there continues to be concern about their application in light of violence within marital relationships, as the following comments attest.

- Livingston (2002) notes, "indissolubility remains a primary mark of the [Roman] Catholic position on marriage" (p. 52). And further: "Church leaders have often colluded with abusive men, minimizing and denying the abuse they see, to the detriment of the women and children in their parishes" (p. 47).

- When the intended "safe, stable and loving environment for adults and children...instead becomes a place of violation and human destruction, the Church has too often opted to preserve the pretense of [the marriage] covenant over the safety of violated people" (Hegen, 1993, p. 93).
- "All too often the preservation of marriage has been exalted as the highest good, even when human life is at stake" (Kroeger & Nason-Clark, 2001, p. 175).
- When divorce is only acceptable on the grounds of adultery or abandonment, and husbands are vested with authority over their wives, women are left with little recourse if they are abused within their marital relationships (Joyce, 2009).

Women interviewed by FaithLink spoke of the confines imposed by narrow theological definitions and strict applications of marriage, noting that it is "hard to reconcile [the abuse experience] with theology." They also discussed how to "reconcile" their beliefs and their experience. Noting that marriage is "a contract," one woman took the position that when "one party is not living up to that [to love and protect and honour each other], I believe that the other party is released....That if there's violence, verbal, emotional, sexual, financial, etcetera, then...and...the party [who is practicing the abuse] is not willing to change, then much better to spare the souls, the relationships with the Lord, the development of the children and the spouse who is being abused...to spare their lives than have the whole ship sink."

Beliefs about repentance, forgiveness, and reconciliation are interconnected tenets and central to the Christian faith. How they are understood and applied, therefore, have significance for victims of abuse, those who have acted abusively, and for Christian leaders. Christians are called upon to forgive those who cause them harm and to do so quickly. But forgiveness is also a part of the healing process for victims of abuse, which cannot be forced, demanded, or rushed. Repentance is acknowledging one's wrongdoing, seeking forgiveness, and changing one's behaviour and attitude so as not to repeat the offence. As such, the

Church has a role in calling for those who have acted abusively toward a partner to take responsibility for their actions, including taking whatever measures are necessary to ensure the behaviour is not repeated. Given the propensity for abusers to deny, minimize, and justify their abusive behaviours, taking responsibility can be a difficult process. Miles (2008) cautions spiritual leaders and congregations to avoid accepting declarations of "instantaneous" change through an act of repentance. Rather, as Hegen (1993) argues, faith communities have a responsibility to support and hold the abuser accountable to take "the necessary steps to assure that his abusive behavior will never happen again...repentance will involve long, intensive psychotherapy" (p. 124). Thorson (2008) connects forgiveness and repentance when she states that "forgiveness [should] occur only after the abuser has changed both attitude and conduct" (p. 73).

The issue of forgiveness is one that elicits strong responses from Christian women. "For people who have been gravely offended...gravely violated, we can re-victimize them by saying 'You know, you need to forgive and you need to do it now. Because if you don't, on the basis of Matthew 6:14 and 15...'"

One woman spoke of her own struggle with the advice she received from her spiritual leaders in the face of abuse at the hands of her father, her process of healing, and of forgiveness:

> When my Dad...beat the crap out of me and lock[ed] me in [for]
> three days...the fourth day I would go to my pastor and the pastor
> [would] say, "Oh...it's your father. The Bible says you need to
> obey....we can forgive". I have forgiven my Dad...because I have to
> make that choice for me....But since age sixteen...and when I was
> forty-nine years old, I got to that point. That's a long time. [A] very
> long time. I went to [the] pastor, I went to people to listen to me.
> Every time I went to talk to somebody, honestly, they would say to
> me "You know what? You need to forgive your Dad."...Forgiveness
> is a very serious thing....A person has to go back. Like I thought,
> okay, I have conditions for forgiveness, too. Because we do. Because
> the victim is so wounded...The forgiveness happened in January
> and the man died in the end of April. And guess what? When I stood
> at the grave I was at peace with myself...we have to allow people to
> get there...[On the flight to the funeral] I wrote down all the things

that I needed to forgive him [for] even though I had said [all] that to him in January, but I felt I needed to bury that with him. So, [alone] at the graveside I would say, "Dad, I forgive you for this. I forgive for this"...And then, I would say "Thank you, God."...I was sobbing. But to get to that point [took] a very long time....[Forgiveness] is a process...It took [from age] sixteen to forty-nine.

The tenets of forgiveness and repentance underlie that of reconciliation, which Miller (1994) defines as the "making of new relationships on new terms" (p. 154). Livingston (2002) maintains that the practice of reconciliation "must be multidimensional" healing on all three levels of human relationality—the individual sphere; the inter-human sphere; and the social sphere (p. 82). Further, he states, "Reconciliation becomes false and perverted when its primary focus and goal becomes reunification, rest, or release from responsibility for one's past" (pp. 79–80).

When IPV occurs within member families, Christian leaders and congregations are faced with difficult practical and theological questions. Instances of IPV can "cause good-hearted people to choose to back away from...the issue of abuse" (Allender, 2008, p. 25). Miles (2008) notes that "leaders and laity are most often ill-prepared to deal with such a complex and repulsive issue as domestic violence" (p. 36). Women congregants are aware of these conflicting concerns, noting that by taking a redemptive stance with the abusive partner, in the

spirit of grace, the victim's experience can be minimized....I think one of the reasons that...violence is more of an issue and harder...to combat within the faith community as opposed to a secular community is because we struggle with wanting to be redemptive as opposed to [holding people accountable]. So [the question becomes] where's the role of redemption and grace for the offender in accountability? So that's why I think when an issue comes up and you maybe know the family, you're scared to put into action...the processes, follow-up that would be justified and that someone outside the church would basically...have no problems [with], knowing what they did was wrong. Christians [minimize the abuser's behaviour]....It's not that you want to spare [the abuser] the consequences, but you [question] that if it goes down this road is there any hope for redemption? [Will the hope for change be lost]...so you enable...the abuser...?

[As a result] victims...may be made to feel like further victims by the church because we're afraid to...validate what they're saying because to really validate someone, you have to call out the offender and call what it is what it is. But we want to...have that spirit of grace for the offender.

Kroeger and Nason-Clark (2001) see the need for Christian leaders not only to increase their awareness of IPV but to grapple with some of the theological questions that arise because of it:

The biblical paradigm is not to conceal abuse but to deal with it... The difficulty arises not because we wish to ignore evil but because we do not know how to deal with domestic abuse biblically. Often we find it easier to deny, ignore, silence or minimize than to address the reality. (p. 120)

"Love says, I love you enough that I'm going to tell you the truth." The church is not being loving or redemptive if it opts to avoid the truth of abuse in favour of not "hurting [the person's] feelings...[or] offending this pillar of the community" (Research participant).

## Jewish Context

Judaism encompasses the religion, race, and culture, with deep historical roots, of the Jewish people. It comprises a number of denominations that variously put emphasis on the importance of culture, religious practice, history, and inter-action with non-Jewish society: Reform—the least traditional with emphasis on culture and spirituality; Conservative—with emphasis on culture, practice, and history; and Orthodox—the most traditional in terms of historical practice. This latter grouping, which encompasses many subdivisions, seeks to live according to Jewish law with a focus on spirituality, practice, and history. Describing Orthodox Judaism, Grodner and Sweifach (2004) state that

the most fundamental value of all Orthodox Jews is belief in the Torah. [Its Commandments] govern a person's relationship with God and fellow human beings. These Commandments determine aspects of daily living, including marriage, divorce, family relationships, sexual behavior, charity and observance of the Sabbath, holidays and dietary laws. (p. 308)

Russian Jewish immigrants comprise a separate group within the Jewish community. Within the context of Soviet Russia, they were forbidden to practice their religion and suffered persecution as a result of their ethnic identity. Hence, they are not grounded in Jewish culture, history, and religious observance.

Marriage and family hold a special significance within Jewish law and culture. This is particularly true for Orthodox believers who hold marriage as one of life's most important milestones (Grodner & Sweifach, 2004). The marriage relationship is entered into voluntarily, is sanctioned through ritual, and is an expression of holiness. A premarital agreement "specifies the husband's responsibility to the wife including what he must provide should he divorce her" (DeVoe et al., 2001, p. 25).

The importance of family is also seen in the concept of *Shalom Bayit*. One of the essential functions of Jewish law is "to guide and enhance marital and family relations in the pursuit of *Shalom Bayit* [which is] supported by both scriptural and rabbinic law" (DeVoe et al., 2001, p. 25). The importance and practice of *Shalom Bayit* is held up as the ideal for Jewish families, regardless of denominational affiliation or level of observance. The significance and value placed on achieving this ideal, Grodner and Sweifach (2004) conclude, "perpetuate the myth that Jewish domestic abuse does not exist" (pp. 309–310). It falls to the wife to ensure peace in the home: "Unfortunately, as Jewish women, we are raised [to accept responsibility] for Shalom Bayit...that it's really our responsibility to keep the family together and the home together." When IPV is present in the home, this becomes, not only an unrealistic expectation but one that causes emotional angst: "And, so that is part of the whole feeling of failure. You know, what could I have done differently?...because my house is falling apart..." "[Family] violence [is]...a very closeted conversation, very private. [T]here is a sense of stigma...and ownership of responsibility..." "[T]here is that sense that maybe I did something wrong in this relationship...maybe I brought it on..." (Research participant).

Given the strong emphasis on marriage and family harmony, it is not surprising that divorce, although allowed, is discouraged:

A strong network of customs and religious law determines the validity of a divorce...In addition to a civil decree, an observant Jewish wife wishing to divorce must obtain a religious decree

or *gett*....Only a husband may initiate a divorce. (DeVoe et al.,
2001, p. 26)

Although the wife can petition the rabbinical court, the husband can refuse his
wife a *gett*, leaving her in a position of no longer being with her husband but also
not free to remarry. Without status, she becomes

> an outcast without a role in the Jewish community. If she
> re-marries without a *gett*, she is committing adultery and
> children from this union will be...illegitimate and prohibited
> from marrying into the Jewish community for ten generations....
> In the context of domestic violence, withholding the *gett* can be
> used by men as leverage, to secure a better settlement or custody,
> or even as blackmail, to obtain money and/or assets in exchange
> for the *gett*. Observant Jewish women are thus increasingly
> vulnerable, left with the choices of staying in an abusive situation,
> becoming an *agunah* (a woman chained but no longer married to
> her husband and an outcast without a role in the Jewish commu-
> nity), or acquiescing to the demands husbands make in exchange
> for the *gett*. (DeVoe et al., 2001, p. 27)

The difficulty in obtaining a religious divorce and the consequences that
may come from initiating a petition before a rabbinic court weigh heavily on
women: "I think a lot of those problems [consequences of disclosing abuse]
stem from some of the...traditions we have, and rituals and laws [regarding]
the divorce system and the gett" (Research participant).

Within the Canadian context, both federal legislation and the Supreme
Court have addressed the concern of Jewish women whose husbands refuse to
consent to a religious divorce. A 1990 amendment to the Divorce Act (1985,
c. 3, s. 21.1) allows the court to take into account any existing barriers hindering
one spouse from remarrying within his/her religion, the removal of which are in
the control of the other spouse. Where such barriers exist and the other spouse
has refused to give his/her consent to a religious divorce, the court can deny the
application for a civil divorce. In her assessment of the effect of this amendment,
Joseph (2008) notes that "this legislation has been enormously successful...

Its mere existence has reduced the use of extortion in gett cases and avoided many long years of waiting for many women....In effect the gett is the mere voiding of a previously entered into contract" (p. 3).

In 2007 the Supreme Court of Canada ruled that a contract dealing with a religious matter is [legally] enforceable provided it has been entered into voluntarily and its object is not prohibited by law or contrary to public order (Moon, 2008). Underlying this judgment, the Court took into account Canadian public policy of gender equality and freedom of choice in marriage. "Underlying [the Court's decision] is a desire to mitigate the harshness of the divorce rules of the Jewish community and a belief that religious community members may sometimes require legal protection from the rules and practices of their community" (Moon, 2008, p. 40). Speaking to the importance of this judgment, Joseph (2008) states, "The court's decision guarantees the obligatory and legal nature of signed contracts. There is no wiggle room in a contract even if the object is a religious item as long as the court is not asked to enter into determining religious value or meaning" (p. 7).

The strong religious beliefs and cultural norms regarding marriage and family influence the community's recognition of IPV and its response to it. Speaking from the perspective of a religious leader, Pesner (2006) comments that

> the great challenge we face in confronting the truth about domestic violence in our own community—among our neighbors and coworkers, among people sitting among us at the High Holidays—is that the majority who have never experienced abuse directly have no idea how widespread and devastating it is. (p. 90)

Similarly, Kivel (2002) identifies

> much denial within the Jewish community [and, even when there is acknowledgement on an abstract level, in] practice, however, when it comes to men we know or know of, many of us inadvertently find ourselves denying, minimizing, or colluding with perpetrators of abuse and withholding support and resources for survivors. (pp. 6–7)

This opinion is shared by women members of the community: "The impression [within] the Jewish community is that...violence doesn't exist. [For victims] it would be...difficult to come out and say it out loud because the impression of the Jewish family is that the family is always strong..." "I think that in the Jewish community, we are all into family and we forget the violence...I think we just don't want to admit it is happening. [It's not a] politically correct [issue]."

But they also worry about the potential consequences of reaching out for help: "Consequences come in many forms...Would the consequences fall against your own family, your extended family, other friends? Would it jeopardize your other relationships, would it jeopardize your employment, would it jeopardize your career, would it jeopardize your children?...I think that all those factors would add up to decisions to make a phone call and where the phone call would go." "With my experience within the Jewish community, I feel like it's such a small community and information about people travels so quickly around the community that people are maybe afraid of coming out in the community.... [T]hey're afraid that even though things are anonymous or that there's confidentiality, that still...somehow it will get around to everyone else."

Kivel (2002) outlines a number of preventive and practical ways Jewish men can begin to address domestic abuse within their communities: by examining their own behaviour to ensure it is nonabusive; by challenging other men when they act abusively; by applying social justice to interpersonal relationships; by modelling and teaching boys and young men nonabusive ways to be men; and by becoming actively involved in addressing the issue of family violence within the Jewish community. Judaism, he notes, has a long history of "drawing on alternative versions of masculinity which are not based on...domination and violent norms...These alternative masculinities have valued learning, critical thinking, caring, concern for justice, and sensitivity to the needs of the community" (p. 12).

## Khmer Canadian Context

The Khmer Canadian ethno-cultural community is founded on refugees of the Khmer Rouge genocide that devastated Cambodia from 1975 to 1979. They arrived in Canada after, for most, spending years in refugee camps. Many came with only their hope for a better future for their children. Their culture and Buddhist faith are closely interwoven. In addition, the immigration experience, the traumatic effects of genocide, and the interplay between these factors and their current socio-economic circumstances provide the context for understanding the IPV experience of Khmer Canadian women (Bhuyan et al., 2005; Yoshihama, 2001).

Cultural and community norms place emphases on male privilege, family values, and the division between public and private relations influences how IPV is experienced, viewed, and addressed within the Khmer community. The value of male privilege is reflected in how women describe their roles as wives: being obedient and respectful toward their husbands; maintaining harmony in social relations; and supporting their husband's sexual entitlement over themselves. Discussing this gender-based double standard, Khmer women describe Cambodian society as allowing "men to do as they please while women must follow strict guidelines for their behaviour...that community attitudes are based on the belief that the husband is the head of the household and women are 'below them'" (Bhuyan et al., 2005, p. 910).

The family is valued, with a corresponding unacceptability of divorce. Bhuyan et al. (2005) report

a strong value on keeping the family together, and divorce...
detrimental to the family and the children. In addition, domestic violence is often viewed as the woman's fault, such that divorced women are viewed with disapproval in the community. (p. 909)

Chung (2001) expands on this element of disapproval, noting that "women who are widowed, separated, and divorced are [perceived as] a threat to one's husband" (p. 119) and are at risk of being rejected by their community and culturally alienated.

Although the customary support systems include family, community, and spiritual leaders, there is also a social norm to keep family problems within the family (Chung, 2001). Bhuyan et al. (2005) also note this public-private division in Khmer social practices. Many of their research participants reported they "would not ask for help or let outsiders help and that talking about your problems with others is at odds with Khmer customs. [To share one's personal and/or family problems with another is to] risk disapproval from others" (p. 913).

These authors further report that without a cultural concept of a developed social service system as is common in Western societies, women have traditionally relied upon family members for help, often being advised to remain in their abusive relationships. Without supports to leave abusive husbands, they relied upon their personal coping skills to get along with their partners: discouraging sad thoughts, talking softly to someone who is violent, doing nothing, being patient, and exercising endurance. These coping skills are also taught within the Buddhist faith, which places emphasis on peacefulness. Additionally, there is fear of being labelled mentally ill, something which is highly stigmatizing and considered as a genetic defect (Chung, 2001).

Both the Khmer Canadian and the Jewish communities have histories of politically initiated genocide and related trauma. Although the Khmer Rouge-initiated genocide is more recent, the long-lasting effects of these traumas continue to be felt by those directly affected, their immediate and extended families, and their communities.

Jewish survivors of the Holocaust experienced persecution and endemic death threats; confinement in ghettos; forced labour and incarceration in concentration camps; living in hiding or under false identities; becoming refugees who left families behind; fighting with partisans; and being sent away on trains to death camps. Children witnessed massive death and destruction; loss of family, friends, home, belongings, and deprivation of the security of childhood; exposure to prolonged and repeated horrors; enduring continuous threats; starvation and humiliation; dehumanization and torture; surviving in hiding, often under assumed identities, in perpetual fear of discovery or betrayal; living in isolation and/or confinement in small and dark places; and for some, abuse by those who were supposed to protect them (Kellerman, 2000; Cohen, Dekel, Solomon, & Lavie, 2003).

Similarly, during and following the Khmer Rouge regime, Cambodians experienced the loss of 20% to 40% of the country's population (an estimated 1.5 to 3 million people) through execution, illness, and/or starvation; forced labour camps or collective farms; brainwashing; physical and sexual violence; threatened asphyxiation; incarceration; re-education camps; witness to killing and torture; exposure to bombing; viewing corpses; and harassment. An estimated two thirds of survivors lost at least one close relative; one third were political prisoners; and one third were assaulted. Children were brutalized, recruited as child soldiers, spies, or formed into an armed national police force. Intellectuals, the educated, and community and religious leaders were targeted for execution. To avoid death or punishment, many developed a survival technique of acting as if they were "deaf, dumb, foolish, confused or stupid, and learned to obey orders obediently without asking questions or complaining" (Chung, 2001, p. 17). Approximately 750,000 fled to refugee camps where they faced ongoing threats and violence; inadequate, unsanitary, and disease-ridden conditions; malnutrition, overcrowding, and lawlessness. Whether in Cambodia or in refugee camps, women were particularly vulnerable with an estimated 95% experiencing rape. Many lost spouses and children (Blair, 2000; Berthold, 2000; Bhuyan et al., 2005; Chung, 2000; Hinton et al., 2005, 2006; Sack, Clark, & Seeley, 1996).

The long-term effects of these traumatic events are profound and are generally subsumed under the category of post-traumatic stress disorder. These effects are evident in both Holocaust and Khmer Rouge survivors. Speaking of Jewish survivors, Kellerman (2001) identified 10 of the most frequently experienced characteristics of trauma: massive repression, numbing of responsiveness, amnesia, and alexithymia; intrusive memories; anhedonia, suicide ideation, depression, and chronic state of mourning; survivor guilt; sleep disturbances and nightmares; problems with anger regulation and in dealing with interpersonal conflicts; excessive worries, catastrophic expectancy, and fear of renewed persecution; suspicion, paranoia, isolation from the community, lack of trust and loneliness; use of survival strategies "from there"; and low threshold for stress in difficult situations (Kellerman, 2001; Schmotkin & Blumstein, 2003).

Studies of Cambodian refugees draw similar conclusions as to the long-term effects of horrors suffered, including high rates of PTSD symptomatology and panic disorders. Some researchers (Berthold, 2000; Sack et al., 1996) report the level of PTSD symptoms in young people who, as children, experienced the Cambodian genocide and/or refugee camps and subsequent resettlement to be comparable with that exhibited by combat veterans. Hinton et al. (2006) note that "given the approximately 30 year elapse between the Cambodian holocaust and the present evaluation, the persistence of PTSD-related symptoms in Cambodian refugees...is noteworthy" (pp. 407–408).

These authors identify a number of possible reasons for these long-lasting effects: the extent of the trauma experienced over a number of years;

the persistent nature of PTSD, even with treatment; the high rates of anxiety and panic disorders experienced; catastrophic cognitions about somatic arousal symptoms that may perpetuate distress; the stresses of resettlement and adaptation to a new cultural context; and continued struggles with poverty, financial worries, and urban violence. Khmer immigrants to the United States are identified as having "a far greater mental health burden compared to other US-born and immigrant Asian Americans" (Marshall et al., 2006, p. 1833). The relational implications of this level of catastrophic trauma are seen in high levels of anger and aggressive behaviour, including violence within the home (Blair, 2000; Berthold, 2006; Catani, Schaver, & Neuner, 2008; Chung, 2001; Hinton et al., 2005, 2006; Kinzie, Cheng, Tsai, & Riley, 2006; Marshall et al., 2006; Sack et al., 1996).

Most refugees were farmers with low education levels and high illiteracy rates, making resettlement into predominantly urban areas very difficult. Sack et al. (1996) summarize the losses the Cambodian people have suffered: homeland, loved ones, property, savings, cultural underpinnings, former status. "These losses are compounded by the need to resettle in a new land, learn a strange language, form new community ties, and engage in new occupations" (p. 107). As a result of the Khmer Rouge regime, the subsequent flight to refugee camps and resettlement, an entire population was traumatized; a culture destroyed, families lost, long-term psychological scarring incurred, and immigration, with its accompanying adjustment, necessitated.

## RESOURCES

Culture, belief, and community influence how and where women seek help and the informal and personal resources available to them. As such, they become contextual factors that inform our understanding of the lives of women victims and thus need to be taken into account in how services are offered and assistance provided.

## HELP-SEEKING PATTERNS

The manner in which we seek help in times of difficulty is informed by cultural norms, personal experiences, and expectations. Within the Canadian context, an array of government-sponsored and community-based resources has developed to assist citizens coping with any number of circumstances. As individual citizens we expect that services will be available and accessible as required. Service providers expect that individuals will seek help as desired and needed. For those of our society whose background and identity is rooted within a different cultural context, this concept of seeking help from services offered by "strangers" may be new and quite foreign. There may be a marked discomfiture with initiating contact with available resources within the broader community (Smith, 2004). Rather, informal networks may be accessed first, followed by more formal connections within one's cultural community. Access to mainstream resources within the broader community may be facilitated through this second-level contact (Raj & Silverman, 2007). In their work with Khmer American women, Bhuyan et al. (2005) identified a similar pattern: Access to specialized services is facilitated through referrals by neighbours, community services, and the police. Depending upon the level of awareness of IPV, the level of denial that may be prevalent, and family-related cultural norms, a victim of abuse could face significant barriers in accessing the specialized services she requires.

Additional factors that may influence how, and if, a victim accesses mainstream services include a mistrust of authority; the fear of losing their children; a lack of awareness of available services; the reluctance to discuss personal and family problems with outsiders; limited host-language proficiency; fear of their abusing partner; pressure from others to stay in the relationship; fear of losing support of family and community; dependency upon an abusive partner; not understanding the legal system, coupled by the length of time the justice system takes to address charges; fear that their partners may be mistreated by authorities if charged and incarcerated; and the fear of placing their immigration status in jeopardy or of being deported (Bhuyan et al., 2005; Menjivar & Salcido, 2002; Smith, 2004).

Christian and Jewish women with whom FaithLink worked also identified in-community networks they utilize when seeking help: spiritual leaders and/ or their spouses; other women; professionals within the community. Although women spoke of the theological and cultural issues that often make it difficult for them to leave abusive partners, they also expressed appreciation for the help and assistance they received from their spiritual leaders and religious communities. "I was lucky. [My spiritual leader] was very open to anything I said and he had both of us to contend with. And you would have never known that he was dealing [with both myself and my partner]." "He [the spiritual leader] doesn't... rush in and fix your problem. He sits and listens to you and...would say, 'If you need to just talk, call me.' I had his phone numbers...I mean I [could contact him] twenty-four hours a day. I could get hold of [him] if I needed to...and if he thought I was in danger, he would suggest to do this or to do that to make sure... I was safe..." "At one point I said to this person, 'You'll have to be my brain for me because...all I can think of is...what do I do next?' And the kids, my mortgage, my job...I was just so overwhelmed with...taking responsibility and actually taking hold of the situation....There was no way I could have handled doing that. I had no one to turn to."

They made particular note of the informal network of women helping women—the offer of nonjudgmental support, caring, trust, and direction to professional services. Investigating these networks within Christian congregations, Nason-Clark (1997) concludes, "Religious women appear to have substantial experience in offering some form of support to an abused woman and her children...practical help featured prominently in the type of support evangelical women offered one to another" (p. 119).

Some communities also have their own formal social service agencies, although some women expressed mixed feelings about accessing these, fearing the community reaction should their confidentiality not be respected. Accessing in-community resources may mean a victim is disclosing her situation to a friend or acquaintance, which brings added embarrassment. Again, when accessing individuals who may not have awareness of the dynamics of IPV, victims may not receive appropriate help in accessing specialized IPV services within the broader community.

## THE STRENGTH OF SPIRITUALITY

Research suggests that spiritual or religious beliefs and practices can be beneficial to one's general well-being and a source of strength when experiencing difficult circumstances. Summarizing research on this subject, O'Hanlon (2006) states, "Having religious or spiritual sensitivities, beliefs, or practices is generally correlated with preventive or positive effects on a wide range of mental, behavioral, emotional and relational issues" (p. 10).

Grams, Carlson, and McGeorge (2007) argue that one of the reasons for addressing spirituality within the therapeutic context is "that people often use their spiritual belief systems to make sense of events and challenges" (p. 148). Gall, Basque, Damasceno-Scott, and Vardy (2007) examined the role spiritual beliefs can play in aiding recovery from childhood sexual abuse and conclude that having "a relationship with God or a higher power can represent an important source, and perhaps the only source, of secure attachment for an individual in crisis" (p. 112). Similarly, Beaulaurier, Seff, Newman, and Dunlop (2007) found that

> spiritual beliefs were an essential part of the coping strategies for women who reported leaving abusive spouses as well as those who reported staying...Women...expressed the importance of their spiritual beliefs in finding the strength to survive in an abusive relationship as well as in finding the power to seek help. (p. 750)

These were themes echoed by women with whom FaithLink consulted as they identified their own spirituality and spiritual practices as sources of strength during difficult times and during their healing process. They spoke of one's spirit as the "essence of who we are," the core of one's being, inseparable from the rest of self and encompassing all of one's parts, that part of oneself that connects us to others and to the Divine—however divinity is perceived. They also identified the deep wounding that can occur through trauma. But it is also our spirit that "reminds us that our lives matter...when we are abused...exploited... oppressed or controlled, the spirit within us rebels [and cries for justice. The spirit] can certainly be crushed...But there is something within us that says, 'My life somehow matters, so this isn't right.'" As such, spirituality is a personal resource for coping and healing. It provided a context within which to see the experience and to find meaning "even in the most rotten of circumstances." For some this meaning is found in helping others: "But it seems to have a purpose now as opposed to just, 'Why did that have to happen?'" "I think every waking moment [when] I wasn't actually having a conversation with someone, I was praying...for guidance, for strength, for direction...And [my faith] just solidified more and more...It brought [a realization that] we have to overcome these things."

## CONCLUSION

Intimate partner violence is a complex and complicated issue. It can, and often does, take many forms, and can occur within any relationship that is based on trust and dependency. Unfortunately, it occurs with relative frequency within our society, with significant cost to those who are its direct victims, those who act abusively, and to those—often children—who are its witnesses. Often its victims are women and it is this phenomenon that is the issue addressed in this work.

But we must also understand the religious, cultural, and communal context in which women live and find their meaning. It is this web of connect-edness, norms, expectations, and potential consequences that come into play for a victim of abuse seeking help and support. We have outlined some of these for three separate religious/ethno-cultural communities: Christian, Jewish, and Khmer Canadian.

· ·

## CO-AUTHORS' COMMENTS
### From the Desk of Michael Rothery

This chapter stresses the need for ongoing dialogue between secular and religious helpers, noting these are people inclined to distrust one another. Reading this chapter, the need for these conversations is reinforced at the same time as some of the inevitable difficulties become clearer.

The opening definition of intimate partner violence is critically important, and it points to issues where dialogue should be relatively easy, as well as to matters about which there are likely to be tensions. For example, people from both the secular and religious paradigms will agree about the importance of intimate relationships and the desirability of supporting them when they are healthy. However, they may not always agree about what "healthy" means, or about how and when to respond to serious relationship problems. When and under what terms do we counsel forgiveness? When and under what circum-stances do we think separation is advisable?

When we define IPV as consisting of a range of coercive uses of power, rather than just concrete physical mistreatment, we take a very important and entirely valid conceptual step. However, we also create a need for dialogue. People from the two paradigms might agree that an equitable distribution of power between adult partners is a good thing and an appropriate goal, but they might *not*—especially if the conversation includes parties from very conservative, patriarchal traditions.

Defining terms like IPV is not at all a tedious, scholarly diversion; rather, it is a very powerful and practically important step. Once we agree about what IPV is, it becomes much more difficult to maintain the "holy hush"[2] that Chapter Three discusses at length. The suppression of information about the reality of IPV is a problem for our whole culture, of course, but can be doubly difficult in religious communities where disclosure can be seen as disloyalty or a betrayal of trust. Defining, or *naming*, abuse is therefore a critical conversation; it is also a challenge to the discussants' sensitivity and skill.

The discussion of different specific religious communities in this chapter is thought-provoking in so many ways. As Chapter One suggests, the ideologies that are an important part of membership in religious communities can be both good news and bad. One of the striking things in Faithlink's research was how aware religious women are of the frequent tensions between aspects of their faith commitments and the realities of IPV. This dialogue is therefore as critically important as it is demanding—in any conversation bridging different world views, an acute, careful attention to language will always be of paramount importance.

### From the Desk of Nancy Nason-Clark

Every week, millions of women across our country attend a house of worship—a church, synagogue, temple, or mosque. Amidst the prayers, the music, the sweet smiles, and the teaching, there is often a very ugly secret. At times, that secret is disclosed to a religious leader—together with the fear, the sense of loss, the tears, and the shame it creates. Sometimes it is whispered to another woman of faith—at a small group meeting, a mother's club, or as women work together in the kitchen during times of food and fellowship within the life of the congregation.

Is it safe for a woman to disclose the humiliation and the pain of abuse within her faith community? Will another religious follower take seriously her plight and walk alongside her as she accesses services and support? Will the leader listen to her cry for help and know what to do in its aftermath? Or will the priest, the minister, the rabbi, or the monk turn away, sweeping the pain and the story under the proverbial carpet?

For almost 25 years, I have been researching issues of domestic violence in communities of faith. Like others, I have considered the world-wide statistics—the prevalence and severity of abuse around the world. We have highlighted these by country on the resources page of our RAVE (Religion and Violence e-Learning) website, and you are welcome to look at them there (http://www.theraveproject.com/index.php/resources/resource/violence_against_women_around_the_world/).

And what is our response to the large number of women (and men) who have been victimized, the men (and women) who act abusively, and the children and other family members who witness the events and suffer on the longer term its devastating consequences? For people of faith, the journey toward healing and wholeness—and accountability and change—includes spiritual dimensions. Religious leaders need to do everything within their strength to speak out boldly and respond with compassion and best practices to all family members—the abused as well as abusers—when violence strikes at home.

So what can one religious leader or one congregation do? Without question, a difference can be made by one person and one congregation. Here are a few suggestions to consider.

- Place a brochure on abuse in every washroom in the facility where you meet (church, temple, or synagogue). Ensure that there is contact information about the local shelter or transition house, and where a woman can call if she needs a place of refuge, or if she has questions. Bathroom stalls are one of the very few confidential places to pick up information without anyone else seeing you do so.
- Choose one week during the calendar year where information on domestic violence is highlighted, as well as how a person who is abused (or an abuser) can receive help. It is important to mention how those who wish to support financially, or with in-kind donations, the work of the local women's shelter can do so.
- During the yearly program for the youth who are connected to the faith community, ensure that there is a set time to talk about abuse in dating relationships and to encourage youth who need to do so to ask for assistance if they, or someone they know, are currently engaged in an unhealthy relationship.

- Offer awareness training for the congregation's leadership team (paid staff as well as volunteers) on an annual basis. Choose someone within the community with expertise in domestic violence to help to facilitate the event.

Reducing all forms of family violence is the work of everyone in our communities, including our communities of faith. Every congregation can be a caring place— where it is safe to disclose the reality of abuse and know that you will receive both practical and spiritual support.

# Collaboration

A poet went searching one day
for the land of collaboration,

journeyed across rocky terrain
strewn with the ruins of old silos
and deserts of fortifications,

finally resting at a spring
that watered the roots of a
towering oak whose great form
danced with the parching sun.

Neck strained to see the symphony
of branches growing into the limitless sky,
the strength of many limbs and leaves
woven into an arch of promise
giving shade and joy to the weary soul below.

Musing how one small acorn had
gone into the ground and broken open its shell
to release the giant oak into the soaring heights of its true home.

he also saw dried husks of many acorns
that had not ventured beyond their shells,
whose survival strategies had become
the tomb of their original intension.

As shadows lengthened across the fields of imagination,
a truth emerged. The land of collaboration is born of sacrifice
and the continual breaking of forms and shells and separate identities
trapped in single vision.

Its work rises from an inner consciousness that sees life whole
and exults at the threshold of infinite relation.
Woven like many reeds and rushes by the bonds of mutual concern
it does nothing alone that can be done together.

This is its renewable power.

A poet went searching for the land of collaboration
and after walking to the outer limits of his mind,
fell into the ground and died.

This one small seed
entered the diverse community of energies,
surging across the web of compassion.

No land was found
outside the inscape of heart
conjoined to the many
who had been called
out of isolation and self interest
by the voice of human need.

The poet's search had found its hidden desire:
a heart of compassion
living out of abundance and congruence.
A heart perceiving life as a spacious whole,
ready to collaborate with its fullness.

—ROBERT PYNN

# 3

# FaithLink

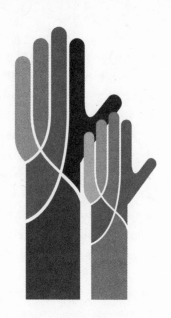

## Building Connections between the Sacral and the Secular

## INTRODUCTION

Addressing the phenomenon of intimate partner violence (IPV)—preventing its occurrence, responding to and assisting its victims, holding accountable and offering treatment to those who act abusively, and arresting its intergenerational continuance—requires a multifaceted and well-coordinated community response. Given that religious communities are affected by IPV, and that they are part of the fabric of our society, the question of whether they should—or can— be included in any broadly based community response raises both fundamental and practical questions. How can they be engaged? What role can they play? What is their level of awareness of IPV? Would their responses to victims and those who act abusively be in line with those of secular service providers? Can the differences between religious and secular perspectives be bridged? Do religious communities in fact have a role in how a secular society responds to social issues?

The FaithLink program arose from discussions aimed at mounting a coordinated community response to IPV and was charged with the task of engaging religious communities in this effort. In fulfilling its mandate, FaithLink came to the conviction that not only can religious/ethno-cultural communities[1] become part of a transdisciplinary response model but that they must. They have a critical role to play in how their communities and individual members define IPV; acknowledge and respond to its occurrence; and develop and/ or access resources. Religious leaders can make a significant contribution by taking a preventive and educative role within their communities; responding to disclosures of abuse by placing victim safety as the first priority and holding accountable the abusing partner; and offering counsel that assists victims find meaning for their experience within their belief and spiritual context.

This chapter outlines the formation and mission of the FaithLink program, and articulates its work with religious/ethno-cultural communities and service providers, its efforts to develop understanding and dialogue and research conducted. It also comments briefly on the results of an evaluation of the program's effectiveness in achieving its objectives.

## FORMATION

FaithLink developed in Calgary, Alberta, from a desire by key religious and service agency leaders to establish a coordinated, systems-wide community response to family and sexual abuse. In 1998 a planning group began the work of developing a dedicated domestic violence court for the city. The proposed model would bring together police, Crown prosecutors and defence lawyers, victim services, probation officers, and those offering treatment services to individuals who have acted abusively. The Very Reverend Robert Pynn, then rector of the Anglican Cathedral Church of the Redeemer and dean of the Anglican Diocese of Calgary, and Karen Walroth, executive director of the Action Committee Against Violence (ACAV), were key members of these discussions. They recognized that to realize the goal of a broadly based community response to IPV, the inclusion of religious communities was necessary.

Events in the next two years would lay the foundation for their vision to become a practical reality. A 1999 survey[2] identified that 16% of Calgarians would seek help from their faith/religious communities if they experienced an IPV incident. In the fall of 1999, RESOLVE Alberta[3] and the YWCA Family Violence Prevention Centre and Sheriff King Home jointly sponsored a two-day discussion forum with Dr. Nancy Nason-Clark. An internationally recognized sociologist, Nason-Clark has conducted extensive research, the findings of which confirm the reality of IPV within religious communities. Further, they suggest that by working together, religious leaders and secularly based service providers benefit from each other's expertise and can thereby augment the healing process for victims. "Religious women who are victims of abuse need the support of secular services to restore their self-esteem; to evaluate their legal, economic and familial options; and to begin to heal the pain of the past...[W]omen of faith [also] want contact and support from their religious network" (Beaman-Hall & Nason-Clark, 1997, pp. 193–194).

To explore the question of how religious leaders could be engaged, a small committee was formed and therein FaithLink was born. One of its first initiatives was to sponsor, in April 2000, a workshop that brought religious leaders and service providers together to discuss the possibilities of working together. This weekend event was sponsored by the Anglican Cathedral Church of the Redeemer and was facilitated by Drs. Nancy Nason-Clark and Lori Beaman. Through presentations and discussions, recommendations emerged that formed the foundation for a long-term initiative whose aim it was to build bridges between religious communities and secularly based IPV servicing agencies. The work of FaithLink was beginning to take shape.

Over the next two years, this small, but growing, volunteer committee realized significant achievements, including

- expanding its membership to include representatives from both religious communities and secularly based service providers;
- choosing of a name—*FaithLink*—to reflect the mission of the work;
- beginning the work of developing a generic response protocol for religious communities;
- publishing and distributing among religious communities a brochure that included quick references for responding to disclosures of abuse; and
- sponsoring two training workshops, with Dr. Nason-Clark as the presenter, for both. One brought religious leaders and service providers together to begin a dialogue aimed at increasing mutual understanding; the second specifically targeted counsel for couples planning to marry.

## TAKING MORE FORMAL STEPS

As the work of FaithLink continued to evolve, the original committee took on the more formal responsibility of a steering committee. Its membership included representatives of, and members from, various constituencies: religious leaders from Christian, Jewish, and Buddhist traditions; members from the Khmer

Canadian, Ismaili, and Hindu communities; representatives from women's emergency and long-term shelters, counselling and IPV intervention services, the Faculty of Social Work at the University of Calgary; and interested individuals. This committee articulated a mission statement: "Spiritual/religious communities and service providers working together to prevent domestic violence and to provide healing and hope to all those affected by it." The term "spiritual/ religious communities" was intended to be interpreted broadly to include a wide variety of religious traditions and spiritually based groups. (As more such communities became involved in the project, it became evident that "religion" and "culture" are inseparably intertwined. Thus, the use of the term "religious/ ethno-cultural" communities became part of FaithLink nomenclature.) In fashioning its mission statement, the focus was placed on the issue of intimate partner violence; it was not on changing religious doctrine.

Five interlocking focus areas gave a practical framework to the mission:

- with religious communities, to raise awareness of the issue of IPV and enhance response capacity;
- with secularly based service providers, to raise awareness of the importance spirituality holds for women of faith who access their services;
- to build collaborative working relationships between religious/ethno-cultural leaders and service providers;
- in recognition of the effects of vicarious trauma, to offer to those who are first responders to traumatized individuals opportunities to enhance their self-care; and
- to conduct relevant research that explores the interface between the religious and the secular regarding IPV.

As the work developed and broadened, it became evident that it could not be sustained through volunteers alone. Funding[4] was obtained and a small staff complement was employed. Robert Pynn continued to act as "advisor" to FaithLink and to cast its vision.

The work began, and continued, with Christian denominations and congregations (Roman Catholic, Anglican, Lutheran, Baptist, United, various evangelical congregations, and Bible colleges). Leaders from the Jewish, Khmer Canadian (Cambodian), and Laos Canadian communities asked FaithLink to help them address IPV in their respective communities and the work again expanded. Connections were cultivated with a number of other groups and communities within the city: University of Calgary Chaplains; a Buddhist student group at the U of C; the Church of Jesus Christ of Latter Day Saints (Mormons); Hindu community leaders; officials, programs, groups, and individuals within Ismaili and Sunni Muslim constituencies; and a Sikh men's group.

FaithLink also engendered provincial, national, and international interest. Its work has being presented at an international conference and its resources accessed from groups across the country. Notwithstanding this recognition, the program remained a community-based initiative.

### ACTIVITIES AND ACHIEVEMENTS
### Best Practices

Each of FaithLink's focus areas were grounded within the following best practice principles.

- As awareness of IPV increases within a given group or community, disclosures will result. Therefore the work of raising awareness within religious/ethno-cultural communities must be done in concert with enhancing the capacity to effectively respond.
- Experiencing abuse affects the whole person, including the spiritual, necessitating a multifaceted response. Given that most service providers are limited in the range of services they can provide, taking a holistic practice perspective requires collaboration across professional disciplines and across secular and religious/ethnic domains. Clients who desire spiritual support and counsel should have access to religious leaders of their own choosing who understand the dynamics of intimate partner violence and can assist victims to create meaning out of their abuse experience.
- Collaborative working relationships are built on trust and mutual respect. Secularly based professionals and religious/ethno-cultural leaders can work effectively together when there is mutual understanding and recognition of the unique contributions made by each.
- First responders to traumatized individuals are at risk of experiencing vicarious trauma. Those responding and giving support to individuals

impacted by IPV are among those at risk. Maintaining personal wellness is therefore of importance to service providers working within this sector.

· When program development and practice are grounded in empirical evidence and a broad knowledge base they are stronger and more effective. When research is grounded within the rich soil of practice the knowledge base is enhanced and deepened.

## Work with Religious/Ethno-Cultural Communities

Research confirms a number of facts: IPV is as prevalent in religious/ethno-cultural communities as it is in the general population; victimized women within these communities often remain in abusive relationships longer than their secular sisters; religious leaders are called upon to intervene in domestic disputes and in so doing they offer counsel to both victims and those who have acted abusively; and abused women report the counsel they receive from their religious leaders is often not helpful (Altfeld, 2005; Beaman-Hall & Nason-Clark, 1997; Beaulaurier et al., 2005; Bhuyan et al., 2005; DeVoe et al., 2001; Grodner & Sweifach, 2004; Javed, 2006; Kroeger & Nason-Clark, 2010; Menjivar & Salcido, 2002; Miles, 2008; Nason-Clark, 1997; Silverman, 2003).

As the work of FaithLink developed, there was increasing awareness of the interconnection between religious belief, cultural mores, and the strength of community. Calhoun et al. (1997) define culture as "the shared, more or less integrated way of thinking, understanding, evaluating and communicating that make up a people's way of life" (p. 28); religion as "a set of beliefs and practices pertaining to sacred things that unite people into moral communities" (p. 377); and community as "a population knit together by common values and interests, relatively dense and enduring ties, frequent face-to-face interactions and a sense of being close to one another" (p. 563). Although this integration is most evident within ethno-cultural communities whose identity may be marked by minority status, a traumatic historical history, or language, it is also true for those who see themselves as part of the mainstream of Canadian society but who also identify with a religious community.

For those affected by IPV, the influences exerted by culture, religion, and community have profound implications: whether to disclose the abuse, when and to whom; whether or not to leave the relationship and if or when to reconcile; how marital disputes are settled; whether secularly based resources, or those outside of one's community, are accessed; the degree of commitment given to secularly based intervention regimes; the extent to which sanctions imposed by the courts are accepted; the status of children and victims within the community should a divorce result (Beaulaurier et al., 2005; Bhuyan et al., 2005; Chung, 2001; Davies et al., 1998; DeVoe et al., 2001; Grodner & Sweifach, 2004; Joyce, 2009; Kroeger & Nason-Clark, 2010; Livingston, 2002; Ware, Levitt, & Bayer, 2003).

The strength of the cultural/religious community influence is exemplified by a woman who spoke of the difficulty of leaving her abusive marriage. She had been raised within a family and community context in which divorce was never an option ("You've made your bed, lie in it"). Though her church gave her permission to leave her abusive partner, the paradigm of her childhood remained on her internal "hard drive" and increased not only the length of time she remained in the relationship but the emotional angst in coming to the decision to eventually seek safety for herself and her children.[5]

With this realization, work undertaken by FaithLink took into account the particular belief, practice, and identity of any given group. Thus, resource persons were recruited to carry on the work within their own communities. Educational and resource materials were developed to reflect religious beliefs and cultural norms. If English was not the first language of the community, these resources were written in both English and the community's first language. Resource materials developed for congregations and/or groups reflected the organizational structure and "internal language" of any given group, e.g., the Salvation Army's use of military structure and designations.

Just as religious/ethno-cultural communities can have negative impacts, they can also play important preventive and practical roles in addressing IPV. Religious leaders have access to individuals across their life span, many of whom may be vulnerable to abuse (e.g., children, the elderly, the disabled, members of minority cultures, women and teenage girls). They are also in unique positions to speak out against, and educate about, intimate partner violence, and to make known the resources that are available within the broader community. They can raise awareness and create a culture of safety for all congregants. In so doing, they signal to victims that the abuse they may be experiencing is not condoned. Within this type of environment victims are more likely to disclose their abuse. When leaders understand the dynamics of IPV they are in a much better position to receive disclosures and to respond in ways that ensure the victim's safety and that hold accountable the abusing partner.

To assist religious and community leaders in addressing intimate partner violence, FaithLink offered assistance in a number of ways. Awareness of the issue was raised through presentations to congregations, groups within congregations and the community, seminary students, and faith leaders. These seminars offered basic information about IPV. They were also geared to the receiving audience (e.g., Roman Catholic deacons and their wives received a presentation on the basics of IPV, plus material on premarital mentoring for their work with soon-to-be married couples; presentations to the Khmer Canadian community were translated to ensure both understanding and cultural appropriateness). Presentations were offered on dating violence and "Raising Safe Kids"—an informational presentation for parents on how to raise children who are safe toward others and safe from the violence of others. Care was taken to insure every presentation was age-appropriate and theologically sensitive. (As mentioned previously, the mandate of FaithLink was to educate about IPV, not to change foundational religious tenets.) "This class has saved me from a lot of mistakes in ministry!" was the comment of one seminary student after hearing a presentation about IPV and boundaries in ministry.

FaithLink developed and distributed informational, education, and resource-based materials for faith communities. A comprehensive manual— *Hope and Healing: Domestic Violence Resources for the Church* (2004–2007)—was made available to Christian congregations in Calgary. This resource has also been accessed by individual congregations from the Canadian west coast to its eastern shores. A portion of this manual was translated into Khmer for use by the Khmer Canadian community (entitled *Planting Peace in Families*). A similar resource, specifically for the Jewish context, was purchased and made available to that community. Brochures, providing basic information about IPV, available resources, and help-line telephone numbers were developed for the Jewish, Christian, Khmer, and Laos Canadian communities within Calgary. As with resource manuals, pamphlets designed for communities whose first language is not English were always done bilingually. Similarly, when resources were developed for specific congregations, care was taken to ensure the language and presentation was appropriately sensitive. When translation work was required, such as with the Khmer and Laos materials, great pains were taken to insure that the information in these respective languages accurately reflected the concepts presented. This work was both labour-intensive and costly.

Raising awareness, however, is only a first step as it inevitably leads to increased numbers of disclosures of abuse. Attention must therefore be given to how religious and community leaders respond when receiving disclosures. Building response capacity was therefore necessary. For Christian congregations and/or denominations, FaithLink developed a generic response protocol, adapted it to the structure and internal culture of individual groups, and offered training in its application to religious leaders and ministry volunteers. Within the Jewish community, training was offered to religious and community leaders utilizing a protocol developed by Jewish Women International. The *Planting Peace in Families* resource manual served as a curriculum base for the training of a group of Khmer Canadian women who expressed a desire to act as resource and support persons within their community.

As connections between FaithLink staff members and religious/ethno-community leaders developed, so, too, did opportunities to build further connections. Staff members offered support to leaders dealing with abuse situations. When disclosures were received following presentations, FaithLink staff members were able to connect those individuals with appropriate resources within their own, or the broader, community. Staff members also acted as liaisons between religious leaders and service providers, facilitating introductions, identifying specific resource persons, and arranging for tours of shelters. Awareness raising and the provision of helpful resources helped break the *holy hush* by openly naming and describing what is a reality in every faith group. Building capacity within religious congregations and ethno-cultural communities to respond to IPV not only assists those directly affected, it acts to engage these leaders in the broader community's multifaceted response to IPV.

## Work with Secularly Based Service Providers

There is well-documented evidence that experiencing violence at the hands of an intimate partner impacts one's physical, mental, and emotional well-being. More recently, research is adding to our understanding the effects IPV has on the spirit as well. Experiencing IPV strikes at the very core of one's being, impacting self-identity and what one holds as sacred and just. It raises questions of belief (e.g., the value of suffering, of forgiveness, and how justice is appropriated). The result is spiritual injury, disrupting personal spiritual development, hindering trust in religious tenets, and reducing involvement in religious practices (Barrett, 1999; Gall et al., 2007; McKernan, 2004; Nason-Clark, 1997).

That IPV negatively impacts the spirit is not surprising. Belief systems frame life with meaning and guidance. Quoting Becvar (1997), Grams et al. (2007) note that spirituality "directs our attention to some of the most basic existential issues: to the meaning and purpose of life and to creating a reality that is supportive of the best interests and highest good of the soul, both of the individual and the world" (p. 150). Not only is this true for those who are members of communities in which religious beliefs and cultural norms are closely woven into the practicalities of daily life (Hodge, 2008; Hodge & Nadir, 2008; Kiyoshk, 2003), it is also true for the general population. A survey by Ipsos-Reid (2003) found that the majority of Canadians, regardless of adherence to, or practice of, particular religious beliefs, identify a sense of spirituality that infuses their lives with meaning.

Thus, when IPV occurs, issues of the spirit—the search to understand, to heal, and/or to modify one's spiritual perspective—can become central for both persons directly affected by the abuse and for those offering counsel. Addressing these issues, however, can present challenges for counsellors trained within a secular, humanistic frame of reference. FaithLink sought, in several ways, to assist service providers to acknowledge and validate their clients' spiritual dimension. First, the program offered workshops to assist counsellors to be more aware of their own spiritual journey, and thus more comfortable in raising spiritual issues with their clients. These workshops provided sound clinical evidence to service providers of why they need to be aware of their own spiritual perspectives, and of the need to be sensitive to the spiritual needs/paradigms of their clients. As a part of this workshop, participants were asked to reflect upon the impact their own experiences have had upon their spirits. For some participants this particular part of the workshop was difficult given their own experiences of trauma. This type of response from caregivers reinforces the depth to which trauma impacts one's spirit, even many years after the event. It also highlights the necessity for "wounded healers"[6] to experience a significant degree of healing within their own souls, as well as to receive ongoing support in the difficult work they do. Workshop participants expressed their appreciation for being "sensitized" to the importance of the spiritual; others reflected on learning new and unexpected aspects about themselves.[7]

To validate, for victims, that abuse impacts the spirit and advise them that spiritual counsel was available, FaithLink developed and distributed a brochure to women's shelters. *Spiritual Support for Victims of Domestic Violence* was written to victims, and stated, "All abuse is spiritual abuse!" It described the impact of abuse upon the spirit, spoke of the power of spirituality to aid in one's healing process, and made clear that spiritual help was available. To this end, FaithLink provided service providers with a list of spiritual leaders within Calgary who understood IPV and would accept referrals from, and work with, secularly based professionals. These spiritual leaders were from Christian, Jewish, Muslim, and Buddhist traditions. A variety of denominations/sectors within each faith tradition were represented. When a woman in a shelter indicated a desire for spiritual support, she could select a spiritual counsellor of her choosing.

Not only was it necessary for secularly based service providers to understand the importance of the spiritual for some of their clients, for client to know that spiritual counsel resources were available, and for those resources to be knowledgeable about the dynamics of IPV, it was also necessary for the secular and religious counsellors to work together. To facilitate these working relationships, FaithLink periodically sponsored luncheons during which service providers and religious leaders could discuss how they could better work together in providing a holistic approach to mutual clients. At one such luncheon, the religious leaders asked for a copy of the list of their colleagues who were accepting referrals from service providers on behalf of victimized women. As Calgary is a multicultural and multifaith city, and as religious leaders encounter violated people of many faiths, they asked for names of leaders from other traditions to whom they, too, could refer victims. This was consistent with the philosophy of FaithLink—to offer victims religious/spiritual support from their tradition—and the list was made available. Program staff members were also asked by secularly based service providers for relevant research regarding the impact of spiritual abuse on children.

## Building Bridges of Understanding and Collaboration

There is often limited trust between religious leaders and secularly based service providers. There are many reasons for mistrust. Religious leaders fear women who access secular services will be counselled to divorce their abusing partners; service providers fear religious leaders will place a higher priority on "saving the marriage" than on the safety of victims (Kroeger & Nason-Clark, 2010; Miles, 2008; Nason-Clark, 1997). Religious leaders express frustration at not having access to women from their communities who enter emergency shelters. Although there may be many reasons for limiting access, religious leaders may assume it is primarily because of who they are and the bias service providers hold toward them (Rothery et al., 2005).[8] Religious women, however, often desire continued connections with their faith communities and the available supports these can offer. They desire spiritual counsel that helps put their experi-ence within the context of their belief paradigm. But they also require that the dynamics of their situations be understood and precautions taken to ensure their safety and that of their children (Giesbrecht & Sevcik, 2000; Grams et al., 2007; Hodge, 2005; O'Hanlon, 2006).

Intimate partner violence involves very complex dynamics and carries with it an inherent lethality. Although they are often called upon in instances of IPV, religious leaders—and their communities—cannot, on their own, respond adequately to these situations (Nason-Clark, 1997). Effective responses call for grounding within the significant body of knowledge and expertise that has developed over years of study and experience and applied through a network of social, judicial, and legal services (e.g., policing, legal counsel, justice services, emergency and long-term shelters, counselling, housing, financial support, and child custody). These services are predominantly secular in orientation and may not take into account the spiritual dimension of the individuals directly affected by IPV.

In the interest of those who are most directly affected by IPV (the victims, those who have acted abusively, and child witnesses), FaithLink sought to bring together the rich resources that are represented by both religious communities and secularly based service providers. It did this through spon-sored conferences and workshops that provided opportunities for participants to learn from each other; discuss issues of mutual interest; and address areas of concern. Each event featured recognized religious, academic, and/or service leaders as keynote speakers. Always the theme of any conference was that of IPV—understanding its dynamics, effects, the services that are available, and the question of how religious/ethno-cultural leaders and secular services can work together to respond.

One of the most interesting conferences demonstrated, through drama and a response panel, how various services within the Calgary community connect in their collaborative response to IPV. A drama presentation portrayed a Jewish family in which child sexual and wife abuse had occurred and the intervention of various services within their lives when the abuse was disclosed. An integral part of the portrayal was the involvement of their rabbi, who not only offered support and counsel but took a strong stand against the abuse, the need for safety for the victims, and accountability for the abuser. Panel members, including a police officer, a child welfare worker, a shelter worker, a victim's support worker, and a domestic violence court judge, responded to the dynamics presented by the actors. When abuse occurs, family members are faced with a myriad of issues, not the least of which are the array of services that suddenly interject themselves into their lives. The result can be feelings of being overwhelmed and of no longer being in control of one's life. Understanding the roles and expectations of the various response services can be challenging for those who work within the domestic violence-related services sector. For those desiring to offer assistance and support to victims and/or those who have acted abusively, "the system" can be confusing and frustrating. This conference was helpful for both service providers and religious leaders. As one participant noted, "As a new clergy, I'm just beginning to gather information/gain an understanding of this whole issue of domestic violence. This conference has given me a great foundation. Thank you!"[9]

Not only did the themes and content of each conference offer opportunities for learning, each event focused attention on opportunities for discussion and networking. Thus, small groups and full plenary discussions were a part of each conference. These times provided opportunities for interaction not only with the information presented but between participants. Conference breaks and lunch periods also offered opportunities for more informal intermingling and networking between religious leaders and service providers. These informal times may have been just as important in building bridges of understanding as the formal events themselves: Both religious leaders and service providers are more likely to access the unique services of the other when there are human faces attached to names and to institutions. When caring, competent people of different disciplines get together, good things happen!

## Providing Self-Care Opportunities for Service Providers

Responding to those who have experienced intimate partner violence—whether direct victims, those who have perpetrated abuse, or child witnesses of the abuse—is stressful, difficult work. It carries with it elements of crises and danger. The impact on the lives of those directly involved is evident, often through physical injury, always through emotional, psychological, and spiritual harm. For those involved in helping victims heal, the details of the abuses perpetrated against them are articulated—often repeatedly and in graphic detail. That first responders and service providers are at risk of vicarious trauma is hardly surprising.

Although vicarious trauma has been recognized for more than two decades, the primary focus of research has been on the effects incurred by direct victims, not on first responders to traumatized individuals. Research that has been done on vicarious trauma experienced by counsellors working within the IPV response field is preliminary. What is clear, however, is that vicarious trauma does occur and is experienced on personal, interpersonal, and professional levels. Further, limiting its effects requires strong self-care practices, careful attention to self-monitoring, social activism, transformation of the traumatizing experience, and work environments that are supportive, flexible, and diverse (Clemens, 2004; Figley, 1995; Iliffe & Stead, 2000; Richardson, 2001; Rosenzweig, Reibel, Greeson, Brainard, & Hojat, 2003; Saakvitne & Pearlman, 1996; Way, VanDeusen, Martin, Applegate, & Jandle, 2004).

That the effects of IPV are broader than individuals and family members directly experiencing the abuse was recognized early in FaithLink's history. Thus, its mission statement expressed the desire to offer "healing and hope to all those affected by it"—including first responders. It took a unique approach to making practical this intention. Through his denominational connections, Robert Pynn was aware of the work of Dr. Cynthia Bourgeault, an Episcopal priest, Christian contemplative, Wisdom teacher, author on the spiritual life, and retreat leader and conference presenter on centred meditation. It was Robert Pynn's conviction that the practice of a centred meditation held important elements that service providers could access in reducing the impact of vicarious trauma and enhancing their personal well-being.

FaithLink sponsored three events that brought Dr. Bourgeault to the city. The first was a series of workshops, over the space of a week, for service providers, the focus of which was participant self-care. Dr. Bourgeault met with small and large groups in sessions that ranged from an hour over lunch to a full day. Her focus was to introduce participants to a centring meditation practice. Those attending ranged from front-line workers to executive directors. The very positive response from individuals and organizations initiated the second event—a one-day conference focused on the theme of collaboration. Participants included professionals working within the IPV services sector and religious leaders from a number of traditions.[10] Again, the response from conference attendees was very positive, so much so that a number of agency directors began to discuss the possibility of utilizing the practice of this form of meditation within the context of their work and agency environments. The idea of conducting a piece of research emerged and FaithLink was asked to provide leadership. Of particular interest was the effect practicing meditation would have for service providers on how they managed the stress of their work with victims of violence; the counsellor-client relationship; and the relationships between colleagues. To facilitate this examination, specific training in centred meditation was offered to research participants over a six-week period. A full accounting of this project is presented in Chapter Six. Suffice it to say here that service providers who participated in all three of these events—the workshops, the conference, and the research—reported finding the practice of meditation personally beneficial.

## Conducting Research

From its beginnings, FaithLink was committed to grounding its work in empirical evidence, practice experience, and program evaluation. Similarly, it was aware that its work was, in many ways, unique and therefore had an opportunity to contribute to the general knowledge base by conducting research. Findings from these endeavours were used to inform program development, have been presented to the professional and academic communities, and have been published.

For a newly conceived program, the amount of research it conducted within its first decade of existence is remarkable. It was fortunate to have the opportunity to join with RESOLVE Alberta and with Dr. Nason-Clark in these endeavours. The findings of three qualitative studies are presented within the context of the following chapters: with women from three religious/ethno-cultural communities regarding the issue of IPV (reported in Chapter Four);

with service providers regarding their handling of spirituality with clients for whom this is an important component of their lives (reported in Chapter Five); and with service providers regarding the efficacy of a centred meditation practice on various aspects of their work (reported in Chapter Six).

The first piece of research undertaken by FaithLink (Rothery et al., 2005) was to gauge the knowledge of, attitudes toward, and responses of Calgary-based Christian religious leaders vis-à-vis IPV. Although there had been previous research addressing these questions with evangelical Christian pastors in Atlantic Canada (Nason-Clark, 1997), it was necessary to have an understanding, within the Calgary context, of the positions held by leaders across the broader spectrum of the Christian tradition. Leaders of Christian denominations made up FaithLink's largest religious constituency. Having an understanding of how they understood the issue of IPV, the positions they held, and how they responded to it would provide important direction in how FaithLink approached its work with them. This knowledge could also serve as a baseline for gauging the impact of FaithLink's work. To these ends, a survey questionnaire was developed and mailed to 333 Christian religious leaders within the city of Calgary. Of these, 114 (34.2%) were returned.[11] This sample comprised 80% male and 29% female respondents. Their denominational affiliations fell into three main groupings: 18% Roman Catholic, 52% evangelical, and 30% mainline denominations (e.g., Anglican, United Church of Canada).

Findings arising from the survey suggested that Calgary's Christian leaders (almost 70%) were receiving disclosures of IPV from congregants. Their confidence level in responding to these disclosures, however, varied depending upon the level of training they had received: 18% identified having had "no training," and 55% identified having "some training"—the majority of whom expressed having "no" or "moderate" confidence in handling situations of IPV disclosed by congregants. Only 27% identified themselves as being "well-trained"—of which 78% expressed being "confident" in handling disclosures.

The majority of respondents held attitudes regarding IPV that are consistent with the accepted professional knowledge: prevalence of IPV within the general population and faith communities (88%); contributing factors and the exercise of power and control (68%); and the priority of victim safety over marriage preservation (73%). Limited training/awareness of the dynamics inherent within IPV relationships and theological positions appear to be significant factors influencing the attitudes of those taking minority positions. Although the majority of respondents identified taking actions within their congregations to raise awareness and/or educate about IPV, only a minority (less than 35%) referred congregants to a family violence service agency. The majority preferred to consult with other pastors or referred to counsellors within their own denominational community.

The following recommendations arising from these findings were offered.

- With Christian leaders:
    - to establish contacts and build trust;
    - to raise awareness about IPV and its relational dynamics through education and the provision of resource materials;
    - to enhance confidence in responding to disclosure through training and information about resources available within the broader community; and
    - to provide opportunities to increase comfort levels with service providers through dialogue and agency tours.
- With secularly based service agencies:
    - to raise awareness regarding the concerns and apparent lack of trust religious leaders have in accessing their services; and
    - to develop a referral list for religious leaders of service providers who would be willing to develop mutually accepting relationships, assist pastors in handling disclosures of IPV, and provide ongoing support as needed.

As is evident from the above review of FaithLink's work, the findings from this initial research project did indeed provide direction to its work.

## A BROADENING INTEREST

As the work of FaithLink gained credibility within the Calgary community, it attracted attention from other communities. In response to requests for resource materials, these were posted on the program's website and made available free of charge. Invitations were received from other communities who were interested in learning about FaithLink, with the possibility of implementing a similar initiative. FaithLink staff and resource persons met with these groups, comprising spiritual leaders and service providers, to discuss the project's development, mission, work, and the lessons learned. The organic nature of the program and the necessity for it to be well grounded within, and owned by, the community was stressed: FaithLink was not a program that could be franchised. Thus, each workshop provided opportunities for attendees to enter into discussion regarding how their particular community could utilize the ideas presented. The commitment to develop a transdisciplinary response to IPV needed to arise from within.

Interest by policy makers and the professional and academic communities resulted in formal presentations being made on both the FaithLink model and its research. Contributing chapters have been included in two books: "It's Everybody's Business" in Kroeger, Nason-Clark, and Fisher-Townsend (2008); and "Finding Their Voices and Speaking Out: Research among Women of Faith in Western Canada" in Nason-Clark, Kroeger, and Fisher-Townsend (2011).

## PROGRAM EVALUATION

FaithLink was committed from its inception to building an evaluative component into its practice. By critically examining its work and achievements, FaithLink sought to inform its decision-making process; examine the effectiveness of its services and the efficiency with which they were provided; identify areas of strength and weakness needing correction; be accountable to funding bodies, constituents, and the community; and add to the extent to which it and similar work could be evidence-based (Pietrzak, Ramler, Renner, Ford, & Gilbert, 1990). To this end, in the spring of 2006, FaithLink contracted with RESOLVE Alberta to do an independent evaluation of its goals and methods. A qualitative methodology, coupled with access to supplementary resource material, was undertaken.

The resulting report (Sevcik & Rothery, 2007) spoke to the program's acceptance within the broader community, and the need for it to continue to expand its work. The report identified FaithLink as a credible, integral part of the family and sexual violence services sector of Calgary, and that it was seen as a significant resource by religious and ethno-cultural leaders. The evaluation noted the strength inherent in taking a flexible but measured approach to needs as they arise and responding to opportunities as they are presented. Individuals interviewed by the evaluators recognized that the task FaithLink had set for itself was daunting and complex. They offered their encouragement to carry on and extend the work, building on the successes already achieved and lessons learned in the process. The evaluation report offered a number of recommendations.

- To maintain the momentum regarding the priority foci of the program but to be careful to not overextend the available resources if that meant the services currently offered would suffer from being stretched too thin.
- To continue to ground the work in best practice principles, enhanced by ongoing research to ensure the program developed in response to reliable information about what needs were paramount and what interventions were effective.
- To continue to disseminate the well-researched and documented information about how the work impacted the Calgary community and to share this information with other jurisdictions.
- To exercise care in responding to the pressures to respond to the need for program services. Those interviewed noted that the program could not attempt to fill the entire need for its services: It could only responsibly expand as resources and opportunities allowed. Relationships with new religious/ethno-cultural communities should only be cultivated when it was clear that the interest was strong and that the program had access to appropriate staff and volunteer resources.
- To consider the growing Buddhist communities within the city as the next focus of expansion, resources permitting. Through the program's then-current work within the Khmer Canadian community, networks and opportunities with other Buddhist groups would present themselves.
- That fundraising would continue to be a time-consuming task.

## CONCLUSION

The FaithLink initiative grew out of the realization and conviction that for a community to implement a multiservices response to intimate partner violence the active involvement of religious/ethno-cultural communities was necessary. To this end, a committee, comprising secularly based service representatives and religious leaders, began the work of making practical this concept. Over the ensuing 10 years, the FaithLink program took shape and effected significant achievements in realizing its mission and mandate. Its work demon-strated that religious/ethno-cultural communities can be engaged with secularly based service providers in addressing IPV. In so doing, it also demonstrated that religious communities do, in fact, have a role in how a secular society responds to social issues. The reality is that those who espouse a religious perspective, and who experience abuse, need not have to choose between remaining, often silent, within their religious/ethno-cultural communities and accessing secularly based services. With awareness, education, trust, and commitment from secular and religious/ethnic leaders, deep resources can be made accessible to victims, to child witnesses, and to those who act abusively within their intimate relationships.

.. 

## CO-AUTHORS' COMMENTS
### From the Desk of Michael Rothery

The keynote speaker at a conference several years ago was the woman who had spearheaded the development of a children's festival in the community where I live. The festival flourished, and she recounted being asked by someone from another city how to replicate her success. Her response: "Give the job to a crazy person who never accepts '*no*' for an answer."

This chapter is a rich narrative detailing things done: tasks, interventions, and strategies employed in the service of Faithlink's goals. At another more important level, it is a story about people with powerful commitments and seemingly boundless energy.

A question behind this exhausting account is: "How does change happen?" As with most, if not all, social service sectors, services targeting IPV have been affected by the hope that successful programs can be understood operationally, and replicated. Thus, strategies for change become manualized, in the expectation that what works to effect change at one time and place can be transplanted elsewhere with similar outcomes.

Bringing secular and spiritual helpers together and inviting them to collaborate, while responding to an issue as complicated as IPV, is enormously complex. One size will never fit all, and what works for a North American Jewish community may not work (or may work differently) with refugees from the Cambodian holocaust.

To be sure, we have much to learn by reading about each other's experiences, and it is safe to generalize about the importance of any number of basic goals and issues. Obvious examples include the importance of network building; the need for public education and consciousness raising; and the desirability of multiple creative interventions, rather than limited, prescribed approaches. That said, the dynamic complexities of spiritual and professional cultures and the uniqueness of families will necessarily render manualized approaches unconvincing. We will need to rely instead on the creativity of highly committed and energetic people, well supported and with ample room to innovate.

## From the Desk of Nancy Nason-Clark

After my first trip to Calgary to meet the people who would form the FaithLink initiative, I was hooked. They were enthusiastic. They understood abuse. They were people of faith. They had a plan. And, as this chapter spells out, they put their plan into action. It is a story of courage and of vision. The road was sometimes fraught with obstacles, but this tenacious group was not to be deterred. The result was success!

I contributed a chapter for a book on religious pluralism that I entitled "Enlarging the Sandbox: Thinking about Cooperation and Collaboration between Diverse Religious and Secular Community Responses to Domestic Violence." Here I argued that many religious people look first to their communities of faith when crisis happens—especially crisis that occurs within the context of family living. Whether a woman or man is assisted first by their congregation, or through a community-based agency, it is imperative that those who are first responders to domestic violence understand both the dynamics of religious faith and the persistence and impact of abuse. Offering practical and emotional assistance without reference to the journey of faith can jeopardize a religious woman's resolve to seek safety and solace in the aftermath of domestic violence. Offering spiritual support without reference to the practical and emotional assistance she will need to ensure her safety can jeopardize a religious woman's life. The stakes are high.

In Calgary, FaithLink helped to enlarge the sandbox. It worked side-by-side with women and men employed in agencies and those within religious communities. It offered support and information; it provided referral advice. It augmented a community-coordinated response to domestic violence through raising awareness and naming best practices. It was, and continues to be, a model to be replicated across the country and beyond. The challenge to religious leaders offered by FaithLink is to take seriously the prevalence and severity of abuse and its long-term impact on survivors and those who perpetrate abusive acts. Its challenge to workers in secular agencies is to take religious faith seriously—a critical part of living in a religiously and culturally pluralistic Canada. But saying the words is a lot easier than putting them into practice.

## CHAPTER RESPONDERS
### Bev Sheckter, R.S.W., Executive Director, Jewish Family Services, Calgary, AB (retired)

I became involved in FaithLink because I am executive director of Jewish Family Service Calgary and recognized the importance of our agency being involved in building awareness of IPV in the Jewish community. I would describe myself as both a service provider and a member of a religious community. I would also say that as a member of the Jewish community, I was raised in an egalitarian home, although traditionally Jewish, and was in denial when it came to accepting intimate partner violence. Becoming better educated on the subject, through FaithLink's many training opportunities, attending a conference offered by Jewish Women International (JWI), and meeting women who have experienced IPV has helped me develop more insight into the subject.

We have had mixed responses by our religious leaders when approached about the subject of family violence. Mostly it has been supportive and two of our rabbis have delivered sermons about the issue. We have also had our most orthodox clergy attempt to solve the problem, although not qualified to do so, and this has actually put some families in danger. For the most part there is a level of trust and the recognition of what each can provide in order to benefit the members of our community. The agency's professionals are very practical about what a woman needs to do to leave an abusive relationship and we always include the idea of the client seeking spiritual guidance from their religious leader. The majority of our counselling clients are not Jewish, so we would encourage them to see their own faith leader.

Jewish Family Service Calgary took responsibility for bringing the issue of IPV to the Jewish community. FaithLink had developed some materials and others we took from JWI, and, with those, we began a publicity campaign. We met with each of the rabbis, we published articles in the *Jewish Free Press*, and then we started a program called *Shalom Bayit*, meaning peace in the home. FaithLink believed that someone who understood the community would best be able to reach the community and this has proven to be accurate. As we have advertised the program, we have been able to access additional funding from the Jewish community and more women are identifying as being at risk. We also go into the schools to teach children about bullying, and facilitate another program in the schools that teaches children about sexual abuse.

We believe that we have developed a preventative program, although some of it is, unfortunately, reacting to women's circumstances as well. Next we plan to have a speakers' series focusing on the topic of family violence and two of the speakers are rabbis. One is gay and one has started a program for children to stay safe. The third speaker is someone who talks about the man's role in family violence. In each case we hope to partner with one of the synagogues in Calgary.

## Reverend Jake Kroeker

*(The late Jake Kroeker was the senior pastor of the First Baptist Church in Calgary.)*
I have been part of FaithLink for most of its 10-year history. The first insight that struck me as I reviewed its history was all that has been accomplished. Our congregation especially appreciated the assistance of FaithLink in the development of a protocol that was presented to our congregation on safety for our children and teens in our various programs. We also benefitted from having Nancy Nason-Clark present at a morning service on intimate partner violence. Through the work of FaithLink, the broader community was impacted by the seminars and workshops it sponsored. Involving both faith communities and services providers opened meaningful doors for not only dialogue and developing trust but also for working together in providing counselling with individuals who desired a faith perspective on their situation.

Another insight that struck me was the work that remains to be done, especially among the faith communities. Only 114 of 333 churches responded to the questionnaire that was sent out, and only 70% of those were receiving disclosures. Therefore, one cannot help but wonder what percentage of the two thirds that did not respond are receiving disclosures. My concern is that IPV is likely not a high priority for them. Furthermore, only 27% of those who did respond identified themselves as confident in handling situations of IPV disclosures. This level of competence may be considerably lower among those who did not respond. The task ahead in raising awareness is huge.

As has been pointed out in this chapter, the trust level between service providers and faith communities is seriously wanting when it comes to assisting people suffering IPV, and yet this trust must be firmly established if clients are going to get the help they require. When this trust is lacking, the client often becomes a pawn between these two powerful influences. On the one hand, the service provider is best equipped to assist a person suffering the effects of IPV, and on the other hand are the influences of faith and culture that can have profound effects on a given client. If these two powerful influences are not working as a team, the result can be added guilt and confusion for the client—rather than providing the help that is so seriously sought and required. This is simply unacceptable. The influences of culture, religion, and community must and should be taken into account and teamed with the service provider who is best equipped to assist clients with the most appropriate and available resources. This can only happen as service providers and leaders within the faith communities determine to work as a team.

# The Good Wife

How can you say
It's just the way things are:

      Born to be violated
      all my loving obedience
      all my heart's desiring
      for naught

I was not created to be your pawn
a victim before I was born

you bend our religion to your will
make it a quisling of abuse

both need release into the unbounded realm
where the core of our core sings freedom.

—ROBERT PYNN

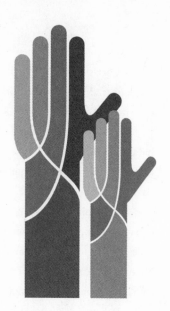

# 4
# Finding
# Their Voices

## Religious/Ethno-Cultural Women Speak about Intimate Partner Violence[1]

**INTRODUCTION**

Women who are victims of intimate partner violence (IPV) often find their choices restricted, their decisions difficult, and the consequences dire. Our understanding of the predicament victims of violence find themselves in has primarily been informed from a secular, humanistic, and predominantly Western European cultural perspective. But what of women who are victims of violence who do not necessarily share this world view? What of women who are members of religious traditions and cultural communities? Do their religious beliefs and cultural norms influence how IPV is perceived and responded to by both its victims and their communities? To explore these questions, we asked women from Christian, Jewish, and Khmer (Cambodian) Canadian communities to tell us how their beliefs and cultures inform how they perceive IPV, the choices they have available to them, and how they go about seeking help. We were also interested to know how their communities responded to the issue of IPV: whether IPV is acknowledged within community families, and what supports are available to women disclosing abuse?

**METHODOLOGY**

A total of 85 women participated in the research project: 44 from various Christian denominations; six from the Khmer Canadian community; and 35 from the Jewish community. They were of differing ages (from teens to seniors) and, for the Christian and Jewish participants, represented different branches of their religious traditions. Of the Christian constituents, 25 were Roman Catholic; six were members of the United Church of Canada (a mainline denomination); and 13 were from various evangelical denominations. Jewish constituents represented Reform, Orthodox, and Conservative affiliations. The majority represented long-standing Canadian families. Three were immigrants from Eastern Europe, having first emigrated to Israel then to Canada. Of the Khmer Canadian women, two were immigrants, having entered into arranged marriages with Khmer Canadian men. The other four participants from this community were women in their late 40s to 60s, who came as refugees and had been in Canada, on average, for 20 years. Participants from all three constituent communities were recruited through personal contacts and advertisements in churches and community centres.

Data were collected through focus and small group meetings and individual interviews. The interviewers were FaithLink staff members, each holding professional credentials. Each, including the translator, was familiar with the issue of domestic abuse. Meetings with Christian and Jewish participants were led by Christian and Jewish interviewers, respectively. The interviews with Khmer Canadian participants were conducted by an English speaker who was familiar with the community, with the assistance of a translator, himself a member of the community. The data were collected during the spring of 2006.

Meetings and interviews with research participants were conducted in an informal and conversational manner. A series of general questions provided themes and were designed to stimulate discussion but were not structured to be presented in any set order. The questions were: "What do women see as being important family violence issues for people in their religious/ethno-cultural community?" "What kinds of help do women see being made available to such families?" "What, if anything, might make it more difficult for family members who experience abuse to find help?" "What changes might improve the ways help is given to family members who experience abuse?" "What ideas do women have as to how such changes can be made to happen?" Participants' names were not recorded, ensuring individual confidentiality. All of the sessions were taped, coded to ensure collective confidentiality, and transcribed. The data were collated across common themes. Each theme was analyzed to further identify commonalities within and across religious/ethno-cultural constituencies.

## FINDINGS

Guided by the broadly based research questions, the women participants often engaged in discussions that provided a richness of context, identified concerns, and offered avenues for change, including their own social action. They reflected on how, as women, their religious beliefs are experienced; the value they place on spirituality; and their personal experiences with family violence. For some, the experience of immigration played a significant role in shaping their situations. Resource availability, whether within or external to their religious/ethno-cultural community, is a critical concern. Throughout their discussions and interviews, participants spoke of how their community's cultural mores and religious beliefs impact themselves and particularly women experiencing IPV.

### Personal Reflections

Participants from each of the three religious/ethno-cultural groups were very clear that IPV occurs within their respective communities. They also expressed concern that the reality of this phenomenon is denied and that a lack of aware-ness pervades the issue: "It [is] still hidden. How often do we really know when someone [is experiencing abuse]...it could be our best friends at our churches and [we] wouldn't know, necessarily." Participants from the Khmer Canadian community referred to IPV as "a silent crisis" and one that remains "a family issue," and, by cultural norm, not openly discussed within the community.

Although attitudes are changing, participants, particularly Christian and Jewish women, noted that denial occurs on both a personal—shame, guilt, and the fear of stigma—"a good Christian [or Jewish] family wouldn't do that"—and communal level. Without awareness, victims do not have the language to name their experience or learn how to seek help. Spiritual leaders, too, lack the knowledge to respond appropriately to disclosures: "[We] do know women who have...gone to the rabbis and they've said you have to go back because...it's your responsibility...And [this rabbinic] advice is not uncommon." If spiritual leaders do not know how to address issues of family violence, they will not ask about it or be alert to indications of abuse within relationships. Communal denial results in leaders not knowing what resources are available, how to help victims access them, and a lack of resource development by the community.

The need to "save face," whether within one's congregation or the community, was another common theme. Women expressed their sense of shame and guilt for not living up to their religious and/or cultural expectations. Christian women identified a theology that downplays our humanness: that Christians "handle life better" and therefore acknowledging any type of "brokenness" places the individual in a position of also acknowledging a spiritual deficit. With the fear that their human failings will be "met with [spiritual] condemnation," congregants are not open about their problems, issues, and/or weaknesses. Participants from the Jewish community, identifying the strong expectations placed on the family unit, spoke of their fear of exposing themselves to "face the reactions of others" if the abusive nature of their families became known: "The last thing you want [is] either people's opinion or people know[ing] your dirty laundry." Similarly within the Khmer Canadian community, a high value is placed on the family and its reputation within the community. Therefore, family issues are not openly discussed within the community.

Participants whose religious affiliations were within the evangelical branch of the Christian church spoke of how the perspectives on marriage, relationship roles, and the application of teachings regarding forgiveness and redemption impact their lives and those women who are victims of IPV. They began by defining IPV as a power and control—not a relationship—issue and argued for a broadening interpretation of Scriptures that address marriage and the role of women within marriage. Only when the marital relationship is mutually submissive, they argued, is safety ensured. They also questioned whether the acceptance of divorce is dependent upon the circumstances: Is adultery a more acceptable reason than abuse; is physical abuse or the abuse of children a more acceptable reason than other forms of abuse; is divorce initiated by the husband more acceptable than if initiated by the wife; is the theological question only the narrowness with which marriage is defined or the unacceptability of divorce?

These women spoke of the practical implications of a theology of submission of wives to their husbands as reducing their (the wives') sense of personal agency and of increasing their individual accountability—just because the husband may "be sinning" by being abusive to her, does not give her licence to also sin (i.e., to not be submissive). This position is reinforced when leaders do not recognize the need to place the safety of the victim as the first priority in abusive situations. Notwithstanding their concerns about the implications of a patriarchal position, these women also made the point that not all men abuse the position and responsibility given to them within this theological frame.

Another aspect of a theology of submission, the primacy of marriage, and the unacceptability of divorce for women who are in abusive relationships is the conflict they experience between belief and reality: it is hard to reconcile the abuse experience with theology. Some described themselves as having a secular self and a theological self. In order to maintain their sanity, they increasingly functioned in their secular self and suppressed their theological self. For them, when every life event is interpreted through Scripture, reality is denied and rationalized. Victims of abuse do not want to hear Scriptures—they want someone to listen to them, to validate their experience. Their advice to other women in similar circumstances was to leave the relationship—for their own safety and spiritual well-being and that of their children.

These women also grappled with the application of the theological tenets of redemption and grace: "Where's the role of redemption and grace for the offender in accountability?" When considering their course of action vis-à-vis the person who has acted abusively, spiritual leaders have difficult choices, participants concluded: Do they emphasize redemption or accountability? If they take a redemptive stance, in the "spirit of grace," the victim's experience is minimized. If they hold the abusing person to account, where does redemption apply? What are the practical consequences of either action—offering redemption, holding accountable? Participants, however, were clear as to their position: There is no conflict between taking a redemptive stance and holding someone accountable for their actions. Congregations and spiritual leaders need to make the difficult choices to face the truth and to walk with people in their "brokenness"—whether victim or abuser. "Love says, I love you enough that I'm going to tell you the truth." The church is not being loving or redemptive if it opts to avoid the truth of abuse, they concluded.

Evangelical Christian participants expressed concern with the application of a theology requiring "early" forgiveness of the abuser by the victim. When a spiritual leader takes this position, they noted, the victim is further victimized and the leader's position is abusive. These women recognized forgiveness as a free act on the part of the victim, as part of the healing process when the victim realizes her own power to act. This position can only be reached within the context of safety. One woman recounted her own healing process, noting that forgiveness, for her, came after many years, when the painful, destructive memories were no longer motivating her actions: "So [alone at the graveside]... [I said] 'Dad, I forgive you for this. I forgive you for this'...And then, I would say 'Thank you, God.'...I was sobbing. But to get to that point [took] a very long time. And it's a process."

Women from different Christian faith perspectives also spoke of the deep spiritual woundedness they experienced as a result of the abuse they suffered. But they also spoke of the strength they gained through their spirituality. Spirituality provides a context within which to view the abuse experience. By utilizing their spirituality as a source of strength, these women spoke of being able to move beyond the question of *why did this happen to me* to finding personal strength, often expressed through helping others.

Women from both the Khmer Canadian and the Jewish communities spoke of the influence of their respective cultural norms and how these impact them individually and how IPV is viewed and addressed. Participants from the Khmer Canadian community identified their culture as male-dominated, with a focus on family togetherness in which arranged marriage is often practiced. Marital relationship conflicts, including acts of violence, are viewed as a normal part of the process of the couple learning to live together. The expectation is that, in time, harmony will be achieved. As a result, violence is not necessarily viewed as a serious matter. Extended family, as opposed to the community, is the primary source of support and assistance. Seeking professional help from strangers is not viewed as an option. Victims of abuse would likely not access shelters, and if they did, would still seek to talk to their husbands to resolve the conflict and return to the marriage. Divorce is not seen as an option. Given the patriarchal struc-ture of the culture, women are placed in dependent roles and therefore find the prospect of being alone foreign and daunting. Value is placed on the strength of the family: "Children who do not have both parents have no future." The need to "save face" within the community also mitigates seeking help. Families remain closed, keeping difficulties within until they "explode." Help is only sought when the situation is at a crisis stage.

Many members of this community still carry the trauma of the Khmer Rouge genocide in their homeland. Family relationships are still impacted by mistrust and fear, resulting in significant rates of family conflict and, despite the dictates of culture, divorce. In addition to cultural norms and the impacts of war trauma, other stressors experienced by Khmer Canadian families include the refugee, immigration, and adaptation process; language barriers; menial employment; and limited opportunities for furthering education and language skills. Some of the Khmer Canadian women, now established in Canada, described their immigration experience as being "very hard." They came with only the hope of a better life for their children. Without language, even basic activities within their new environment posed significant struggles. Many refugees who fled the Khmer Rouge regime were illiterate in their own language, so learning a new language was exceedingly difficult.

Other participants were more recent arrivals. They were completely dependent upon their Canadian-established husbands, often without extended family or community connections to turn to when their relationships became abusive. With young children to care for, often employed in low-paying, physically demanding jobs that required long commutes, these women found themselves in positions where separation from their abusing partners was not an option. One participant, who had separated from her partner, was unable to continue to care for her son and work at the same time. She lived under the constant threat of her ex-partner, who also threatened to have her killed if she returned to Cambodia. She questioned whether she had the strength to continue in her current circumstances.

Within the Jewish context, culture and religious observance are closely intertwined. This religious-cultural context was reflected as women from this community discussed the many interconnected expectations, constraints, and potential consequences for women experiencing IPV. Not only is there high value placed on the strength of the family, the wife is charged with the responsibility for *Shalom Bayit* (peace in the home). Many participants challenged this expectation as unrealistic when abuse is present: "If you are being beaten, then it's not peace in the house...there isn't Shalom...and [the wife should] leave and take her family with her." These women also spoke of "feelings of failure" when they have not met the cultural and religious expectations: "It's shame, but it's also a feeling of failure to keep the family...and home together....what could I have done differently?"

They also spoke of the expectation to marry within the community and the personal and familial consequences that can ensue if the relationship becomes abusive. One woman, who had married a non-Jewish man, spoke of her family's reaction ("My father sat Shiva [a seven-day mourning period that follows the death of a close family member] for me"), her sense of self-blame when the relationship became abusive ("I was wrong, I couldn't turn around and tell my parents. I could never, ever tell them, so...I hid everything....nobody knew what was behind closed doors"), and her difficulty in accessing resources for fear that the abuse would become known within the community ("You hide it because it's your fault or...because I went against my religion...I went against my parents").

Notwithstanding the cultural and religious expectations for the family, these participants estimated the current divorce rate within the Jewish community as 50%, even though it is seen as unacceptable, particularly among the older generation. One of the significant concerns raised by participants is the difficulty women from some sectors of their community face in obtaining a divorce and the potential consequences that may follow. In addition to a civil divorce, obtained through the justice system, a religious divorce—a *gett*—is also required. Because it is only the husband who can initiate a divorce before the religious court, a wife wishing a divorce must have her husband's agreement. Thus, he is in a position to exercise control over his wife. His refusal to grant her a divorce was viewed by participants as another form of abuse. A wife can petition the religious court on her own behalf, but this is "very, very difficult because it is a very humiliating and very demeaning experience." Participants also expressed other concerns including having the necessary finances that may be requested by the husband to break the marriage contract; the negative social consequences that children may experience and that their future opportunities may be jeopardized; and knowing what resources are available to assist women through the process. As one participant noted: "[There] is not [an] easily accessible answer [for] getting out of an abusive...situation...[I]t's all the circumstances that filter into that. [It's] the jeopardy for children. It's...about knowing what is accessible and if you have the means, how you take advantage of [what's available]...you can try to secure all sorts of things but to secure...independence is a bigger factor than anything. Trying to secure independence [is the biggest hurdle]."

Some Jewish interviewees who were immigrants from Eastern Europe, or were Canadian-raised children of immigrants, had varying opinions regarding IPV. Some noted that for their parents who had lived in Russia, they "live[d] everyday with abuse...everyone in the neighbourhood was experienc[ing] the same thing. There was no way you could get out of it." Others questioned the assertion that IPV was prevalent within the Jewish community, noting the strength of the family, a lack of agreement on what constitutes abuse, and a belief that if the family was well-educated and financially successful, abuse would not occur. A Russian-based cultural orientation also influences immigrants' expectations of noncommunity intervention into family life. The assumption is that the family will address the situation appropriately: "They know what they're doing." Nor would the victim view seeking help from a counsellor as acceptable. As a child of immigrant parents noted: "Always the answer to every single problem is, 'Get over it, move on.'"

Those participants who work with recent immigrants and with senior members of the Jewish community identified specific cultural and/or experiential impediments to addressing the issues of IPV. For those who had survived the Holocaust, the family unit became very closed, with issues remaining within the family. This norm has continued to influence post-Holocaust families. Immigrants from Russia are hesitant to integrate into the general Jewish community, preferring to "congregate amongst themselves, within their own homes," making it more difficult to raise awareness through public, community-based information. Other impediments include a narrower definition of what constitutes abuse (i.e., that it is physical but not other forms); an acceptance of abuse as part of the marital relationship; a lack of awareness of the resources that may be available; and concern by women for financial stability should they leave the relationship. The value placed on self-reliance is still strong. If services were accessed, they would likely be secularly based (e.g., a hospital's emergency department). Those of the younger generation may access a Chabad House (an outreach centre, targeted at Russian and Israeli immigrants, set up by Jews from the Ultra-Orthodox sect of Lubavitch Judaism).

## Accessing Current Resources

Both Jewish and Christian participants identified in-community resources available to victims of abuse: spiritual leaders and their spouses, other women, social agencies, and other professionals. Some participants expressed concern that their spiritual leaders may not have the awareness to respond appropriately to disclosures of abuse, necessitating referrals to other service providers. Others expressed appreciation for the positive and supportive responses of their leaders. Roman Catholic participants noted that priests who received disclosures of abuse within the context of the confessional were bound by strict confidentiality. They suggested that victims choose to disclose their abuse either outside the confessional or to another resource person within the congregation. Of interest is the support that is given to women victims by other women. As one participant noted, women know that the abuse "is not the victim's fault." The support offered is often through women's groups, where the trust and nonjudgmental attitude among members facilitates disclosures. Participants also spoke of the support, or lack thereof, that extended family can provide. When the nuclear and extended families are strong, problems can more easily and effectively be addressed. When families are separated by geographic or emotional distance, support may not be as easily accessed. If one's family has been lost through war, even "long-distance" support may not be available.

In contrast to the in-community resources available to Jewish and Christian participants, the Khmer Canadian interviewees expressed concern about the lack of resources available within their ethno-cultural community. They noted that their community is relatively small, with members focused on meeting basic needs and on establishing some level of economic security. Many face language barriers and are still adjusting culturally. For some, the trauma of the Cambodian genocide still negatively affects their individual and familial lives. Collectively, they do not have the time, financial flexibility, or energy to give to others, resulting in a limited number of community helpers or resources. Additionally, the cultural norm is to seek assistance from one's family, not from the community. Establishing community-based services, fashioned on a Western model, is a culturally foreign concept.

A consequence of the life circumstances faced by the Khmer Canadian community was expressed in interviewees' concern for their children. With parents working long hours, often in physically labourious jobs and without the support of extended family members, they are not able to give enough care or proper supervision to the activities of their children. Parents do not always know where their children are or who their friends are. As a result of children and youth being left on their own while their parents are working, they do not attend school regularly and are vulnerable to being recruited into gangs: "Then they get killed."

Notwithstanding the in-community resources available to Christian and Jewish women, there are barriers that can often make accessing these difficult. In close-knit communities, accessing in-community resources may mean that the disclosure could be made to a friend or acquaintance, which would add to the sense of embarrassment and sense of failure. They also raised concerns that their confidentiality may not be maintained, resulting in them then facing the reactions of the community. Some noted they would choose to access external-to-community services to maintain their anonymity. Others expressed a fear that even if they did access in-community resources, they would be referred to other services—that the awareness and capacity of in-community resource persons to respond to disclosures of IPV would limit their ability to fully address the situation.

Jewish participants particularly identified their own sense of vulnerability in disclosing within their community. Family violence is still a closed subject, they noted, especially among immigrants. With the strong expectations placed on the family unit, openly discussing domestic abuse is not a "politically correct" topic. Not only must victims acknowledge that the abuse is occurring, and overcome their sense of responsibility for it and the desire to "try harder... stay longer...[make] amends," there is also the fear of exposing themselves to the opinions of others. They do not want to face the reactions of others.

For immigrant families, the stigma of making family issues public and the mistrust of counselling adds to their reluctance to access any type of service. The cultural norm of "what happens in the family stays inside the family" is a strong deterrent for victims to disclose abuse and seek help. The religious position of some Jewish women may limit their in-community resource to that of their rabbi, who, hopefully, would have the knowledge and capacity to respond appropriately to a disclosure of abuse.

Others from the Jewish community spoke of the potential multilayered repercussions within the community: "Consequences come in many forms... reprisal...from a spouse, your own extended relationships...Would the consequences [of making a disclosure] fall against your family, your extended family, other friends? Would it jeopardize your other relationships...your employment... your career...your children?" Faced with the lack of acceptance of divorce and the difficulty in obtaining a religious decree, many Jewish women feel pressure to justify to their community why they desire to end their marriages. This pressure becomes another deterrent for them in seeking help and in accessing in-community resources.

When addressing the question of accessing external-to-community services, the comments of Christian and Jewish participants were limited to concerns that services may not be readily available or responsive. They noted the importance of shelter beds being available, the importance of quick and sensitive responses by the police, readily available information, and knowledgeable counsellors. With the limited in-community resources available to Khmer Canadian women, this group is reliant upon external-to-community services. Understanding and accessing these, however, pose significant challenges. Given the complexity of IPV, the broader community has developed an array of response services: shelters and counselling services; law enforcement and legal services; justice and correction services. How these work together can be confusing for members of mainstream society. For those whose background is rooted within a very different cultural and legal frame-work, the complexity can be insurmountable. This confusion was evident in how participants spoke of their experiences with various services.

Additionally, for some the lack of fluency in English poses a significant barrier in seeking any type of service without the assistance of a translator. For those who experienced the Cambodian genocide, there is also a lack of trust in the police service and fear that if family members are arrested they will be abused. It was evident from the participants' discussion that resources are only accessed in times of crises, and then with the expectation that "the authority" will act decisively and quickly to end the abuse. Thus, they look to the police, immigrant, or government services to intervene, often with unrealistic expectations. There is very little utilization of follow-up or longer-term services. For women of this community who lack self-confidence, trust, or a sense of their own ability to act on their own behalf, and faced with a confusing array of external services, an attitude of helplessness can easily develop.

## Resource Development

Across each of the religious/ethno-cultural groups, participants presented a range of ideas about how their communities, and the broader community, could implement preventive and practical responses to IPV. Although each constituent group spoke to their respective communities, their ideas can be categorized as follows: clarifying definitions of abuse; addressing denial and challenging cultural norms; affecting attitudinal change; building response capacity; developing resources; and taking collective action.

Participants began by addressing the question of a common definition for what constitutes IPV. They noted that although the external community, particularly those agencies responding to domestic abuse and serving those affected, may share a common definition of what constitutes "domestic abuse," this definition is not necessarily understood in its breadth within given ethno-cultural/religious communities. Thus, there is need, participants noted, for raising awareness in these communities regarding a *complete* definition. They also advocated for spiritual abuse to be recognized within the definition utilized by the broader community.

Participants from the Christian and Jewish communities expressed the need for systemic and attitudinal change. Of significant concern was the need to address denial and challenge existing cultural norms—be they within congregations or communities. They felt strongly that old attitudes of hiding family violence "because it was not supposed to happen" have to change. Communities need to move out of denial and recognize that domestic violence is a community issue—not just a private family matter. They suggested that the cycle of abuse within families would only be broken when religious and ethno-cultural communities recognize, and change, structures of power and domination, including the role expectations for husbands and wives. Unless these positions are challenged and changed, they will continue to be perpetuated from one generation to the next. Rather, communities should take measures to support victims and assist them in leaving abusive relationships. An authoritarian stance is not helpful in these circumstances.

In order to affect such change, these participants focused on changing attitudes through raising awareness and education. Suggested avenues for raising awareness and education within Christian communities included addressing the issue in sermons; open discussions within congregations; inclusion within ministerial and theological training venues; the witness of women victims to various groups; and implementing a social justice focus. Speaking from a United Church of Canada perspective, which has a social justice agenda, one participant commented, "We recognize [domestic violence]. It's a human condition and we need to tackle that in ways that are helpful."

Jewish women spoke strongly for children and youth to be educated about family violence as a preventive measure and suggested venues through which this could occur: private Jewish schools, beginning with administrators, board members, parents, and educators; bar and bat mitzvah classes; youth activities; and social groups. They also suggested that premarital counselling curricula developed by other faith traditions could be adapted to the Jewish context and form the basis for rabbis to initiate discussion about husband-wife relationships: "The Kullah classes [premarital classes for brides]...didn't focus on anything that had to do with marriage. It was all just about the Halakhah [laws]...family purity." Other suggested avenues through which information could be made available to the community at large included common meeting places, articles in local newspapers, and inclusion in sermons. Women could also be reached through the *mikva* (ritual baths).

The Khmer Canadian participants also identified the need to educate both children and adults within their community on the issue of IPV. They identified the need for educational materials about family violence for use within the community and for information about resources within the broader community and how these can be accessed.

Building the capacity of spiritual and community leaders to respond to disclosures of IPV was also identified as a necessary course of action. Specifically, these leaders need to know how to help a victim through the recovery process and how to ensure places of worship are safe for women. Participants noted that educational and practical resource materials would also be helpful. Evangelical Christian participants also identified the need for women within their constituent community to gain a perspective of Scripture, which places specific passages within a broader context. Without this awareness and understanding, women will continue to accept a submissive position and therefore continue to be vulnerable in abusive relationships.

Suggested ways of enhancing resources within communities were also made. The Khmer Canadian participants focused on very practical needs: direct intervention with families experiencing difficulty and crisis—someone who can provide direct services that are practical and hands-on. Noting language and cultural barriers to accessing external resources, they suggested the establishment of "a little shelter for women and children" within their community, with Khmer-speaking counsellors who could provide culturally and religiously sensitive and practical advice on family, relationship, and parenting issues. Other participants expressed a desire to help other women experiencing abuse, even though they felt overwhelmed by the prospect. How, they asked, could they begin to offer assistance? Without a cultural norm of seeking assistance outside the family structure, they lack models for developing community resources.

Christian participants from the Roman Catholic and United Church denominations offered ideas for enhancing resources within their own communities and to link to the broader community. They suggested their respective dioceses employ a female social worker or nurse, who was not identified with a specific congregation, to work with congregations. Having this employee at arm's length from the parish would engender a higher level of trust and comfort for women experiencing abuse. In addition to responding to women experiencing abuse, this person could offer education and support to spiritual leaders and to congregations. She would also represent the diocese within the broader community, working collaboratively with services and programs. Another resource suggested was that of a dedicated telephone line as an avenue to assist victims of IPV in finding resources and seeking help: "Maybe the community is just too closely knit for someone to come in and [disclose their abuse]....So, if there was a number that could be used...[it would facilitate disclosures]."

Both Christian and Jewish participants identified that they, too, needed to take individual and collective action to effect change. Women within the evangelical branch of the Christian tradition need, these participants noted, to "find their voices." With a broader interpretation of Scripture, they need to exert their equality with men and thus begin to change the subtle cultural message about women's and men's roles. Jewish participants, too, identified the importance of speaking up for themselves: "So, it goes back to what you were saying about...self-esteem, empowerment, being able to stand up with your own voice and say, 'You can't talk to me like that, you can't treat me like that.'" Roman Catholic participants offered encouragement that change is possible: With a more liberal attitude toward divorce, the younger generation does not have this same expectation and is therefore less likely to stay in abusive relationships.

Jewish participants also discussed ways in which they could take collective action to challenge old and existing norms and religious laws, particularly as they relate to women's roles and obtaining a religious divorce. They suggested the establishment of a national, 1-800, confidential, support telephone line, similar to the Kids Help Phone, which would give Jewish women a broad range of advice.

Although the focus for most participants was on the needs of their own communities, some also addressed themselves to resources available in the broader community. Participants from all three religious/ethno-cultural constituencies expressed concern for culturally and religiously sensitive resources available for men from their communities who were in need of abuse-related services. Khmer Canadian participants noted the difficulty men from their community face in seeking help for themselves. They may not understand that there are consequences for their abusive behaviour, and struggle to comprehend the complexity of the Canadian legal and justice system. Without in-community resources, they can only rely on friends when they find themselves confronted by the police and the courts. Estranged from their families, they may also find themselves isolated within the community. If mandated into treatment by the court, they may face additional barriers: limited English language proficiency; employment schedules; services that may not take into account their cultural or religious context. The need for treatment services that take into account religious, cultural, and immigrant contexts was also identified by participants from the Jewish community.

Noting the prevalence of IPV within the general population, including religious and ethno-cultural communities, participants advocated for a coordinated response. They took the position that there is need for a united stance against violence and support through the healing process for those affected by it. Participants suggested that if religious and ethno-cultural communities had designated employees who could work more closely with external services, a broad community response could be facilitated: "It would be great if the...churches had somebody who was specifically trained...[They could have a] connection [with] the secular [service sector] and then you're really saying, 'we're all together on this violence issue.'"

Participants who spoke from an immigrant perspective asked that external-to-community services have patience with them as they adapt to a new culture. The immigrant experience requires significant adjustment and can increase the vulnerability of families to domestic abuse. As one participant explained, fear and a lack of confidence hindered her initial contact with the police and with a lawyer. Once, however, these connections were made, her confidence increased and she was able to give her lawyer information he used to protect her. Other participants noted the need for understanding on the part of service providers of the larger life context for some ethno-cultural and immigrant victims of abuse. Obtaining a divorce from an abusive partner is not necessarily the answer if it results in the victim then facing insurmountable financial, emotional, cultural, and parenting concerns. Without understanding of, and assistance with, these issues, obtaining a divorce may add to the victim's struggles, they suggested.

Recognition of the spiritual was another aspect participants saw as enhancing secularly based services for men and women affected by IPV. There is need to provide avenues through which victims can deal with the shame and guilt they feel within the context of their faith. Women would be comforted if service providers inquired of clients as to whether spirituality was important to them and facilitated connection with appropriate spiritual guidance. Men also would benefit, they posited, from counsel that had a spiritual component to it. As a potential answer to this need, some participants suggested that religious communities make spiritual counsellors or chaplains available to secular services: "What if the diocese were to hire a spiritual [counsellor] like they do chaplains [who] go to the different hospitals? Someone who could [be a connection with] the shelters."

## DISCUSSION

The findings of this study provide richness and variation specific to each of the three religious and ethno-cultural groups represented. There are also surprising commonalities across all three constituent groups. The ideas and concerns of Jewish and Christian women were articulately expressed. Khmer Canadian women, notwithstanding language barriers, the continuing acculturation process, and a significantly different world view, spoke, at times poignantly, to the challenges faced by victims of violence within their community. The findings of this study also share commonalities with those of many other researchers, as well as adding new insights to our understanding.

Three different religious traditions were represented by study participants: Judaism, Buddhism, and Christianity. Jewish and Christian women further identified themselves as belonging to differing divisions within their religious traditions. Three different cultural contexts were also represented. The Jewish and Khmer Canadian communities are ethnically defined within the larger Canadian society, with their own unique histories, traditions, and languages. Participants of Russian descent form a subgroup within the larger Jewish community. Those participants who comprised the Christian constituency identified primarily with mainstream Canadian culture. However, within their respective congregational and denominational contexts, they, too, are part of distinct communities and cultures. It is within these contexts that women gain their sense of belonging, meaning, support, connection, and, often, explicit behavioural and social expectations. Notwithstanding the supports that derive from community connections, for women victimized through intimate partner violence, community ties can also bind (Calhoun et al., 1997; O'Hanlon, 2006; Nason-Clark, 1997; Jenkins, 2002, Sevcik, Reed, Pynn, & Silverstone, 2006).

The strength of culturally and religiously grounded identity is evident in what these findings do not express. Regardless of the concerns participant women have about the constraints they experience in the face of IPV, and how their communities respond to their being victimized, there is little in the data that suggest a desire to distance themselves from their communities. Rather, they advocate for changes on both religious and cultural levels and clearly identify their own role in effecting these changes.

For the women who participated in this study, the reality of IPV within their respective communities was not in question. Their collective witness confirms the conclusions of others who have researched the prevalence of IPV in Christian, Jewish, and South Asian communities within the North American context. There is general agreement that IPV occurs at rates that are similar to those in the general public (Altfeld, 2005; DeVoe et al., 2001; Grodner & Sweifach, 2004; Hyman et al., 2006; Kivel, 2002; Kroeger & Nason-Clark, 2001; Menjivar & Salcido, 2002; Miles, 2000, 2008; Nason-Clark, 1997, 2008; Raj & Silverman, 2007; Statistics Canada, 2008).

The complexity of the interconnectedness of religious beliefs and cultural norms is reflected in how IPV is defined, viewed, and responded to by both women and their communities. For women, cultural norms and religious beliefs often determine how they perceive themselves, their roles in family and community, choices available to them, and how and where they seek help. On a community level, religious and cultural influences are evident in the degree to which the reality of IPV is acknowledged, the availability of resources, and the supports offered to victims in accessing in-community and external-to-community resources (Allender, 2008; Bhuyan et al., 2005; DeVoe et al., 2001; Grodner & Sweifach, 2004; Heggen, 1993; Joyce, 2009; Kivel, 2002; Kroeger & Nason-Clark, 2001; Livingston, 2002; Miles, 2008; Miller, 1994; Nason-Clark, 1997; Pesner, 2006; Thorson, 2008).

The incongruence between the ideal of religious belief and the reality of IPV serves to foster denial on both the individual and the communal level. The shame, guilt, and sense of failure many victims of abuse experience are compounded for women of faith. They desire to live by the principles of their beliefs and to fulfill the expectations of their communities. But, in the face of violence, their desire cannot be fulfilled. As women of this study testified, they either must deny the reality of their lives or deny the practicality of their beliefs. For example, the special significance given to marriage and the value placed on achieving the ideal of Shalom Bayit (a responsibility carried by the wife) combine to perpetuate "the myth that Jewish domestic abuse does not exist" (Grodner & Sweifach, 2004, pp. 309–310).

The reality of IPV poses challenges for religious leaders as well. The theological positions they take on how religious tenets are applied to everyday life significantly impact their response to a victim's disclosure and to the larger issue of acknowledging the reality of family violence within their communities. For example, within the Christian tradition, beliefs about repentance, forgiveness, and reconciliation are strongly held and inter-connected doctrines. Responding to disclosures of IPV requires ensuring victim safety, recognizing forgiveness as part of the healing process, holding accountable the abusing partner, and accepting that divorce may be neces-sary. A Christian pastor, desiring to be responsive to congregants experiencing domestic abuse, may thus be faced with the prospect of reconceptualizing the interpretation and application of basic tenets of his/her belief system (Allender, 2008; Heggen, 1993; Kroeger & Nason-Clark, 2001; Livingston, 2002; Miles, 2000, 2008; Miller, 1994; Nason-Clark, 1997, 2004; Thorson 2008; Ware et al., 2003).

Each of the constituent groups included in this study also identified cultural factors that serve to reinforce communal denial of IPV and make it difficult for victims of violence to seek help. These include the primacy of marriage; the integrity of the family unit; saving face within the community; and the noninterference by the community into the family's affairs. The influence of cultural norms on how domestic violence is acknowledged and addressed within specific ethno-cultural communities is also noted by other researchers (Bhuyan et al., 2005; Chung, 2001; DeVoe et al., 2001; Grodner & Sweifach, 2004; Kivel, 2002; Pesner, 2006).

Again, the influence of religion and culture is evident in the detrimental influence patriarchal family and cultural structures have on women and particularly victims of violence. When women are placed in subservient positions vis-à-vis men, they define themselves in gender-dependent terms, thereby increasing their vulnerability to being abused and decreasing their ability to consider the strength of their own personal agency in living independent lives. For those women who are in arranged marriages, or who are recent immigrants, their dependency is increased.

Taking the step to separate from, or divorce, an abusive partner poses significant challenges and can carry long-term consequences for women and their children. Not only must they overcome the effects of being victimized, they must also redefine how they see themselves, and be prepared to face the disapproval of family and isolation within the community. Some will face religious scrutiny, the severing of the father-son mentoring of religious rituals and culture, and the potential of lost opportunities for their children's futures. For some, the breaking of wedding vows may require a rethinking of religious convictions (Beaulaurier et al., 2005; Bhuyan et al., 2005; Chung, 2001; Davies et al., 1998; DeVoe et al., 2001; Grodner & Sweifach, 2004; Hathaway et al., 2006; Javed, 2006; Kivel, 2002; Kroeger & Nason-Clark, 2001; Menjivar & Salcido, 2002; Pesner, 2006; Rothery et al., 1999; Silverman, 2003; Tutty, 2006; Williams & Poijula, 2002; Yoshihama, 2001).

The interconnected and complex nature of religious and cultural influences is again evident when resource availability and access are considered. When strong systemic forces inhibit recognition of the presence of intimate partner violence, victims experience constraints rather than support; spiritual leaders misinterpret the dynamics at play within abusive relationships; and communities fail to develop resources to assist family members affected by IPV. If the community is immigrant-based, there may be additional socio-economic and adaptation considerations. Even when there is recognition of the issue of IPV, and concrete action is taken to raise awareness and to develop resources, victims still face challenges. They may be hesitant to access in-community services out of concerns for confidentiality, embarrassment, their own sense of failure, and/ or mistrust. Women whose cultural context does not include seeking help from strangers may not be comfortable in accessing any of the range of services available within the broader community. Language, fear, the effects of war trauma, and confusion pose additional barriers for them. Yet, in the face of violence, these women do seek assistance on an emergency basis. In so doing, their expectations of crisis services may be unrealistic. With divorce not an option for them, service providers may have unrealistic expectations of them as well.

The women who participated in this study were very aware of how their respective beliefs and/or cultures affect them and the issue of how IPV is viewed and addressed. Nor were they hesitant in voicing their opinions and ideas for change, including resource development. Although Jewish and Christian women were most vocal in expressing their ideas, Khmer Canadian participants also had suggestions for how resources could be made available within their community.

Women advocated for clarity of the definition of IPV. They made the point that although there is an accepted and comprehensive definition within the professional community, it cannot be assumed that this definition is understood or accepted within religious and ethno-cultural communities. Depending upon experiences in their countries of origin, emotional, financial, and other more subtle forms of control may not be seen as abusive behaviours. However, gambling, extramarital affairs as a humiliation tactic, inhibiting the acquisition of skills designed to increase independence, and the harassment of extended family members may be seen as abusive (Bhuyan et al., 2005). The need for spiritual abuse to be recognized and included as a form of abuse was also noted.

Women identified the need to challenge patriarchal structures, cultural norms that reinforce authoritarian perspectives, the literal interpretation of Scriptures, and the denial of family violence within their communities. Change would not occur, they recognized, if they remained silent and subservient. Women must find their individual and collective "voice." Through speaking up for themselves, challenging the roles assigned to them, and building support systems among themselves, women in this study concluded that they can affect attitudinal change and help those who are being victimized. The necessity for family violence-related education and building response capacity on the part of spiritual leaders was noted as critically important. The mentoring of their sons was also of concern for study participants. Unless mentors were men who took an egalitarian view of male-female relationships, the generational transmission of patriarchal attitudes would continue. The strength of their collective action was also recognized in the development of resources and supports.

Nor did these women confine their vision for change to their own religious and/or ethno-cultural communities. They offered ideas of how their communities could collaborate with the broader community in addressing intimate partner violence. Intimate partner violence is an issue, they noted, that is bigger than any one community and therefore requires a comprehensive and coordinated response.

They also had some requests of the broader community. Through this research study, they advocated for service agencies to be sensitive to the religious and cultural contexts of their clientele. They expressed particular concern for the men of their communities, advocating for religious and/or cultural contexts to be acknowledged. Similarly, they requested that service providers servicing victims of abuse recognize the effects of spiritual abuse, the strength victims gain from their faith, and the need for their abuse experience to be processed within the context of their belief system.

When asked for his reflections on the findings of this research study, particularly as they relate to Khmer Canadian women and their community, Pol Ngeth, a social worker and member of the Khmer Canadian community, offered the following comments:

> [Immigrating] to Canada brings not only an opportunity for economic growth, but also challenges...such as issues related to cultural differences and conflicts, especially those concerning violence against women....Many people who live in Canada but come from different cultures have different experiences with regard to dealing with issues involving family violence. Some look to their religious leaders for help; others may follow other norms of marital relationships which view IPV as the process of the couple learning to live together. Another may continue to hide the abuse because of shame and guilt associated with revealing it to others in the family or community.
>
> Services that address IPV must be culturally competent and sensitive as newcomers may be struggling with cultural barriers such as language, the legal system in Canada and accessing external resources. A number of books have been written on changing the status of women within different faith/religious societies. But very little interest has been shown by these

researchers with regard to women in Buddhism, especially in the Khmer-Buddhist community.

This chapter has opened my eyes to the different interest groups, such as religious leaders, service providers and especially the Khmer-Canadian women themselves, that must understand the issue of IPV to make life safer for Khmer-Canadian women in Calgary and elsewhere. There is need for [Khmer-Canadian] women [to "save face"] due to cultural norms...[especially] cultural expectations of being submissive to the male's dominant role in society and in the family and [not having] independent financial resources. The impacts of war trauma, other stressors such as the adaptation process, and economic security may add more difficulty to family situations. This chapter has raised [the need for] awareness within the Khmer-Canadian community to begin to develop new insights [into] IPV where we dispel the myth of the cultural norm of violence, and begin to fulfill the teachings of Buddha to provide his followers with happiness, peace and salvation and to live together in harmony.

...Some people may find discussing IPV not only to be diffi-cult but also challenging: it can bring back painful memories. IPV has an impact on the whole community, not just the family and the victimized partner. Women in the Khmer-Canadian community are still struggling to get answers to questions about violence in their own lives and those of other women they know. Most challenging, for me, as I...read this chapter is the commu-nity and spiritual leaders' lack of knowledge of how to respond to family violence, and therefore the finding that these leaders are not well equipped to have a direct influence on the occurrence of IPV. Secondly, the cultural norms of not seeking help from service providers and/or strangers hinder women's ability to access appropriate services. This is made more challenging by the way IPV is dealt with here [in Canada]—a culturally foreign concept in our [Khmer-Canadian] community. Thirdly, despite the inter-connected and complex nature of religious and cultural influences, and the lack of available resources that need to be addressed,

as [the findings reported in this] chapter have found, Khmer–
Canadian women are still experiencing confusion, not knowing
how to go about seeking help for issues related to IPV.

The closer we can get to women in [ethno-cultural] communities the more likely they are to open up to us, and help us to
dispel the myth [related to] violence [which is embedded within]
their cultural norms. As we all know, if we are working together to
end the circle of violence, and help[ing] individuals to be safe, the
whole community might be able to live in harmony.

## CONCLUSION

This study sought to gain an understanding of the influences religion and culture
have on how intimate partner violence is perceived, the choices available to
victims of abuse, how they go about seeking help, and how their communities
respond to them and the issue of IPV. What emerges from the discussions with
85 women drawn from Jewish, Christian, and Khmer Canadian communities is a
complex, interconnected web of religious and cultural influence that affects both
women and community. It is within this web that women define themselves,
their roles within family and community, and whether and how they take action
to extract themselves from abusive relationships. This interconnected influence
is also evident in the incongruence between the idealism of belief and the reality
of the abuse experience. A community's denial of IPV limits the resources and
supports made available to victims of abuse. For victims to acknowledge their
experience and seek help, they may need to move out of the patriarchal paradigm that has defined their lives and face both religious and social disapproval.
These barriers are increased for women of refugee/immigrant-based communities who may hold a differing world view and have access to very limited
internal-to-community resources.

But the women who participated in this study also recognized the
strength of their individual and collective voices in challenging religious
tenets and patriarchal structures. They recognized the need for greater education, capacity building, and collaborative efforts in addressing IPV, both within
their communities and within the broader community of which they are a part.
Notwithstanding the concerns they voiced about religious and cultural influences, they were clear about the strength they gain from their own spirituality.

## CO-AUTHORS' COMMENTS

## From the Desk of Michael Rothery

In Chapter One we recounted how, 1,600 years ago, St. Augustine reported that his mother dealt "successfully" with IPV in her life through forbearance—in some ways sacrificing herself on the altar of family peace. The women who we interviewed have had to wrestle with similar options, and it is painfully common for abused women to feel guilty and ashamed, as if they have let down their families (indeed, their entire spiritual community) by taking a stand against violence.

"Finding Their Voices" is the most striking chapter in the book for understanding the relationship between theology and the family—especially when families are not working well. The women's voices that comprise this chapter are culturally and spiritually diverse, with marked differences between their belief systems or world views, cultures, and ideologies. And yet, there are commonalities in their concrete experiences. Be they Jewish, Cambodian Buddhist, evangelical or mainstream Christian, they would have no trouble understanding each other respecting the theological challenge of reconciling their spiritual obligations with their experience of IPV.

In Chapter One considerable attention was given to how ideologies are both good and bad news. At the same time as ideological commitments give focus and meaning to life, they can create conditions in which violence can take root and grow. We further noted that religions, as ideologies, promote complex systems of values. To the extent that they are utopian, they also set the bar high—living with good enough adherence to spiritual values is something to strive for but seldom achieved. The women we interviewed made the struggle clear: How does one reconcile the experience of being abused with a commitment to potentially utopian values like love, compassion, forgiveness, and submission?

Of course, one can be a strong Christian, Jewish, or Buddhist woman while refusing to accept mistreatment. It is precisely this that the women whose voices comprise Chapter Four are accomplishing through theological reflection on their circumstances and options. Properly understood, ideological commitments to values like forgiveness (even submission) can be made into sources of strength and resistance, and the testimony of the women participating in our research shows this to be a difficult but feasible task.

### From the Desk of Nancy Nason-Clark

If you want to know the impact of abuse in the lives of ordinary women of faith, all you need to do is ask them. They are ready to talk. Not surprisingly, it almost always brings new insights to the discussion of any topic when you ask those involved directly to offer their opinion or their experience. And that is certainly true as you listen to the voices of the women highlighted in this chapter. The women offer the reader a window into the discussion of abuse in families of deep religious faith.

As I read the chapter, I was drawn to three particular findings: the need for faith communities to stop denying that abuse exists; the difficulty of reconciling the experience of abuse with theology; and the deep spiritual woundedness that often accompanies abuse in religious families.

A *holy hush* has permeated churches, synagogues, and other houses of worship for too long. It is now time to shatter the silence and to offer compassion and resources to those who have been impacted by the devastation of abuse in the family context. In our recent book, *No Place for Abuse* (2010), Cathie Kroeger and I argue that the *listening ear* of another woman of faith is a central ingredient to help religious victims begin their journey toward safety, healing, hope, and renewal. Religious leaders also have an important role to play—in raising awareness concerning the frequency and severity of domestic violence; offering spiritual insight and practical resources; and dispelling the myth that religious families are free of abuse. By their words and their best practices, pastors, priests, monks, and rabbis can journey with a woman or man as they cope with the aftermath of violence in the family context. They can challenge the erroneous religious thinking of a victim or an abuser. They can speak the language of hope; that tomorrow can be a new day.

Reading the voices highlighted in this chapter reminds me once again how important it is to talk about domestic violence in communities of faith, to offer resources, and to work together to ensure that every home is a safe one. There is no place for abuse. And all of us have a role to play to assist our communities and our congregations. As part of our work, we have developed a web-based series of resources and we invite you to access these online at http://www.theraveproject.org.

## CHAPTER RESPONDERS

### Pol Ngeth, Social Worker, Member of the Khmer Canadian Community

There is a need for more research to inform and improve the work with all people across cultures, especially among women in minority groups such as in the Khmer Canadian community. The chapter highlights the challenges of these women's lives in the shadow of the patriarchal culture, the cultural norms that reinforce authoritarian perspectives, and the denial of family violence in the community. Especially, I find there is the need for voicing their opinions, their ideas for changes, and the need for more supports and resources within our community when Khmer Canadian women are unable or unwilling to seek help from strangers and resources with which they are not familiar.

Thinking of the results discussed in this chapter, I would suggest that we need to enhance additional services for Khmer Canadian women in order to provide them with more education or educational materials in their own language; in-home support services (i.e., social workers, cultural brokers, or first-language counsellors) to build some trust with them so that they can voice their concerns; and there is a need for interpreters and translators who can help Khmer Canadian women to further connect with the broader community and community-based services (i.e., women shelters, police, or legal services).

### Miriam Mollering, Ph.D., Pastor of Life Care Ministry, Centre Street Church, Calgary, AB

As I began reading, I was immediately struck with the thought that women who are victims of IPV are often victims of spiritual abuse in a church/faith community setting. Their choices are restricted. Their voices are silenced. Their cries go unheard. What do spiritual/religious leaders need to be doing that we are not doing?

The understanding by leadership as to the impact of IPV is often seen through the eyes of male leaders as, historically, male leadership is the prevailing presence in most faith communities/churches. Therefore, how are we, as females in leadership within the church or faith community, called to respond and to give voice to victims?

The information in this study has brought clarity to the reality that there is not a common definition of what constitutes IPV. As a result, I have been challenged to ensure that my conversations with colleagues about cases of IPV be more explicit so that when we discuss IPV we are doing so with the same understanding of its definition.

In a recent situation in my church this became very clear as a male colleague was providing spiritual support and guidance based on his definition of IPV, which was somewhat different from mine. I must admit this was an eye-opener for me as I had wrongly assumed that someone trained in helping victims of abuse would "naturally" have the same definition as me. That is not necessarily true. I will now approach such situations by first making sure of the definition we are working from if I am collaborating with a colleague to provide support to a victim or to a family where abuse has occurred.

The insights regarding the unique needs of immigrant women in this chapter are timely and helpful. With the diversity of cultures represented within the faith community and churches, it is imperative that those of us who are offering support must seek to understand the impact of culture and spiritual beliefs when responding to cries for help. The same can be said about the application of theology. Sadly, some religious leaders are more concerned about advancing their theology as they understand it rather than advancing the safety and protection of women. Abuse is wrong: That is the most *redemptive* message a woman can hear from a religious leader.

I serve in a multi-ethnic church. This study has caused me to be more diligent in understanding the cultural influences and beliefs of females who are breaking the silence of abuse in their lives. I may have 20/20 vision on what I believe is domestic violence. However, if the mistreatment (abuse) of a female within another culture is not viewed as abusive, then the message of hope can be lost. Help will be hindered or denied. The cycle will continue.

The study has correctly called IPV a "silent crisis." The silence can only be broken by those who will give voice to what IPV is—a violation of human dignity. It is wrong. It is always unjustified. Always unacceptable. The perpetrator is always responsible, not the victim. At the very core, the truth is that IPV is a sin against God.

God calls us to be "imitators" of Him. As reflected in John 3:16, He would never cause harm to those He loves.

# Mutations of the Heart

In the early hours of the morning,
when the cloak of evening still
holds the morning light hostage,
your mind races through conflicting
thoughts bound in menacing fears.

Nagging questions take up residence
in the place where you cry for peace.
The ordered landscape of solid belief shifts
under the impact of abuse that sears the soul.

Spirit longs for inner unity but walks a divided path.
What was inviolate now wars with a deep need for release
and the irrepressible demand to free your children, yourself
from its body of death.

In the early hours of the morning there is a light that moves
across the face of darkness uniting dark and light in its shimmering presence.
What seemed to be opposites vying for control
now give their energies to the emergence of a new day.

In the light you come to see hope beyond your mind's divisions—
faith rewires belief in the unitive perceptions of the heart.

Once the puppet of personal desires,
doctrines give themselves up to the freedom of compassionate relations.

You have asked the question: there is no going back.

The answer burning at the depth of your pondering will not harm.

The path of its wisdom leads to transformation in the fires of Sacred Love.

—ROBERT PYNN

# 5

# Incorporating Spirituality into Practice

## How Service Providers Address the Spiritual Needs of Clients

### INTRODUCTION

North American human service professionals are schooled in therapeutic theory and practice that flowed from the European Enlightenment—humanism, secularism, feminism, individualism, and scientific inquiry. Religious beliefs and spiritual influences have no place within this world view. Rather, therapeutic modalities reflect the values of independence, self-actualization, self-expression, egalitarian gender roles, explicit communication of personal opinion, identity rooted in work and love, insight strategies, and self-understanding. Within this frame of reference, religion and/or spirituality raises a number of concerns: the lack of a clear, practical definition, making scientific inquiry difficult; the lack of therapist training in how to address spirituality with clients; the fear of imposing one's own beliefs and values onto the client; and rituals and practices that reflect patriarchal values and are therefore counterintuitive to women (Baskin, 2002; Besthorn, 2002; Canda, 2002; Coholic, 2002, 2003; Funderburk & Fukuyama, 2001; Hodge, 2008; Hodge & Nadir, 2008; O'Hanlon, 2006).

Notwithstanding the skepticism with which spirituality[1] has been held, the past number of years have witnessed a resurgence of interest in revisiting the question of whether spirituality has a place in practice and therefore in educational curricula. This discussion has been informed through conceptual writings, several research studies, the adaptation of treatment modalities to be more responsive to client cultural and/or spiritual realities, and a broadening definition of the construct of spirituality to make it more inclusive and honouring of diverse traditions. There are a number of themes emerging from this discussion: the need for a more holistic practice in recognition of the importance spirituality holds for some clients; an increasingly diverse population; recognition that personal spirituality influences practice; the lack of training models and practice guidelines; recognition that therapeutic benefits can be realized; that for some cultural groups, spirituality and culture are inseparably intertwined, both forming part of individual identity; and that finding meaning in trauma is fundamentally a spiritual process—that spirituality is about making meaning (Baskin, 2002; Beres, 2004; Besthorn, 2002; Canda, 2002; Carlson, Kirkpatrick, Hecker, & Killmer, 2002; Clews, 2004; Coholic, 2002, 2003; Funderburk et al., 2001; Gall et al., 2007; Grams et al., 2007; Hodges, 2008; Hodge & Nadir, 2008; Kiyoshk, 2003; Nash & Stewart, 2005; O'Hanlon, 2006; Robinson, 1998; Todd, 2004).

The issue of intimate partner violence (IPV) places the question of addressing spirituality at the forefront for secularly based service providers working with women who identify with and/or belong to spiritually influenced communities. These are women who not only bring practical, physical, and emotional needs when accessing services, they also bring spiritual needs that need to be addressed. How do service providers begin to understand clients whose life meaning may be derived from world views very different from their own? How do they apply helping skills that have derived from a frame of reference not shared by the individuals they are attempting to help? How do they—or should they—address the question of spirituality with clients?

As researchers, we were interested in exploring these questions. To do so, we posed a number of questions to secularly based service providers: How do they view the issue of spirituality relative to their work with clients? Should spirituality be addressed and/or incorporated into the counselling process? If spirituality is considered an important component to be addressed, how do they go about including it into their work with clients? Is there a role for spiritual leaders and their communities in assisting victims of IPV? What resources should be available within the broader community for addressing the spiritual needs of clients?

## METHODOLOGY

Using a nonprobability availability sampling method, 21 front-line and management staff members of agencies offering services to victims of IPV were recruited to participate in this study. Agency directors were contacted and asked to identify staff members who may be interested in being interviewed for the study. Most participants were identified through this process. Some were recruited through professional connections with members of the research team. It can be assumed that those who chose to participant did so out of their personal interest in the subject at hand. The opinions expressed arise from their own experiences and observations and do not represent the agencies for which they worked.

Participants represented a range of IPV service-related agencies: women's emergency and second-stage shelters (9); general counselling agencies offering family violence-related programs (6); a specialized IPV coordinating agency (3); agencies serving immigrants and/or ethno-cultural populations (2); and a crisis service (1). Most participants were female (19); two were male. Fourteen were involved in providing direct client services, including one who was an in-agency spiritual counsellor; seven held management positions. Client groups included female victims of violence; individuals who had acted abusively within their intimate relationships; child witnesses of IPV; individuals accessing crisis services; gay, lesbian, bisexual, transgendered clients; individuals desiring spiritual counsel; and immigrants and/or members of ethno-cultural communities. Participant employment service ranged from one to 25 years, with the average being eight years. Seventeen held professional training in the fields of psychology, social work, and/or pastoral counselling. Thirteen had attended some form of training related to the issue of spirituality.

A semistructured interview format provided the parameters to the interview discussions while allowing interviewees the freedom to express their ideas, practices, and opinions. Research interviewers were knowledgeable of the dynamics inherent in IPV. Each interview was coded, taped, transcribed, and handled in a manner to ensure confidentiality. To assist in analysis, the data were collated across common themes. Specific points and/or concerns were noted.

## FINDINGS

### Definition of Terms

Given that the constructs of "religion" and "spirituality" are not always seen as interchangeable, and that there are often distinctions made between them (O'Hanlon, 2006), it was important to gain the meaning(s) research participants applied to these terms. As researchers, it was important to allow a free discussion of the questions we posed to participants: We did not want to hinder the flow of ideas by imposing terminology with which participants may be uncomfortable.

All of the participants defined "religion" as an established set of theoretical concepts and traditions; a set of beliefs, rules, procedures, and rituals that are based on sacred texts. They saw religions as grounded historically and culturally and as forming the foundations upon which morals are based. The intent of religious rituals, they noted, is to assist individuals to translate their spirituality into practice. Beliefs, rituals, and expectations connect believers to the spiritual part of themselves. For adherents, religions provide a sense of identity, behavioural norms, and expectations, and an avenue for community membership. With these understandings, participants viewed religious traditions as influencing the decisions made by individuals affected by IPV.

In contrast, research participants defined "spirituality" as a very personal experience that is not necessarily dependent upon religious practice. Rather, spirituality was defined in terms of an internal process of reflection and connection: as one's personal search for meaning, the wrestling with questions of the meaning, the source and origin of life, and living out the beliefs that arise from this wrestling. Spirituality was seen as an innate sense of being, as the core of one's identity, as an important part of what people are about, whether they acknowledge it or not. One's spiritual understanding may be understood within the context of a religious tradition, but not necessarily so. For these participants, spirituality is not bound by predetermined precepts. Rather, it is equated with the freedom to explore concepts from a variety of traditions and perspectives and is therefore broader in scope than any particular religious tradition. It is a personal choice regarding one's faith and beliefs and the living out of these personal tenets.

## Spirituality as Part of the Counselling Process

*The Influence of the Counsellor's Spirituality on Practice*

"As counsellors," one of our participants said, "we are never neutral—we all bring our own life perspectives to the counselling relationship." For those participants who identified themselves as having espoused a religious and/ or spiritual perspective, their spiritual journeys influenced their professional practice. A common insight was the recognition that one's self-perception, personal values, and beliefs influence if and how issues of spirituality are defined and addressed within the counselling context. One participant took the position that there is a close connection between psychology and spirituality. In his/her opinion, the separation between the secular and the spiritual within the therapeutic context is artificial and not helpful: "Psychology is part of spirituality, not vice versa." Not having a religious tradition or spiritual life perspective was identified, by some participants, as both an advantage and a disadvantage. Being concerned with the danger "of imposing one's biases upon the client," they noted that not having a personal spiritual perspective allowed them to be more open and respectful of their clients' beliefs and practices. However, others noted they were hindered by not having a conceptual context for discussing spiritual matters or for offering guidance to clients. The question of professional ethics was a theme throughout participants' discussion. Although all were careful to uphold the practice principle of not imposing their beliefs and values onto their clients, they also spoke of the importance of bringing personal and professional integrity to the counselling process: recognizing how one's own spiritual perspective is part of personal integration and professional integrity.

*The Importance of Spirituality to Clients*

The majority of participants agreed that spirituality was an important aspect for those clients who identified themselves as prescribing to a religious faith or to spiritual beliefs and practices. Their comments ranged from the very practical to the philosophical, from the positive aspects spirituality can bring to the healing process to concerns when religious precepts are given preference over client safety.

In regard to the client's healing process, the negative impact of abuse on the spirit was a common theme. Participants described this impact as spiritual brokenness, affecting both the victim and the abusing partner, as a disconnection with self and the sense of the divine. When these connections can be regained, spiritual strengths can be accessed and can form the basis upon which other personal strengths can develop. It is through the spiritual domain that, for some participants, clients gain the strength to cope with their circumstances. As one noted, immigrant/refugee groups "come with nothing, only their spirituality—their own beliefs, attributes and culture." Other participants spoke of how victims of abuse grapple with the "why me" question and how their beliefs provide a sense of hope that the future will be better for them and their family.

One participant likened the process to that of the Alcoholics Anonymous program—there is a release in the act of "surrendering, giving over, leaving" the struggle with a higher power—if only for a time. Not only does this "act of surrender" provide a sense of relief from the burden of the current situation, it also infuses a broader life perspective—the abuse experience can begin to be seen as part of one's life, not the totality of one's existence. Another participant observed that often the issues presented in the counselling forum are spiritual in nature.

There was also recognition of the struggle clients experience when IPV is not acknowledged within their religious and/or cultural communities and when a patriarchal perspective is taken by leaders. Victims' decisions about their circumstances—how the abusive behaviour is understood, whether to leave the abusive relationship, from whom to seek support, whether to access secularly based services within the broader community, the fear of being ostracized—are impacted by feelings of failure, guilt, and/or anger arising from the incongruence they experience between their religious beliefs and cultural expectations and their current situation. These are concerns, participants noted, that need to be addressed with the client within the context of her/his belief structure.

Some participants identified the importance, for the counselling process, of gaining an understanding of the client as a whole person, including the importance placed on spirituality. As the counsellor understands the importance the client places on spirituality and/or religious practice, needs can be better identified and appropriate resources identified. Perspectives taken by spiritual leaders (e.g., the primacy of the marital relationship, not holding the abusive partner accountable, counselling patience and prayer) may need to be challenged. Most participants recognized that religious communities can offer instrumental, social, and moral support to their members. If a client is attached to a spiritual community, the availability of assistance and the advisability of ongoing connections are important to explore and access if appropriate.

## Addressing Spirituality within the Counselling Context

*Counsellor Comfort Level*

Although spirituality was identified by most participants as important to clients, and a topic that often arises during their clinical work, their own comfort level with including it within their work varied. One participant noted that a discussion of religion or spirituality has no place in family violence-related counselling—the focus should be on education, empowerment, and responsibility taking. Another expressed the strong opinion that it was not appropriate for a counsellor to raise the issue of spirituality, seeing such an approach as both an exercise of power and control and as unethical. There is, this participant noted, a professional tension between counselling and religion: "We are led by our personal values and beliefs, and these need to be held in check within the counselling process. [The] higher need is the therapeutic alliance with the client, and the professional ethic of 'do no harm' takes precedence," with spirituality a part of the counselling discussion only if it is initiated by the client. Participants from one service agency noted the availability of an in-house spiritual counsellor. Clients who had questions or concerns of a spiritual or religious nature were referred to this specialized individual.

Most research participants expressed a level of comfort with addressing spirituality within the context of their work but were divided between those who were prepared to engage the discussion if it was client-initiated and those who took the initiative to introduce the topic. Regardless of how they approached the topic, there was recognition of the importance spirituality held for clients and for the counsellor to be open to its discussion. As one participant noted, "When the counsellor is comfortable with the topic, clients are also more comfortable in raising the discussion." Notwithstanding their willingness to engage in discussions with clients about issues of the spiritual, these participants also expressed their concerns about doing so in an ethical manner. A commonly expressed concern was that of not wanting to give the impression they were putting forth a particular religious position. Clients, however, they noted, need to feel they have the freedom to initiate whatever issues they wish and to be heard and respected by the counsellor.

*Client-Initiated Discussions*

Counsellors within the client-initiated subgroup expressed openness to addressing spiritual matters if the discussion was initiated by the client, or if the topic arose naturally in the course of the counselling conversation. Their intent was to understand the client's religious belief and/or spiritual perspective, the meaning these held for the client, and to explore how the client could utilize their spirituality within the current situation. The focus, however, remained on family violence—safety for the victim, educating and encouraging clients to make their own decisions. One participant noted the importance of teaching regarding IPV, particularly with immigrant clients, some of whom do not have a concept of abuse: "Without the concept, there is no learning."

*Counsellor-Initiated Discussions*

Participants who were comfortable with initiating spirituality-related discussion with clients represented over one half of research participants interviewed. They voiced the opinion that it was important for the counsellor to raise the question of whether spirituality was important to the client and to then take their cues from the client's response, noting the importance of being client-centred. If the client indicated that spirituality was not of interest, the topic would not, and should not, be pursued. These participants described their clinical work as taking a holistic approach and therefore spirituality, if important to the client, should be incorporated.

With spirituality identified as important to the client, the counselling question then becomes one of how their needs can be met. For example, if the client is the victim, needs include her safety, respect for her choices, identifying the choices she has available to her, and practices and cultural norms that need to be respected by service providers (e.g., prayer times, dress). The discussion also allows the counsellor to explore a number of questions: Are there supports that may be available to the client from their spiritual community? What is the response of the client's spiritual leader to the issue of IPV? How does the client's beliefs impact her/his feelings and decisions about her/his circumstances? The discussion also allows the counsellor to provide the client with resources that are available for spiritual counsel if it is desired. Presenting an accepting and respectful approach, participants noted, can enhance the client's willingness to access services, be they family violence-related, spiritual, or medical.

A number of participants spoke of the relief that clients expressed when the topic of spirituality was introduced by the counsellor. Clients appreciated being given permission to grapple, within the counselling forum, with their questions and feelings of guilt. For one participant, including spirituality gives an opportunity to work with clients in a different way, to assist them "in finding peace, in finding their own meaning of life experience." It provides an opportunity to invite clients to look at life in a different way and can be very rewarding for both the client and the counsellor. Given the responses these participants have had from their clients, they concluded that spirituality should be recognized as a legitimate part of the counselling process. Some participants noted their practice of introducing the client to techniques and practices they may find helpful in their own spiritual search and/or reconnection.

The work of several participants focused on specific client groups. They noted that, with each client group, the issue of addressing spirituality varies. One participant spoke of the "spiritual woundedness" clients had experienced by being raised in religious traditions that were not accepting of who they were as individuals. Although the counsellor may recognize the need for healing, unless the client is prepared to re-open these deep wounds, or if religion/spirituality is no longer considered important in their lives, the trauma cannot be addressed. Other participants, whose work is primarily with immigrant/refugee clients and/or members of ethno-cultural communities, expressed concern for the vulnerability these clients face. By virtue of their age and sponsorship arrangements, they may be completely dependent upon family members, and be isolated from support systems by language and/or transportation barriers.

Clients who are members of ethno-cultural communities that are sacral in nature presented particular concerns for these research participants. The need to be sensitive to the client's religious/cultural perspective was a common theme when describing their work with members of these communities. Participants spoke of being cautious not to impose their own values. However, they were also very conscious of the struggle clients find themselves in when there is incongruence between their religious beliefs and their personal experience. When, for example, the belief is that marriage is forever, regardless of the circumstances, it becomes very difficult for a victim of abuse to reconcile her abuse experience with the religious/cultural perspective and her desire to be obedient to these expectations. In these situations, the counsellor, too, is placed in a difficult situation.

There is the desire to both respect the client's belief system and cultural context and to challenge the limitations and potential danger these impose. One participant described assisting a client to move to another province to ensure her safety. In so doing, it was necessary to locate a religious/cultural community with which the client could identify and in which she would be accepted and safe.

Participants also expressed concerns about the struggles they themselves have in working with clients whose religious beliefs and cultural mores restrict clients' consideration of other perspectives and/or choices. Some of the questions they posed were: How do they, as counsellors, not impose their own values but work for the safety and empowerment of clients? How do they respect religious beliefs, on the one hand, and challenge a culture of patriarchy on the other, when the two are so closely intertwined?

All participants in this grouping identified their awareness of professional ethics and the requirement to respect the beliefs held by the client and his/her receptivity to entering into any discussion of spiritual-related issues. Participants who introduce the topic were very clear that their intent is to explore meaning and to provide clients with tools they may find useful in their healing process—it is not to use the session as an opportunity to put forth a particular religious/spiritual perspective.

## Incorporating Spirituality into the Counselling Process

Fourteen of the 21 research participants identified incorporating spirituality into their work with clients. In so doing, they spoke of the need for sensitivity, openness, and alertness on their part. The topic needs to be introduced carefully. One participant spoke of the client's right to know the counsellor's life perspective and his/her practice. At the end of the first session, they tell clients "a little bit about my views on things....I just present who I am...I've got to constantly acknowledge my spirituality...into the equation...[as counsellors] we cannot claim neutrality."

Others noted being alert to how clients presented themselves and the context in which they describe their situation. How clients may approach different situations, solve problems, or define the problem all give clues as to their world view, and offer avenues through which issues of a spiritual nature can be raised. Taking a broad perspective (e.g., exploring life's purpose and living by one's values) can address spiritual issues without directly raising the issue of "spirituality" per se.

A number of participants within the counsellor-initiated group identified the strategic use of questions to explore the client's spiritual awareness and/or how spiritual and/or cultural perspectives impact the presenting situation. Questions also serve as introductions to broader discussions (e.g., strategies for coping with stress; access to supports from spiritual communities; and spiritual practices). A series of four questions were identified as being particularly useful: "What does culture say about this?" "What do others say about this?" "What does self say about this?" "What does religious tradition say about this?" Other questions were designed for reflection, asking clients to consider the congruence between their spiritual/cultural reality and their individual circumstance: "Is that going to work for you?" "Is that something you believe in?" "Is that okay for you?" "How does your gender fit with your family, culture, religion?" Still other sample questions were framed around issues of the fit between personal circumstances and scriptural teaching, the value to the client of specific belief tenets, and the roles ascribed to husbands and wives. Posing questions such as "What would God say about this?" "What advice would He give you?" can stimulate a re-examination of personal perspectives and incongruence between teaching and practice, between expectation and experience. Questions, participants noted, can also be utilized to gain an understanding of supports that may be available through a spiritual community, the client's safety in accessing these, and the supports s/he would like to have and how these can be accessed.

A number of participants identified the importance of listening for, and responding to, "spiritual undertones." Attitudes of helplessness, hopelessness, guilt, shame, and negative self-worth are common to IPV victims. These are also issues that may be reinforced by religious perspectives and thus have spiritual implications. With a better understanding of the client's perspective and position vis-à-vis her beliefs, these participants noted, a counsellor can open discussions ranging from how safety can be enhanced to how spiritual practices can be utilized to facilitate the healing process.

A few participants described their deliberate efforts to make their offices comfortable places by displaying religious symbols from a variety of traditions. This was their way of making the client feel comfortable and to initiate the topic of spirituality if they wished.

## Involving Spiritual Leaders and Their Communities

Given that most of the research participants recognized the important part spirituality can have for women victims of IPV, it was of interest to know their thoughts in relation to the role, if any, spiritual leaders and/or their communities have in assisting women in their healing process. Following the pattern established in regard to addressing the question of spirituality within the counselling forum, we asked research participants to comment on their comfort level in referring clients, who desired spiritual counsel, to spiritual leaders; their practice of doing so; the degree to which collaborative working relationships developed; and how a spiritual leader's involvement influences their own work with a client. We were also interested in knowing their experiences with, and ideas about, how spiritual communities respond to clients experiencing IPV.

### Referring to Spiritual Leaders

Research participants expressed varying degrees of comfort with referrals to spiritual leaders and working collaboratively with them, ranging from being "very comfortable" to having "no comfort" in doing so. Participants who voiced discomfort expressed mistrust of how spiritual leaders would approach the issue of IPV, fearing that female victim safety would be jeopardized and her experience not validated. The motivation and approach of the spiritual leader were also questioned. There was concern that the client would be manipulated into complying with religious/cultural expectations and that she would be silenced. This assumed authoritarian approach was viewed as being hurtful and potentially dangerous to the victim. One participant questioned the credentials spiritual leaders have as counsellors, noting that "clients have a right to know the credentials of any professional, to be treated competently, and to seek out the most competent services available. Without specialized training, spiritual leaders may not be in a position to offer competent counselling services, particularly to those individuals experiencing family violence."

Participants who expressed having some level of comfort with referring to spiritual leaders noted the benefits to clients in exploring their faith. Their referral practice was, however, not without reservations. These participants only referred at the client's request and then only to spiritual leaders in whom they had confidence would respond appropriately to the client's experience and safety needs. This confidence was grounded in either their direct knowledge of the spiritual leader's position or his/her reputation in the community as someone who understood IPV. For some, referrals were only considered for the instrumental support the spiritual community could offer the client, or for interpretation of specific sacred texts.

Of the 15 research participants who spoke to the question of referring clients to spiritual leaders, 11 had made at least one referral, while four had made none. The referrals that were made were to specific spiritual leaders who were known to the participant, or the client had chosen from the resources available to her. One participant noted her close working relationship with spiritual leaders from her own religious/cultural community. Another spoke of her utilization of Aboriginal spiritual resources available through shelter services or community Elders and the benefits Aboriginal clients receive when the healing process includes their culture's spiritual practices. One participant identified having received a referral from a spiritual leader, noting "attitudes are changing."

*Working with, and the Influence of, Spiritual Leaders*
Mistrust was a dominant theme in the attitudes participants held regarding working collaboratively with spiritual leaders. Some participants acknowledged, in principle, the benefits of professional collaboration, but on a practical level they were not initiating discussions with individuals from whom clients were receiving spiritual counsel. With collaboration, they noted, understanding would be enhanced and the potential for the client to be triangulated between differing counselling approaches—one from a secular, theoretical base, one from a theological, cultural base—would be decreased.

Of the 11 participants who had made referrals, most did not initiate contact with the spiritual leader receiving the referral. They were concerned that clients would be torn between differing advice received from the secularly based and the spiritually based counsellors. Others took a more pragmatic approach, noting that they inquire of the client about the perspective of the spiritual counsel they are receiving and, where possible, support it; inquire as to whether the spiritual counsel is useful to the client; and ensure safety needs are being taken into account. If the spiritual leader understands the dynamics of IPV, and does not take a patriarchal position, his/her involvement with the client can be helpful, these participants noted.

For those who did collaborate, they did so both formally and informally. Two participants within this subgroup noted they support, as much as possible, the client's continued connection with her/his spiritual community, recognizing that these connections will be a longer-term support system for the client, regardless of the beliefs or tradition.

*Spiritual Community Responses*

Research suggests that subgroups within spiritual communities often respond to victims of violence by offering practical help, even when IPV is not acknowledged by leaders (Nason-Clark, 1997). It was thus of interest to learn how secular service providers experienced the responses of spiritual communities to victims of violence. Not only did research participants share their experiences, they also offered suggestions regarding the role spiritual communities could—or should—play in addressing the issue of IPV.

Again, participant responses varied and, in some instances, were harshly critical. Those who found spiritual communities beneficial identified specific communities. They spoke of the instrumental, practical, and emotional support provided to victims; of being a source of personal strength for victims—a place of stability and belonging in the midst of personal crises; of victims receiving support from individual community members and leaders even when the community itself was not necessarily supportive. They also spoke of the importance of a community to the children affected by family violence and how, in keeping children connected to friends and activities, these communities can provide a "haven of normalcy" in the midst of being uprooted from home and school. With understanding of the dynamics of IPV, participants noted that the spiritual community's support of the victim can not only offer significant support and aid to the victim, it can also free the secularly based counsellor to focus on emotional issues rather than also having to be attentive to the practical needs of the victim. Examples included escorting them to places of worship to ensure their safety and providing interpretation services.

Most participants, however, did not see the responses of spiritual communities as helpful or appropriate to victims of IPV. They offered a list of concerning examples, including imputing a sense of failure and guilt in women victims; counselling clients to return to, or remain in, abusive relationships; condoning the abuse and not taking threats to kill seriously; extorting money from, and manipulating, the vulnerability of victims for ulterior motives; counselling marriage even with the knowledge of a history of abuse on the part of the man; counselling patience on the part of the victim in the belief that the abusing partner would change his behaviour; attending court in support of the abusive partner and offering character witness statement—even after hearing the testimony of the injuries caused to the victim—with no comparable support offered to the female victim; pressuring the victim to withdraw her disclosure and not testify against her abusive partner; attempting to provide counsel to family members instead of referring to specialized domestic violence services. When the religious/cultural norm is one of not "airing one's family troubles" outside the family unit, there are additional constraints placed on victims. Immigrant members of these communities, who are sponsored by and dependent upon their families, are particularly isolated and vulnerable, participants noted.

Participants offered their opinions on the role spiritual communities could have in addressing IPV. They spoke of the degree of influence community leaders have and how this influence could be exercised in preventive and practical ways by leaders: speaking out against IPV; challenging abusive relationship patterns and holding those who act abusively to public accountability; taking moral stands on issues that impact people's lives, including IPV; addressing sexism, whether within their own structures or the general public; ensuring their places of worship are safe for all members; ensuring personal and corporate integrity by "practicing what is preached"; acknowledging that IPV occurs in every community; and confronting denial and fear by openly and directly addressing the issue of IPV.

Clearly, these research participants recognized the influence spiritual communities have and the contributions they can make to individuals affected by IPV and to the larger whole through preventive and practical—but appropriate—responses to IPV.

## Increasing Capacity for Responding to the Spiritual Needs of Victims

The final group of research questions posed to participants related to what resources or capacities were needed to adequately address the spiritual needs of victims of IPV, whose identity and affiliation is within a spiritual context. Response needs fell into three groupings: professional training; the needs of specific client groups; and the inclusion of spiritual communities.

Participants identified their desire for increased understanding of religious traditions/spiritual perspectives and practical approaches to enhance their capacity to appropriately incorporate the spiritual as a component part of their work with clients. They identified the need for enhanced professional training in a number of areas: a more in-depth understanding of spirituality; the effects of abuse on the spirit; the importance spirituality can hold for clients; how to address spirituality within the counselling context; and the need to be respectful of clients' beliefs. One participant spoke of the richness to herself and to her practice of being part of an agency that set out to create a workplace culture in which staff members were challenged to reflect on their own assumptions, to broaden their understanding of spirituality and religious traditions, and to integrate client-centred practice principles into their work.

A variety of suggestions were offered as to how these learning opportunities could be provided. To establish a base of understanding, many suggested that traditional religious beliefs and spiritual practices be included in college and university professional curricula. Spiritual leaders from various religious/spiritual/ethno-cultural communities could be accessed as resource persons to speak about their own beliefs and cultural norms and how these impact the issue of IPV, they suggested. Continuing professional educational forums were also suggested within abusive situations; the importance of responding to disclosures in ways that place victim safety as the first priority; to confront abusive behaviour as unacceptable; and to assist victims in accessing services without retribution.

The need for dialogue between secularly based service providers and members of spiritual/ethno-cultural communities was also identified. Participants voiced the struggle and the challenge. One noted:

> Religious/spiritual communities and secularly based service
> providers need to get beyond seeing each other as the enemy. Each
> needs to recognize that they are both working for the common
> good of individuals and families. Dialogue needs to be established
> and maintained. There does not need to be agreement on the
> theories, foundations, or beliefs held by different individuals or
> groups—the only agreement is that family violence is wrong and
> that we all need to address it. Religious/spiritual leaders—priests/
> pastors, rabbis, imams, monks—have to say that violence is wrong
> in society, but first of all in the home." Another participant voiced

hope for the future: "It's a confusing mess to try to figure out how to best meet the needs of such a diverse city, it's a little bit easier to just let it sit. But it isn't going away, and it shouldn't. The conversations are beginning to happen—it will take time.

## DISCUSSION

Participants in this research study were employed in agencies providing services to clients affected by IPV—victims of abuse, child witnesses, and/or individuals who had been abusive to intimate partners. Their clientele included individuals from mainstream society, members of spiritual and ethno-cultural communities, and immigrants. Most participants held formal professional training in social work, psychology, or related human service fields. Collectively, they held significant experience working with clients affected by IPV. Their definitions of, and distinctions between, "religion" and "spirituality" were very similar to those presented in the literature (Baskin, 2002; Coholic, 2003; Funderburk & Fukuyama, 2001; Grams et al., 2007; Hodges, 2005; O'Hanlon, 2006; Nash & Stewart, 2005).

Participants were asked to respond to three general questions: whether spirituality should be explored within the context of counselling and, if so, how; the role, if any, spiritual leaders and communities have in assisting those affected by IPV; and resources required for meeting the spiritual needs of clients. Although their responses were grounded within their own practice, collectively, their discussion highlighted a number of issues: the importance and efficacy of spirituality for clients who espouse a spiritual life perspective; the importance of a client-centred and holistic practice; recognition of their own need for increased understanding of, and skill development in, appropriately addressing spirituality with clients; and identification of the challenges presented by a multicultural and spiritually diverse society. These are also issues currently under discussion within the professional literature.

That spirituality is important to clients was not in question for those participating in this study. Many also identified its importance to their own lives. These positions are in harmony with others who have addressed this question from conceptual, research, or practice perspectives. Spirituality is identified as a human need (Nash & Stewart, 2005); as a process of making meaning (Coholic, 2002); as being positively correlated with mental, physical, emotional, and relationship well-being and a powerful resource in meeting life's challenges; and as being an important component of both personal growth and professional practice (Besthorn, 2002; Fisher-Townsend, 2008; Gall et al., 2007; Hodge, 2005; O'Hanlon, 2006).

Notwithstanding the importance with which spirituality is viewed, its inclusion within the counselling context raises ethical concerns and the danger of infusing the therapeutic process with personal bias. Although most participants in this study identified the need to respect professional ethics, only a few articulated the ethical conflict that is inherent—the danger of not recognizing the power imbalance that exists between the therapist and the client and therefore the danger of manipulation. Introducing the subject of spirituality requires a high level of self-awareness. Of concern is that personal and professional perspectives often go unspoken, yet significantly influence the therapeutic relationship (Coholic, 2002; Nash & Stewart, 2005). Respecting client autonomy and self-determination requires continuous monitoring by counsellors of their own, and the client's, responses. Guarding against personal bias, as Hodge (2005) notes, is particularly important when working with clients from faith traditions that are different from that of the counsellor, or when a counsellor carries their own historical and unresolved religious/spiritual issues. The question of whether to disclose one's personal spiritual perspective is also of concern. Some may view, as Coholic (2002) notes, disclosing personal information as unethical. However, given the subjective and influential nature of spirituality, is it unethical not to advise clients of one's position?

As is evident from this study, whether or not counsellors have considered the inherent concerns and have taken the appropriate safeguards vis-à-vis their professional practice, spirituality is being included within the counselling forum. This inclusion arises from a desire to be client-centred and holistic in one's practice approach. It is also in recognition that spirituality can be a source of strength for clients (Gall et al., 2007) and of the need to work with clients within the context of their own traditions and world views (Besthorn, 2002; Hodge, 2005, 2008). The openness to explore issues of spirituality reflects recognition that matters of the spirit are important to clients. As others have noted (McKernan, 2004; O'Hanlon, 2006; Gall et al., 2007), such discussions open avenues to an exploration of existential questions, to individual sources of strength, and to communal support. Many clients desire to integrate their beliefs into the counselling dialogue (Hodge, 2005). In doing so, the therapeutic work can be deepened (Nash & Stewart, 2005). Not all clients, however, view spirituality within a positive light. Some have experienced deep wounding as a result of religious and/or spiritual teachings. There is need for healing. Here, too, the topic of spirituality becomes relevant to the therapeutic discussion (Funderburk & Fukuyama, 2001).

The approaches utilized to facilitate the inclusion and discussion of spirituality vary with the comfort level of the counsellor, the counsellor's own professional exploration of the topic, and his/her personal spiritual interest. As such, how spirituality is approached and addressed tends to be counsellor-specific, and therefore open to subjective bias and manipulation. However, the use of questions—to gain understanding of the client's cultural and/or spiritual context, their existential perspective, their use of spiritual resources in the management of stress—are in line with approaches suggested by other practitioners and those developing practice guidelines and methodologies for including spirituality into one's practice (Coholic, 2002; Hodge, 2005, 2008; Hodge & Nadir, 2008; Kiyoshk, 2003; O'Hanlon, 2006).

Given the importance spirituality has for some clients, and their desire to place their life challenges within the context of their beliefs and practices, counsellors have a responsibility to explore these issues with clients (Grams et al., 2007). The need for enhanced professional training is evident. Not only are counsellors identifying their own need for increased understanding of different religious/spiritual systems and for increased skill development to address client spiritual issues, there is obvious need for professionally developed modalities, self-awareness vis-à-vis spirituality, and clarity regarding ethical practice. This is a recognized need by educators and social work practitioners (Baskin, 2002; Canda, 2002; Clews, 2004; Coholic, 2002, 2003; Hodge, 2005).

The challenges of addressing the issue of IPV within a pluralistic context, such as Canadian society, are significant themes in the findings of this research. While those working with victims of IPV articulated their professional commitment to being sensitive to the client's spiritual/cultural context, they also expressed their grave concerns for how spiritual beliefs and cultural norms may be applied in situations of IPV. These concerns highlight a clash of perspectives. On the one hand, values arising from the European Enlightenment are dominant within mainstream Canadian society, most therapeutic modalities (Funderburk & Fukuyama, 2001; Hodge, 2008; Hodge & Nadir, 2008; O'Hanlon, 2006), and our understanding of IPV and our responses to it. On the other hand, spiritual/

ethno-cultural communities are often grounded in different perspectives and world views (Hodge, 2008). The issue of IPV brings these differing value systems into sharp focus. Values that uphold patriarchal relationships, vest sole responsibility for the happiness of the family with the wife, and expect conflicts to be resolved within the family unit all raise concerns within the context of IPV. How do family violence service providers respect the victim's world view when the values inherent within that perspective place her in danger, fail to validate her experience, and/or do not hold accountable her abusing partner? The factors inherent within these tensions are complex and highlight some of the divergent forces inherent within feminism, multiculturalism, and spirituality (Funderburk & Fukuyama, 2001).

The mistrust by family violence service providers, as represented by the participants, of spiritual leaders is a dominant theme arising from the findings of this research study. Examples of how some of these leaders have responded to disclosures of abuse from community members reinforce this skepticism. Concern was specifically expressed for ethno-cultural and immigrant women in dependent relationships. Participants also suggested a lack of understanding of the dynamics and potential lethality inherent within abusive relationships, a reliance on spiritual beliefs to effect behavioural change, and an adherence to cultural norms over the safety of the women who are the victims.

Participants also raised concerns regarding counselling credentials and a fear of the counsel victims would receive. Given the level of mistrust exhibited, it is not surprising that most participants did not view working collaboratively with spiritual leaders as a viable option, although exceptions for specific spiritual communities were identified.

Notwithstanding this predominantly negative perspective, there is recognition of the influence spiritual leaders have, and the strength of supportive connections members have to their communities, concepts supported by others (Hodge, 2005, 2008; Nason-Clark, 2006, 2009). Participants offered suggestions that, if implemented, would enhance their willingness to engage these leaders and/or communities: an openness to exploring the implications of doctrines and cultural norms; acknowledging counselling limitations regarding IPV; utilizing their position to educate about, and take a preventive stance vis-à-vis, IPV. There is within the findings recognition that some spiritual leaders are aware of, and respond in helpful ways to, IPV. However, the practice of utilizing one's own spiritual leader as a referral source may increase the ethical concerns of counsellor subjectivity and client manipulation.

The value of collaboration is acknowledged, although there is hesitancy in doing so, and indeed a lack of knowing how to initiate collaborative connections. There is evident need for spiritual leaders—across religious traditions— to address the issue of IPV from a position of awareness, victim safety, and accountability of the abusing partner. There is also a need for service providers to be open to engaging spiritual leaders in the process of education, awareness of resources, and building levels of trust. The need for open dialogue is evident: We cannot afford to build and maintain silos when it comes to IPV. Addressing the clash of values between a European Enlightenment-grounded counselling and service sector and values held by varying spiritual/cultural communities is a significant challenge. As Hodge (2008) notes, "As societies become more multicultural, growing recognition exists that helping procedures should be consistent with clients' understanding of reality" (p. 180). Doing so within the context of IPV poses significant challenges, as the findings of this study attest.

## CONCLUSION

Not only does experiencing abuse affect one's physical, emotional, and mental well-being, it deeply wounds the spirit (Barrett, 1999; Nason-Clark, 1997; McKernan, 2004; Gall et al., 2007). For those victims who espouse a spiritual life perspective, their beliefs and practices become a reservoir of strength and healing. It is not surprising, therefore, that they desire this important component of their lives to be included within their work with counsellors. Although there is recognition by professionals of the importance of being client-centred and holistic in their practice, there is still a hesitancy to incorporate spirituality into the counselling process. There is need, within professional schools of learning, for continued discussion, research, and the development of practice guidelines to ensure that when spirituality is addressed, it is done so within the bounds of ethical principles.

When an IPV victim's spiritual perspective is embedded within a religious and/or ethno-cultural context, as it often is, counsellors are faced with very practical challenges, which are in effect a clash of values arising from differing world views. As Funderburk and Fukuyama (2001) observe, secularly based professional perspectives, multiculturalism, and spirituality represent convergent and divergent forces. Those experiencing domestic violence are caught up in the vortex. On the counsellor–client level, sensitivity to the client's context is good practice—however restrictive the choices may be. On the broader community level, responding to IPV requires continued efforts to understand differing ideologies, research inquiry, education, and the building of collaborative connection. "Breaking the cycle of violence...requires both the input of secular culture and support from the religious community and its leadership" (Nason–Clark, 2009, p. 389).

. .

## CO-AUTHORS' COMMENTS
### From the Desk of Michael Rothery

As noted in Chapter One, the relationship between secular helpers and religion has seen significant recent change. Until relatively recently, professional helpers were predominantly also spiritual leaders; help for the psyche was inseparable from help for the soul. With the scientific revolution and the Enlightenment, religious thinking and practices were dismissed from the consulting rooms and offices of most social workers, psychologists, and psychiatrists, most of whom claimed (or at least desired) scientific credibility and many of whom regarded religious practices as outdated superstition.

We also noted in Chapter One, however, that there has been a recent resurgence of interest in, and respect for, spirituality and religion. We argued that this reflects a shift in Western cultures generally, where for many people secular humanism has proven too narrow. It also recognizes that for many consumers of social services, especially with a dramatically increased representation of people from diverse cultures, religion and spirituality remain fundamentally important. Simply setting spiritual needs and concerns aside as issues peripheral to the helping enterprise is no longer always possible. There is a renewed recognition of the need for effective dialogue between religious and secular paradigms.

The material in this chapter is an important part of a larger conversation, comprising the thoughts and experiences of professionals in secular agencies respecting their responses to the spiritual dimension of their clients' lives. These workers do not speak with one voice, which is scarcely surprising given the complexity and richness that the dialogue taps into. The distrust in the relationship between the paradigms is present, but so, too, is a genuine interest in collaborating more. The familiar traditional view that matters spiritual and religious should be carefully bracketed and not allowed to influence the helping relationship still has its proponents. However, other voices suggest new ways of approaching the issue, ways to accommodate or even proactively invite relevant spiritual questions into the therapeutic conversation.

In part, the discussion concerns technical questions regarding what one can practically do to provide clients with more diverse supports. Strikingly, ethical concerns seem even more prominent: How can a professional engage clients around spiritual questions while remaining properly neutral about the moral values those questions contain? We accept that some questions are not ultimately fully resolvable, even as they deserve our continued careful thought and deliberation—and note that this is a perfect example of questions where both secular and religious thinkers have much to offer.

## From the Desk of Nancy Nason-Clark

Over the years, I have thought a lot about collaboration between the secular and the sacred. It is very difficult work, the task of building bridges between faith-based communities and community-based agencies. At times, when I have been engaged in speaking to audiences where both religious leaders and community-based professionals are present, I ask directly: Is your church or house of worship a safe place for a woman to disclose that she has been abused? Is your community-based agency a safe place for a woman to disclose that she is religious? Often the answer to both of these questions is a resounding, "No."

Building bridges between various first responders to the needs of families impacted by domestic violence involves trust, respect, and a passionate commitment to peace and safety in every home. Finding and maintaining common ground is not always easy. There are disciplinary boundaries, differences in values and world views, various professional practices, and the matter of personal egos. Walking through these troubled waters requires skill, tact, and determination.

Sometimes I think of these issues in terms of paving the pathway between the steeple and the shelter, a reference to the notion that in an ideal world, there would be the *potential* for a bidirectional referral process between women of deep religious faith who seek help in the aftermath of domestic violence. Sometimes

I think of these issues in terms of shattering the *holy hush* that operates in many communities of faith regarding the prevalence, severity, and longer-term impact of abuse. Sometimes I think of these issues in terms of shattering the *secular silence* operating in some agencies or among some professionals where there is an unwillingness to understand—or to respond to—the deep spiritual needs of families impacted by abuse.

I wrote a paper entitled "Referrals between Clergy and Community-Based Resources," together with a pastor, an executive director of a community-based agency, and a private practice clinical psychologist (Nason-Clark, McMullin, Fahlberg, & Schaefer, 2010). Here we reported that one thing that leads clergy to make referrals includes personal feelings on the part of a religious leader that a case is too difficult to deal with single-handedly. A further factor involves their level of training. Pastors with more preparation, knowledge, and experience about domestic violence were more likely to refer parishioners that sought their help than those with little or no training. In fact, where referrals are needed most (among those religious leaders who have little prior training or understanding of domestic violence), they are least likely to occur. Interestingly, the overwhelming majority of pastoral counsellors report that they have been satisfied with the counsel parishioners received when they followed through on advice to seek the help of a community-based professional.

One of the pieces of advice for religious leaders in our article was to begin to establish relationships in the community, where you learn the names of some people who work in the various agencies and begin to establish a working relationship with them. Ask for them to send you brochures of the agency. Acquaint yourself with their programs and their services. Ask how your community of faith could support the agency and their work. And make yourself available to meet or discuss work of mutual interest. Collaboration is a two-way street.

## CHAPTER RESPONDERS
### Christine Berry, Director of the Family Violence Prevention Initiative, Calgary Counselling Centre

I found it troubling that the issue of incorporating spirituality into the counselling process became for so many an ethical dilemma. As a service provider in the counselling profession, my commitment is to the ethical position of "Do No Harm" that trumps all other considerations. With this edict in mind, to dismiss my client's spiritual views puts me at risk of ignoring important information when the matter is safety planning or support that may prove harmful or helpful to my client and thus involve me in unethical practice. The questions provided in 3(d) [Incorporating Spirituality into the Counselling Context], which articulated how one might ask about cultural/spiritual matters in an open, straightforward manner, were, in my opinion, very good, simple questions that could prove very useful to counsellors and help inform a client-centred, ethical approach. I appreciate and support the notion that professional training should include how to address spirituality within the counselling context and how abuse affects spirituality and wellness.

### Cynthia Wild, Director of Client Services, YWCA Sheriff King Home Emergency Shelter, Calgary, AB

I think Sevcik, Rothery, Nason-Clark, and Pynn make an understandable overstatement, at the beginning of Chapter Five, when they suggest, "Religious beliefs and spiritual influences have no place within this [post-Enlightenment] world view." I would argue, instead, that there is a certain ambivalence in those of us involved with counselling practice in a postmodern era when it comes to spirituality and, more especially, religion. We have not really been able to collectively determine the socially acceptable place of spirituality and religion within our professional ethos. We are still trying to find where it fits, and for whom that goodness of fit is actually for. We want to be open to the range of human experience, but we also want to practice from a scientific and objective framework. And therein lies the ambivalence. There is a professional and hegemonic dynamic pushing for self-determination, best practices, rigorous evaluation, individualism, and choice, while, at the same time, a grudging recognition that much of community-based social service provision comes from religious foundations, particularly as the social welfare state continues to be under attack, ironically, from the quasireligious basis of neo-conservatism. It is a fine line that we need to walk, and a line that is in many ways countercultural.

However, we also need to put much of this existential angst aside and focus on the needs of the person before us. And this is where the strength of the chapter comes through. In 1957 Felix Biestek, a Jesuit priest, wrote a relatively short book called *The Casework Relationship*. In this book, he argued there are seven principles of the therapeutic relationship: individualization, purposeful expression of feelings, controlled emotional involvement, acceptance, the nonjudgmental attitude, client self-determination, and confidentiality. And it is within the context of the therapeutic alliance that issues of spirituality and/ or religion can be considered. We come to the core of this when the authors of this book write: "For those victims who espouse a spiritual life perspective, their beliefs and practices become a reservoir of strength and healing." Ultimately, we need to be there for the client; to be able to offer hope over fear and build upon the lodes of strength that each person actually has within them. And this requires counselling professionals to overcome their own views on spirituality and religion and be firmly and intentionally there for the well-being of the person.

But what does this actually mean? I am not suggesting that counsellors become intimately familiar with the tenets of all the major religions nor be aware of the breadth of spiritual experience. Rather, it is important that in the tuning-in phase of the therapeutic relationship that space be given to an assessment of what, if anything, religion and spirituality means to the person. Then, if it does fit, how can it be leveraged as a source of strength? This not only helps the person but could also provide links to larger supports and structures.

Ah, but if only it was so simple! As a society, we tend to avoid discussions of spirituality and religion. Indeed, watching *Hockey Night in Canada* on Saturday night is more likely to be readily admitted to than going to Mass or a service on Sunday morning. People might not feel as though they are given permission to speak about these issues in the assessment phase; after all, these days, it is truly countercultural. The question, then, becomes when is the issue introduced and by whom? I believe that addressing the spiritual realm within the context of a holistic assessment for all victims of IPV is critical to mapping the future course of case planning and, ultimately, to providing the best service. As part of their clinical training, counsellors are introduced to many techniques, approaches, and therapies in order to ensure that they are equipped with an array of therapeutic tools they can apply and match to the unique elements of each counselling situation. Unfortunately, this training has excluded how counsellors can introduce and become comfortable with the language of the "spirit" in their work with victims of IPV. The concept of "spiritual woundedness" is a very powerful description of the spiritual impact of hurt and betrayal that occurs for many of the women who seek services for domestic violence. I would argue there is an ethical imperative that counsellors have some level of competency in supporting women who relate their experience in spiritual terms, or are able to refer these clients to someone who does.

Finally, as noted by the authors, there is the bigger role that spiritual leaders can play in terms of dealing with complex social issues, including IPV. Years ago, I worked with a church-based domestic violence program (and that is when I first met Nancy Nason-Clark). A central part of the job involved information sessions with clergy to let them know some of the signs of domestic violence and what resources there were in the community. It was to show that it was not the duty or "cross to bear" of a good and faithful spouse to put up with violence but rather a crime (and let us face it, a "sin") that should be dealt with in a manner that supported the inherent dignity and choices of the victim. This was not always easy. Some clergy have peculiarly odd views regarding the dynamics of private relationships! But the point was that religious imperatives and contexts could be used to advocate for changes in how clergy and spiritual figures responded to domestic violence within their communities—at both the pastoral and structural levels.

Overall, the space for an authentic consideration of the place of spirituality and religion in the course of the therapeutic relationship must be determined by the client. If imposed, it can be a further layer of oppression. If freely chosen, it is a wonderful, healing, and important dimension.

# Meditation

You are the circle
of a thousand
riding the centuries
of holy longing,
opening your hearts
to the counterintuitive,
embracing
the zero point
from which
the all possible unfolds,
walking barefoot
on sacred coals
ablaze with primordial fire.

You torch
the ordinary
in its self reduction.
Amidst the compression
of the times, you rise like
a cloud of compassion
hallowing mutations
of the mind
that dance
the stillness of its
own surrender.

*A voice says:*
"Only a small number"—
No! Only a universe of love
multiple in its unfolding.
There is nothing
foolish here
save the holy
waste of a soul
giving up
to the abundance
of its own heart.

You dare touch
the hem of wisdom
at the virgin point of
your soul's becoming—
heart bursting
in the wager
of love's union
with its source.

And as for me,
I come,
a beggar,
in awe of the power surging
from the wealth of your poverty,
the gold pouring forth
from the deep
mines of your care,
the courage wrapped
in the risk of service
on the crest of an uncertain sea.

In the silence,
eyes closed
to the light stealing
through drawn blinds,
I am aware
of your burning
like points of light
coming together
in the face of being itself.

Only a small circle:
No!—the gate
of heaven flung wide open.

—ROBERT PYNN

# 6

# Contemplative Meditation

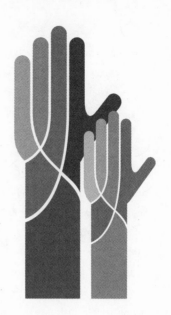

## Its Efficacy with Service Providers Working with a Victimized Clientele

### INTRODUCTION

There has been a growing scientific interest within the medical and mental health fields as to the efficacy of various meditation modalities in alleviating symptoms arising from a variety of illnesses and psychological conditions. In a review of more than 1,000 peer-reviewed scientific articles on meditation, Unger (2005) reports that research inquiry is focusing on understanding the correlations between meditation and improved mood and/or decreased disease symptoms. Neurological research identifies meditation as one of the top four activities for keeping the brain healthy (Newberg & Waldman, 2009). Other studies are exploring the hypothesis that meditative brain changes are at the heart of claims, by practitioners, that meditation induces improved health, well-being, and emotional balance. Given the findings of experimental studies and outcome research within the clinical setting, mindfulness stress reduction techniques are being incorporated into numerous treatment modalities for various psychiatric and behavioural conditions. Reporting on the efficacy of mindfulness-based stress reduction (MBSR) with medical students, Rosenzweig et al. (2003) conclude that MBSR is "relevant throughout the lifetime of the physician and is arguably a core characteristic of clinical practice" (p. 90). Addressing the practice of a contemplative meditation practice, Finley (2005) opines that meditation practice has the potential of playing a powerful and decisive role in the healing process. Through meditation we can learn to be less...subject to all the ways in which we as human beings suffer and, in our suffering, contribute to the suffering of others. (p. 6)

Further, Bourgeault (2004) concludes that a contemplative meditation practice can result in "a profound healing of the emotional wounds of a lifetime" (p. 96). (See also Bonadonna, 2003; Kabat-Zinn et al., 1992; Mason & Hargreaves, 2001; Majumdar, Grossman, Dietz-Waschkowski, Kersig, & Walach, 2002; Newberg & Waldman, 2009; Reibel, Greeson, Brainard, & Rosenzweig, 2001; Rosenzweig et al., 2003; UCLA Semel Institute, 2011.)

Those who respond to, and provide ongoing services to, individuals traumatized by intimate partner violence (IPV) are exposed not only to highly stressful work environments but are also at risk of experiencing vicarious trauma. Figley (1995) sees this as an understandable consequence of caring. Given the benefits of meditative and mindfulness practices reported within other fields of inquiry, we questioned whether a contemplative meditation practice would be efficacious for those working within the intimate partner violence services sector. Specifically, we questioned whether it would offer them some protection against the risks of vicarious trauma and assist them to better manage the stress experienced within their work environments; affect how they related to their clients within the counselling context; and affect how they worked with and related to their colleagues. Given that meditation is an inward focused practice, we were also curious as to what effects it may have on the more personal level.

## METHODOLOGY

The research project comprised two distinct components: training and support, and data collection and analysis.

### Phase I: Meditation Training and Support Groups

Developing a practice of meditation requires instruction and discipline. To facilitate the implementation of such a practice, training and support were offered over a six-week period. Three full days of training in the theory and implementation of a contemplative meditation practice were offered in weeks one, three, and six. Weekly, 30-minute support groups were arranged for the intervening weeks. The training sessions were led by Dr. Cynthia Bourgeault and Robert Pynn, both practitioners of contemplative meditation. The intent of the support groups was to encourage the discipline of practice. A designated leader arranged the time, place, and space and facilitated practice and discussion.

Thirty-one participants, recruited through general advertising within family violence and general counselling agencies, completed the three days of training and availed themselves of the support groups as their schedules allowed. They also committed themselves to private meditation practice. Participants included those working directly with IPV victims (19) and employed in general counselling agencies (3); supervisory, executive, and management personnel (6); and a child abuse prevention educator, a pastoral care coordinator, and an interested individual.

## Phase II: Data Collection and Analysis

To facilitate the collection of relevant data, a survey questionnaire and two semistructured interview schedules were developed. All instruments were coded to ensure participant confidentiality. Interviews and focus groups were taped, transcribed, and coded. Data was collated across common themes. Each theme was further analyzed to identify commonalities.

The survey was administered to all 31 participants on the first day of training. The survey data provided an understanding of why participants chose to be involved in the research and established a baseline for the information provided through interviews and focus groups as to changes, if any, that were experienced as a result of the meditation practice.

Each of the interview schedules was designed to guide the discussion, with flexibility to pursue questions as they arose. The first interview focused on three general themes: understanding how participants viewed the issue of vicarious trauma and their own self-care practices; understanding how the participant experienced the meditation training and practice; and, finally, understanding the impact, if any, of the meditation practice. Of particular interest was the impact the meditation may have had on how participants handled the stress of their work, their work with clients, and their involvement with colleagues. Twenty-one of those who completed phase I participated in the first set of interviews. These interviews occurred within 10 days of the last phase I training day.

The intent of the second interview was to gauge the degree to which participants continued the meditation practice and to capture further reflections participants had on its effects within the context of their work environments. The three focus areas identified in the first interview were addressed again. Eighteen, second interviews were conducted. These interviews were conducted six weeks following the completion of the first interview set.

Following the initial analysis of the survey and interview data, two focus groups were held. The purpose of these discussions was for participants to respond to the general themes researchers had identified as arising from the data. These groups were held six weeks following the completion of the second set of interviews. Seven participants attended.

Collectively, those who participated in phase II represented 122 years of direct work in the family and sexual violence field, with each averaging 7.63 years of direct service.

### DEFINITIONS

Within the context of this research project, a number of terms were used and it is worthwhile to clarify their meaning. Some terms are drawn from secularly based literature, some from meditation-related literature, and some are the common vocabulary of research participants.

- *Vicarious Trauma*: The transformation of the therapist's or helper's inner experience as a result of empathetic engagement with survivor clients and their trauma material. It results in physical, emotional, and spiritual exhaustion and difficulty separating from one's work. These effects can be subtle or pronounced, are uniquely applicable, can extend to all realms of the helper's life, and are unavoidable. Effects are experienced in one's personal relationships, view of the world, and perception of safety. Those working with IPV victims describe having visual images of abusive events described to them; experiencing physical reactions (churning stomach, nausea, feeling shaken); and being angry, sad, and unsupported by the legal and justice systems. They describe becoming immune as a self-protection method—of withholding or limiting their emotional availability to clients, of avoiding hearing traumatic material. Further, because most IPV victims are women, vicarious trauma effects appear to be more intensely and frequently felt by female counsellors (Clemans, 2004; Costa, 2005; Figley, 1995, 2002; Iliffe & Steed, 2000; Richardson, 2001; Saakvitne & Pearlman, 1996; Way et al., 2004).

- *Stress*: In *Webster's New Dictionary and Thesaurus* (MacLeod & Pauson, 1989, p. 682), stress is defined as "Pressure, urgency, strain, [or] violence... producing or sustaining a strain." Within the context of the discussions with research participants, the terms "stress" and "vicarious trauma" were occasionally used interchangeably. They are, however, different in that "stress" is a general term, whereas "vicarious trauma" is directly viewed as a secondary effect of being exposed to traumatized individuals. Stress, therefore, can be seen as part of the vicarious traumatizing experience. The research project focused on vicarious trauma.

- *Self-Care*: Strategies employed to maintain one's general well-being. Saakvitne and Pearlman (1996) identify three strategic categories: self-care (relationships, healthy habits, implementing limits, creating balance); nurturing (self-gentleness, comfort, relaxation, play); and escaping (activities that allow forgetting work, fantasy, getting away from painful feelings).

- *Being "Present"*: The deliberate focus of attention on the present, the act of being conscious of the present moment, of being aware and open to the immediate, whether thought or experience. The state of being consciously aware. Within the counselling context, presence is the giving, by a counsellor, of his/her full cognitive and emotional attention to the information and experience of the person being counselled (Finley, 2005; Helminski, 1992; Rosenzweig et al., 2003; Tolle, 2004).

- *Collaboration*: To work jointly with, to cooperate with, or willingly assist others to achieve particular goals.

- *Contemplative Meditation*: Meditation is a spiritual practice common to all religious traditions that hold a vision of human transformation. Within the Christian West, meditation is most commonly identified with the Christian tradition of contemplation. Contemplation is the closest Western practice to Eastern meditation traditions. Contemplative meditation is intentional silence, the fostering of an attitude of listening and receptivity; a listening within, a function of consciousness, not intellect. Bourgeault (2004) describes meditation as the deliberate effort to "restrain the wandering of the mind, either by slowing down the thought process itself or by developing a means of detaching oneself from it" (p. 8). Centering Prayer is described as a preparatory method for contemplation by "reducing obstacles caused by the hyperactivity of our minds and of our lives" (Keating, 2002, p. 11). The meditative stance is that of being present, open, and awake to thoughts (including feelings, memories, interior dialogue, physical sensations, and/or stimulation), not clinging to or rejecting anything as it may arise, and maintaining a nonjudgmental and compassionate attitude toward oneself and others. The goal is to develop a detached attitude toward one's thoughts, letting them go as they are noticed, not engaging in self-reflection. This letting go of thoughts is also referred to as "surrendering."

Contemplative meditation takes us "closer to the spiritual level of our being" (Keating, 2002, p. 81). It has the effect of shifting our awareness from "surface, matter-of-fact levels of consciousness to more interior, meditative levels of awareness of the spiritual dimensions of our lives" (Finley, 2005, p. 5). It is a shift of perception: from ordinary awareness (a subjective–objective perceiving of ourselves and the world) to that of spiritual awareness, a perception of self and the world through an intuitive grasp of the whole and an innate sense of belonging. Spiritual awareness is perception based on harmony, as opposed to dichotomy, and a sense of selfhood not plagued by a sense of isolation and anxiety (Bourgealt, 2004, pp. 10–12). It is through this shift of consciousness that, as Finley (2005) maintains, meditation has the potential for healing.

## FINDINGS

### Vicarious Trauma and the Stress of the Work

The majority of both front-line and management personnel who participated in this study described effects of their work that are consistent with vicarious trauma. They spoke of their own experiences and their observations of colleagues. Specifically, they noted the cumulative effect of vicarious trauma and offered personal, relational, and workplace-based examples, including

- a high level of stress;
- the inability to "leave work at work" (sleep disturbances, nightmares);

- relational tension (edginess, denial, rudeness, anger);
- mistrust of, and a skewed perspective of, men;
- male bashing;
- hyper-vigilance about their own safety;
- ill health;
- the need to vent frustrations;
- desensitization to client situations as a defence mechanism (participants spoke of needing to take a detached position from clients; some identified their inability to continue to listen to the stories of abuse experienced by those accessing services); and
- staff turnover as a result of being "burned out."

Only one participant voiced disagreement with this majority opinion. This person's assessment was that with experience in the field, people develop good coping techniques to block the negative impact of the work.

Participants identified the focus of the study as a factor in heightening their awareness of the effects of vicarious trauma. Through their meditation practice, they also became more aware of their own feeling states and of the impact of working with traumatized individuals within a crisis-oriented environment. They also identified their increased advantage of being able to recognize the symptoms sooner and to more readily take action to relieve the stress and limit the traumatizing effects.

The workload carried by participants, its nature, and its demands were identified as significant contributing factors to their level of stress: "The workload is so high, and we're into it, and meeting goals and meeting deadlines...doing so much that sometimes we forget about us." The constancy of being available takes its toll: "You cannot not respond to a crisis call or someone arriving at the door." From the perspective of someone who had had experience responding to the crisis line in an emergency shelter, one participant noted, "But that front line-office, forget it. I've been in there and it is go, go, go, go. I don't know how they do it. I just don't know how they do it!" With the tight budgets many agencies experience, workloads tend to increase during times when regular staffing is decreased (e.g., vacation times, on statutory holidays).

The element of danger is an ever-present preoccupation, whether working within a shelter or within a community-based counselling program with victims

of violence. A shelter worker remarked, "We are a secure site, [but] I still remind myself that I am working in a high-risk situation." Those working in community-based counselling programs identified the level of vulnerability they feel when visiting victims: "We are working in family violence. So I may not talk about it, but I am very mindful. Depending on the day, anything can happen. [When you do home visits] you're always on guard, and you're always at risk.
It's one thing to be in the building [i.e., the shelter] it's another thing to be in the home...Maybe there's a restraining order, but whoop-dee-do." The reality of the danger inherent within the work is heightened when a victim is murdered: "I thought it was one of my clients and it triggers so much...I was really conscious when I was going out from the office yesterday because I was leaving the grounds at 7 p.m. and I started to be more conscious of my surroundings—like, oh my God, this is not exactly what I want."

The need for constant vigilance for one's safety also takes energy and becomes, as one participant noted, "normal for us....Because we know the work we do...we need to be alert....I didn't realize that I'm always [alert for my safety]...but now I'm more conscious....I have to watch."

All of the research participants identified self-care practices they and their colleagues use to maintain personal well-being. The specific practices are as varied as the individual interests and abilities. There is, however, a common theme—they find themselves in a Catch-22, struggling to maintain the very practices they know they need. It seems that as the demands of the workplace increase, their ability to implement self-care practices decreases.

The busyness of the workplace, with its multitasking demands, contributes to the crisis atmosphere and stress-inducing impact. The comment of one participant captures her struggle, as a supervisor, to implement helpful management techniques: "It's just that everybody's so busy, in terms of the job, it's like: 'Wow, there's so much to get done, and there's so much to do.' And it's like, 'How do you take care of your staff when all this is happening, and how do you check in with your colleagues, when all this is going on?' and you hear mostly the same thing: 'Going good, really, really busy, gotta go.'"

Even when there is support for staff members to take time to meet with colleagues at worksites, the demands of the work hinder consistent attendance. Time demands squeeze out self-care intentions. When workers do access on-site opportunities or take time for themselves, they find it hard to "turn off" the immediacy of the situation and to become centred and calm: "So when push comes to shove, your self-care in the workplace just is a lower priority."

## Effects of Meditation

Having identified the reality of vicarious trauma and the high degree of stress encountered in their work environments, we were particularly interested to know what, if any, effects the meditation practice had in mitigating these deleterious effects participants experience. Participating in the research project raised participants' awareness of the importance of self-care and the need for intentional and consistent implementation of self-care habits. Many identified the contemplative meditation practice as an additional self-care tool. One management group participant, who came to the research project with an established meditation practice, spoke of her experience:

> [It's] just that calmness...a feeling of control, more power, for myself and my own decisions.... I feel so much more able to deal with larger...issues because it's been a clarity for me....When we've had...conflict, I've had to go to the person and maneuver or facilitate it. I did a meditation on that, to get some answers on how to approach that situation. And I write that down and so before I go in, I take that time, I just take a minute or two to have my paper, think about it, get grounded, and deal with it. It's become much better, for myself, because I walk into those meetings and I've had some where it just works. It's so successful.

The meditation practice did not help participants, however, with the Catch-22 in which they regularly find themselves. Only a few noted they have made it a priority to practice daily by scheduling a regular time each day and intentionally maintaining the routine. With this disciplined approach, it becomes easier to be consistent with the practice. Most, however, experienced difficulty in finding the time to fit it into their day. They spoke of not having enough time in the day, of being too tired, and of the busyness of life as factors that limit their meditation practice.

Even given a rather sporadic utilization of the meditative practice, participants still reported significant and positive effects. They spoke of an increased sense of well-being and that it had influenced how they relate to their work environments.

It has [had an impact on how I handle the work]. I think I'm able to step back, I'm able to be more objective and to allow people their own process....That's really freeing. I've changed a lot...I find myself doing a lot more asking questions and less information giving, letting people find their own solutions....It's trusting that everybody's capable...I don't have to run around trying to fix it all by myself.

Allowing myself to feel stressed...acknowledging the stress and the few minutes' break seems to help and you're able to come back and go right into the next thing that is happening.

The biggest [impact]...is just continuing to notice that when I'm [meditating] I'm more able to let go of the outcomes of things, whether it's a meeting or wondering about how things are going to come down, or what I'm doing in session with a client. I think that makes me more present and able to go with what needs to happen rather than what I think should happen and trying to make it happen.

I think I'm dealing with things a lot better. I think I feel a lot more grounded and calm. I'm not having as many jaggedy edges around my mind, my emotions...I don't feel as anxious.

I think it [has impacted how I handle stress] because I know that I can step back and do something, because I'm becoming more and more conscious of how I'm feeling...and I think, "I know that I can do this [meditation] and it's gonna change how I think. [It's going to impact] the person that I want to be...." This is a way that I can look at [larger systemic perspectives] differently, and that's profound.

Actually, yes it has, yes it has [impacted how I handle stress]. I was having a heck of a time with this situation with my boss and I was feeling angry about that. And all of a sudden it hit me, I need to move this along. I'm saying that I'm stuck here and I wanna go over there. What do we need to do? We have to let it go. Let it go. I had a good laugh about the silliness of my behaviour and thought, "here's the thing: you've got a whole new solution. You can change the dynamics of this whole situation." And that's been bugging me for two years. And it broke through and I went, "Yeah, I like this.... Why didn't I think of that before?" I suffered for so long.

I feel more present, particularly after the support group. I feel in a better place.

The protective shell we all develop is a little less hardened.

The themes that emerge from these and other comments suggest that a contemplative meditation practice has beneficial effects for those working in highly stressful situations and with traumatized individuals. Participants identify an increased sense of calm, being more emotionally grounded, and increased objectivity and trust that others have capabilities. With "permission" to acknowledge the stress they experienced came also the permission to take time to reflect—even if for only a few minutes. Participants credit the meditative practice with giving them a more objective perspective, with being able to let go of their own anticipated outcomes to hear the perspectives of others. They are more able to be present with others and to allow decisions to flow from the collective discussion. With an increased sense of awareness and well-being, participants also gained a broader perspective of their work situations and their own place within them. They felt their own work was more effective.

Another common theme reported by participants was their ability to better handle the stresses they encountered. They attributed this to their changed perspective, particularly as it related to the importance of self-care. They reported being more conscious of finding ways "in the moment" to better shield themselves from the effects of constantly working with people experiencing multilayered distress and the potential danger to their own person. They spoke of using meditation techniques to "become centred in the midst" of handling a crisis; of giving themselves permission to "not need to know every-thing"; of creating space and time to take a few minutes to "slow down and regroup." Some spoke of consciously assessing situations relative to the impact they felt they could have and not assuming responsibilities that may be better assumed by others.

Most participants identified a number of specific personal changes they attributed to their increased ability to handle work environment stress:

- an increased ability to set boundaries, which decreased the impact of clients' situations and experiences;
- an increased ability to accept their own limitations;
- an increased awareness of the good intentions of colleagues;
- an increased awareness of one's own feeling and physical states "in the moment," of having become able to step back from the situation, of meditating "on the spot" to lessen frustration and stress levels, of utilizing the meditative technique of surrendering thoughts.

Participants also identified changes within their agency's culture. As one participant noted, "When workers can deal better with stress, it has a positive effect on the workplace environment."

### The Client–Counsellor Relationship

In responding to the question of whether the meditation practice impacted their work as counsellors, most participants identified changes in how they approached their counselling role. They made a correlation between their own self-awareness and their work with clients. As has already been noted, participants equated an increase in their self-awareness and their effectiveness within the work setting. When asked to be specific about this connection, participants spoke of an increased ability to "be present," being more aware of the client's attitude "in the moment" and their own sense of calm and confidence, and of a decreased tendency to "rescue" the client. The following statements are representative.

I've noticed that...I'm not as tense, I'm not as
results-oriented...I'm calm with it and I think things get
processed faster, somehow, or certainly more effectively.

I think it [the meditation practice] has [impacted my work with clients] in terms of continuing to not react to clients when they're in such severe trauma. Because you want to...make it all better versus trying to continue to step back and empower them to work things out for themselves.

I think it helps me stay more focused, more available.

I feel a lot more calm. I feel that when a woman [is] sharing her story, or experience, with me, I feel a lot more calm. Like I'm not ready to jump in and rescue or save. I think to listen more and listen better to what she's telling me.

The meditation technique of surrender or letting go of thoughts, which a number of participants identified as helpful in their handling of the stress they experience, was also identified as an important factor in work with trauma-tized clients. As one participant noted, she can "be more open to [her] clients' abuse experiences because [she] knows [she] can 'surrender' the effects after the sessions." Others commented on an increased objectivity and awareness of the agenda they bring into the relationship. A few felt they had an increased confidence when handling difficult situations. A number of participants noted they were more conscious of the spiritual component and more comfortable in discussing spiritual issues with their clients.

Some participants noted their attempts at introducing some aspects of the meditation practice into their work with clients. Some had introduced times of quietness; others were working with the centring and surrender techniques: "I had an opportunity [with a colleague to do] some teaching of [a mindful meditation practice] to a senior that I work with and it was one of the coolest things that I've seen, because this woman had huge resources and just had all sorts of insights....That was one of the places, with a client, I saw that it was really helpful."

Others found themselves changing how they conducted the session itself: "Possibly asking more questions and knowing I'm not here to fix everything, but certainly pointing out possible resources that may not have come up at times."

For some participants, their own meditation practice and learning shifted the perspective they took in working with clients. Not only were they viewing their clients more holistically, (i.e., there is more to the person than the experience of intimate partner violence), they had deliberately shifted their counselling focus. Rather than a focus on mourning the past, they were now placing a purposeful and intentional focus on the future. As one participant noted, "Hope leads to empowerment, which in turn leads to action." Others noted a shift in how they viewed the work itself: "There is a creative and spiritual component to working with traumatized individuals. This work cannot be grounded only in the intellectual. To be effective, we have to connect with our core components."

Not all participants felt the meditation practice had impacted their work with clients. Some noted there had been no discernable impact they could identify. There was an assumption by some that because they went into their counselling sessions more relaxed and calm, there would have to be an effect, but they were not able to identify specific changes. Others noted that it was too early to tell—they needed a longer period of time to practice the meditation before they could expect to notice any differences.

*Relationships with Colleagues*

Given the effects of the meditation practice participants experienced relative to their work environments and their work with clients, it was not surprising that they also identified positive changes in their relationships with colleagues. Their increased self-awareness made them more flexible within their collegial relationships. Some participants identified a change in perspective, noting an increased ability to "hear" colleagues as opposed to a former tendency to take a defensive posture. Of note were comments that suggested that conflicts were more easily resolved as former grievances were surrendered. An increased willingness to move away from their own agendas and to be more patient and accepting of colleagues was noted. They were now more accepting of differing approaches presented by coworkers. Participants also identified that having ways of dealing with stressful situations helped them better cope with stressors arising from relationships with colleagues. Their increased sense of personal "authenticity" allowed for more genuine relationships. The following comments reflect these attitudinal changes.

I think so...just letting something go. I'm getting to the point where I can see the value in living a life where you don't have to be right. You don't have to agree. You can have an opinion and you can express that opinion and that's okay. And so I think when I go forth like that, I get that back. And that makes for much nicer relationships—where it's not the power, the control, one of [us] has to win, one of us has to be right. You can talk about what you're thinking and feeling and believing and that's okay. And I think the [contemplative meditation] will really help with that.

That's where the letting go [surrendering technique] is big. I hang onto those things, and I need to apologize and go on, instead of berating myself all day for saying something stupid.

It has [impacted relationships with colleagues] just in terms of continuing to not get hooked and learning to provide support for them and just really stay focused, to listen better. Because I find if I meditate, I can listen better. So I think somehow it goes together.

Oh yes [it has impacted work with colleagues]...I'm not going to stress about [not doing things in the same way as my colleagues]. I'm going to do it my way, how I feel I can [be] most effective.... When it comes down to it, it doesn't matter how we cross our t's or dot our i's, as long as the bottom line's covered. And once I realize that, and allow my colleagues the same, then [we're] more accepting of each other and more supportive of each other.

No, I have great coworkers. Let me think. I guess maybe again, being able to hear what they're saying, to listen more, more intently, than having to figure out what I'm going to say next.

A few respondents did not identify any discernable changes in their collegial relationships.

### Effects of Meditation on the Personal

Throughout our discussions with participants, it was evident that the changes in how they dealt with work-related stressors, their work with clients, and their relationships with colleagues were grounded in changes, insights, and learning they experienced on a very personal level. To explore these effects in more detail with participants, we first inquired as to their pattern of, and general experience with, the practice. We then turned to understanding the impact it had on them as individuals. In an effort to apply some structure to these latter inquiries, we asked participants to comment on insights that were "intellectual," "emotional," and "spiritual" in focus. We recognize that these are arbitrary demarcations and the data bear this out, particularly across the intellectual and emotional categories; the spiritual was more distinct. There were, however, some very common themes that emerged. It was also evident that learning took place on more than one level. It is worthy to note that although most participants reported positive personal changes related to the meditation practice, a very few did not. Rather, they spoke of being uncomfortable with the inward focus of the practice and the potential that it could result in emotional crises.

*Patterns of Practice*

Most participants reported patterns of practice that varied in frequency from several times a week to daily. They identified a more consistent practice during the training phase of the project than during the weeks following. The support offered by the groups during phase I was helpful to this end. When this support ended, some found it difficult to incorporate a regular practice into their schedules and life patterns. A few participants reported they were not practicing at all or were doing so "on an as-needed basis" (e.g., when feeling particularly stressed).

Participants spoke of the importance of a disciplined meditation practice. They related feeling better and having "better days" on the days they meditated. A repeated comment was the value of the technique of surrendering thoughts. Through the conscious exercise of this technique—whether part of the formal meditation practice or "in the moment"—participants noted they were able to "let go" of "stuff as it arises." Some used the surrender exercise to deal with sleep disturbances and nightmares when the stress of work intruded on their ability to get proper rest. They described the effects of this technique as freeing, even as having a sense of "cleansing." By "letting the little things go," the ability to handle stress increased.

*The Importance of Self-Care*

Most participants noted an increased awareness of the importance of nurturing and caring for themselves—to not burn out; to be prepared for crises; and to be mindful of how one responds to crises. They also identified giving themselves "permission" to care for themselves—to take personal time. A few spoke of implementing a disciplined practice.

> I've certainly learned and made that commitment to be kind to
> myself. That's very, very important. No matter how busy my day
> gets...[It's important to take] some form of time out for me.

> [I'm] a lot more intentional [about self-care]. I've made it
> a priority. I'm less apt to abandon myself, which is kind of
> wonderful.

*A Different Perspective of Themselves*

Throughout their responses, there is a consistent theme that the meditation practice had a positive effect on how they felt about and viewed themselves. Participants spoke of:

- being more accepting of themselves—their value, equality, that they had something to contribute;
- being more in control of themselves—their time, how they saw themselves, their responses to situations (one participant's comment captures this sentiment: "We have choices for how we spend our time, what we allow to influence us, and what we become involved with");
- an increased awareness of the importance of one's inner self and acknowledging that some difficult issues may need to be addressed;
- an increased awareness of the need to maintain boundaries between one's own emotional states and those of one's clients; and
- the need to respond to others from a less defensive position: "The knowledge around what Cynthia [Bourgeault] talked about and how...

with all our experiences, all the things that have hurt us, we've developed this hard shell [but] we have this pure centre that's soft. So trying to find a way of responding from here [the heart] rather than from this shell."

*Changes in Feeling States*

Most research participants spoke of changes to their feeling states as a result of their meditation practice. They spoke of the calming effect the practice had and the accompanying sense they gained of being more centred and grounded within themselves. They used a variety of phrases to describe their emotional experiences, such as:

- a sense of peace and serenity;
- being more relaxed;
- the enjoyment of "being quiet"; and
- an increased ability to regulate their level of activity—to deliberately "slow down" the pace of their lives.

Accompanying the changes in positive feeling states was a corresponding decreased level of anxiety, anger, and stress. Some spoke of gaining the ability to "let go" of fear, of self-judgment, or always feeling they have to "perform."

Some participants spoke of gaining awareness that they had been assuming responsibility for situations that rightly belonged to others or for which they could not effect change. With this awareness came the capacity to view situations within a broader perspective and an ability to set limits on the degree to which they took on unrealistic responsibilities. They identified the importance of setting stronger boundaries between their "work lives" and their "personal lives": "I'm very aware of limits now, and I'm very aware that...I tend to think about [difficult cases] quite a bit. So I'm aware, even more so, about going home and trying to shut it off. I don't pick up my cell phone, like I used to, on weekends. I realize there's got to be a balance between home and family and so the little time I have off, I have to put it towards the family."

Participants reported that by participating in the research project, they gave themselves "permission" to pay attention to their feeling states. With this self-granting and the meditation practice came an increased self-awareness. Participants noted an increased awareness of their ongoing coping level and the ability to take quicker action to self-correct when their level of stress escalated. Others spoke of being less "self-driven"—of placing fewer expectations upon themselves, of being more comfortable with "being" versus the need to be focused on "doing." They spoke of gaining increased clarity of thought and ability to concentrate. They spoke of increased openness to the perspectives presented by others.

### A Sense of Connectedness with Others

For some, there was a realization that they are not alone in experiencing stress as a result of their work. The "learning" that others had similar experiences broke their sense of isolation. Others spoke of the importance of the trust that exists among colleagues and that this level of trust only develops when people are prepared to be vulnerable with each other: "A sense of belonging and connection to some other people...I don't have a lot of peer support...so it's very wonderful to get together with people and to be orientated to the moment and to be calm, peaceful, and not talking about work and...about what happened there."

### Impact on Other Areas of Their Lives

The insights and emotional changes participants reported had influences beyond their work environments. A number noted positive changes in their personal relationships and lifestyles as well. They noted that as they themselves became more aware of, and dealt with, their "own stuff," they were able to respond differently to others: "And once I started looking more inward and acknowledging the feelings and emotions that were happening, I think I had more patience as a mother, I had more patience as a coworker, and more patience with my husband....Knowing, acknowledging who we are, and we can't be everything to everybody." Others spoke of an increased ability to handle stressful events within the family setting. Some reported that when both partners made a practice of taking personal time and space, the marital relationship was enhanced.

The involvement in the meditation training and practice highlighted, for some, the need to make changes in their lifestyle. They spoke of a heightened awareness of the busyness of our culture (and their lives), with a focus on "doing." They expressed a desire to consciously take time "to be" and to "be with," to move away from the need for intellectually based answers by allowing other options to emerge through quietness and contemplation.

*A Sense of Spiritual Connection and Awakening*

A number of participants mentioned an increased sense of the spiritual as a result of the meditation practice. They spoke of being more conscious of the spiritual journey they are on; of a deeper spiritual awareness; of a sense of connectedness to a transcendent power—the divine, the creator, God, a higher power. "Spiritually? Oh, now I'm tingling. What have I experienced spiritually? I feel a sense of confidence and a sense of guidance and I'm not alone….I feel like I'm connected to something bigger, I'm not frantically searching in my head for this." Others identified a confirmation of an established spiritual foundation, a validation of personal beliefs, an awakening quest to re-establish religious practices. "A sense of coming home. They're [the trainers] speaking in my language. They're talking about the stuff that's influencing me, my values."

*Finding the Philosophical*

A few participants spoke about the insights they gained from considering the deeper concepts upon which the centred meditation practice is founded. Their responses suggest they found these principles deeply meaningful. Comments regarding the concept of vulnerability included

- working from a defensive stance is always destructive;
- working from a position of vulnerability allows for a different way of dealing with issues;
- the concept of vulnerability fosters respect and understanding between people; and
- the call to view others with compassion and acceptance is difficult given the effects of abusive behaviour.

Other comments included awareness that the meditation practice is essentially a journey of personal growth, a process that allows for intellectual and emotional knowledge to be congruent. The contrast between our dominant culture (with its emphasis on domination and self-centredness) and the principles underlying the contemplative meditation practice (such as connectedness, acceptance, and the awareness that we do not have control over everything) was striking.

## DISCUSSION

This inquiry sought to examine the effects a contemplative meditation practice would have for professionals providing services to individuals victimized
through intimate partner violence. Areas of specific concern were whether the
meditation practice influenced how research participants managed the risk of
vicarious trauma and related stressors encountered in their work environments;
how they related to clients within the counselling forum; and how they related to
colleagues. Also of interest was the question of what impact the meditation
practice had, if any, on participants' feeling states.

### The Cost of Caring

That there is an emotional cost borne by those who work with IPV victims is
confirmed by this study. Although the body of research examining the effects
on service providers working with this client group is limited, the personal
testimonies provided by the participants of this study leave little doubt that
they are impacted in significant ways. These effects are consistent with the
findings of other studies and with the general symptoms associated with
vicarious trauma (Figley, 1995, 2002; Clemans, 2004; Way et al., 2004; Iliffe &
Steed, 2000). The variation of effects reported by participants is also consistent
with the findings of Saakvitne and Pearlman (1996), who conclude that not all
first responders to traumatized individuals are affected to the same degree.
Rather, it is the interplay between the personal and the situation that determines the specific impact. Mitigating factors include the strength of one's
professional identity; personal history; current life circumstances; one's coping
style; the number and type of clients and their trauma; the length of time
working with traumatized individuals; and the nature of the trauma.

The emotional cost arising from the nature of the work—its constant
demand for compassionate responses, crisis-focused work environments, the
implicit danger in IPV—is also seen in the struggle service providers have in
caring for themselves. The more the demands of the work indicate the need to
exercise consistent self-care regimes, the less time and energy they have to
actually implement these practices. In order to maintain their emotional well-
being, it is critical for service providers to exercise self-awareness as to the risks,
self-assessment as to the ongoing impacts of their work, and to be diligent for
their self-care to both prevent and ameliorate the effects of vicarious trauma

(Richardson, 2001; Saakvitne & Pearlman, 1996). Without consistent monitoring and attention to the personal effects experienced as a result of their work, service workers are at risk of withholding or limiting their emotional availability to clients. As Iliffe and Steed (2000) found, this self-protective stance can manifest itself in the tendency for counsellors to "avoid hearing" traumatic material and thereby limit the effectiveness of their therapeutic work.

## The Impact of Contemplative Meditation

The findings of this research study suggest that a contemplative meditation practice can significantly enhance the well-being of service providers, positively affect the efficacy of their work with clients, strengthen collaborative working relationships with colleagues, and change the perspective in which they view their work. As such, contemplative meditation can be viewed as an important practice for those responding to traumatized individuals.

The meditation practice had the effect of increasing practitioners' awareness of their own feeling states, making them more alert to the impacts of their work environment and to the symptoms of vicarious trauma they were experiencing. They were then in a position to more quickly take action to relieve stress and thus decrease the overall impact of their work with traumatized clients and the demands of the workplace. That participants were more aware of their feeling states as a result of the meditation practice is not surprising. Keating (2002), speaking of Centering Prayer, notes that positive effects can be realized soon after starting the practice. Finley (2005) notes that "you do not have to meditate very long to begin experiencing more interior, meditative states of awareness. There is something about simply sitting still, quietly attentive to your breathing, that tends to evoke less agitated, less thought-driven modes of awareness" (p. 42). Similarly, Newberg and Waldman (2009) report that even a few minutes of meditation can be beneficial to one's health.

With increased awareness also came changes in how participants approached their counselling role. As they experienced increased internal calmness, they were able to be more emotionally available to their clients, more alert to the client's presentation, and more "in the moment" with the material presented by the client. They found themselves approaching the counselling forum with a more positive and future-oriented perspective. As they experienced more confidence, and moved away from a "rescuing" position with clients, they felt the effectiveness of their work increase.

A similar pattern is seen in how participants described changes in their relationships with coworkers. As they themselves gained self-awareness, they were able to move away from more rigid positions resulting in more cooperative and flexible working relationships. Not surprisingly, they reported less conflict and more open decision-making processes.

In describing the changes they observed in their work with clients and their relationships with colleagues, participants spoke of the benefits they gained through the meditative method of surrender. Within the context of contemplative meditation, surrender is the letting go of issues, thoughts, hurts, and anxieties as they arise. Keating (as cited in Bourgeault, 2004, p. 92) describes this "relaxation of attention" as a purification process at work. Bourgeault herself identifies this gesture of release as the central power of the contemplative meditation form. The effects are realized in daily life: increased calmness and ability to cope with life circumstances, increased emotional and spiritual strength, and increased flexibility and compassion toward oneself and others (Bourgeault, 2003, 2004; Finley, 2005).

The meditation practice was also identified as affecting how service providers viewed the work of responding to IPV and their part in it. They reported moving from a more subjective to a more objective and broader perspective. This shift allowed them to see themselves as part of a larger whole and to place their contribution and responsibility within this broader context. With this shift also came a more holistic frame of reference; a decrease in personal agendas, defensiveness, and need for control; and an increased confidence in the capabilities of others. This shift is exemplified in the challenge some participants experienced in changing their perspective toward individuals who have acted abusively. Working with victims of IPV can reinforce a dualistic perspective that sees victims only in a positive light and the abusing partner only in a negative light. Some research participants noted the challenge they encountered in viewing the abusing partner as an individual requiring compassion and acceptance, even if the behaviour cannot be condoned.

Proponents of contemplative meditation would explain this broadening of perspective as a shift in awareness—from an "ordinary" or "egoic" awareness to a more "spiritual" or "unitive" awareness. Ordinary awareness is described as a way of perceiving that which arises from the functioning of the mind— our sense of identity, thoughts, memory, associations, sensations. This way of perceiving is dualistic, self-reflective, separating self from others, win-lose, and subjective-objective in nature (Finley, 2005; Helminski, 1992; Keating, 2002). Spiritual awareness is also a way of perceiving, but one that arises

> through an intuitive grasp of the whole and an inner sense of belonging....And since spiritual awareness is perception based on harmony, the sense of selfhood arising out of it is not plagued by that sense of isolation and anxiety that dominates life at the ordinary level of awareness. (Bourgeault, 2004, p. 13)

With an increased sense of being grounded and settled within ourselves comes a decrease in defensive responses to life's circumstances: "Action flows better when it flows from...that place of relaxed, inner opening" (Bourgeault, 2003, p. 75).

Notwithstanding the significant changes reported within the work setting, perhaps the more significant are those that occurred on the more personal level of participants' lives. It would appear that these personal changes, in .fact, underpin the more overt changes in how participants handled the stress of their work environments and related to clients and colleagues. The changes participants experienced on a psychological level (how they saw themselves; an increased sense of being grounded in their own identities; changes in feeling states; being less driven by a need to do, more focused on being, and finding more meaning in who they were rather than through what they did; and an openness to solutions that arise through quietness and contemplation rather than intellectual consideration) were for them the foundations for changes in how they handled stress at work and at home, and how they related to their partners, children, and colleagues.

Yet there is need to be cautious to not overstate this correlation. Although meditation is a "transformative process of shifting from surface, matter-of-fact levels of consciousness to more interior, meditative levels of awareness of the spiritual dimensions of our lives" (Finley, 2005, p. 5), it also is a discipline requiring commitment and consistent practice. Finley (2005) further states that "it is in committing yourself to daily meditation that you stand to benefit the most from the ways in which meditation can revolutionize your life" (p. 72). And Bourgeault (2004) notes that the transformative process is not necessarily an easy one: "Centering Prayer is a psychological method and will produce results in that realm, some of them initially painful" (p. 98). Keating (2002) notes,

"Centering Prayer will reduce anxiety for perhaps the first three months. But once the unconscious starts to unload, it will give you more anxiety than you ever had in your life" (p. 115).

But the changes research participants describe are consistent with, although not as profound as, the transformative changes arising from a cultivated habit of contemplative meditation. Keating (2002), Finley (2005), and Bourgeault (2004) attest to this psychological transformation. "Meditation practice has the potential of playing a powerful and decisive role in this healing process [of the violations and compromises of our ego consciousness]" (Finley, 2005, p. 6).

> The fruits of this [Centering Meditation] prayer are first seen in
> daily life. They express themselves in your ability to be a bit more
> present in your life, more flexible and forgiving with those you live
> and work with, more honest and comfortable in your own being.
> These are the real signs that the inner depths have been touched
> and have begun to set in motion their transformative work.
> (Bourgeault, 2004, p. 30)

In identifying the results of a dedicated practice, Keating (2002) speaks of the realization of new levels of freedom, faith, hope, charity, creative energy, humility, and trust (p. 90).

Meditation is fundamentally a spiritual quest, a process with which some participants identified. Keating (2002) describes this quest as plumbing the depths of one's consciousness:

> Beneath the ordinary psychological level of awareness, there is a
> spiritual level of awareness where our intellect and will are func-
> tioning in their own proper way in a spiritual manner. Deeper
> still, or more "centered," is the Divine Indwelling where the
> divine energy is present as the source of our being and inspira-
> tion at every moment...Personal effort and grace meet at the most
> centered or inward part of our being, which the mystics call the
> "ground of being" or the "peak of the spirit. (p. 66)

The quest is that of transformation, something Bourgeault (2003) refers to as

> a kind of sacred alchemy. And it is precisely this alchemy that
> defines our essential human task. The secret of our identity does
> not lie in the outer form or in how successfully we manipulate the
> outer forms of the sensible world. Rather, it lies in how we are able
> to set them (and ourselves) aflame to reveal the inner quality of
> their aliveness. (p. 55)

Contemplative meditation is one method of entering into this transformational quest. "[Meditation is] a way of entering into a more interior, meditative awareness of oneness with God" (Finley, 2005, p. 4).

## CONCLUSION

Meditation is a transformative interior discipline that has the effect of changing perspectives, increasing spiritual awareness, and motivating compassionate living. That service providers participating in this study reported positive changes in how they experienced their work, the people they worked with, and themselves is consistent with the emerging research regarding the efficacy of meditation in other physical and mental health fields. As participants gained congruence between their intellectual and emotional selves, they experienced increased capacity to accept themselves and others, to let go of personal agendas and control. They found their viewpoints broadening as they gained a more objective perspective of themselves, their work, and how their contributions fit within a larger whole. The changes they reported suggest that a contemplative meditation practice increases and fosters emotional health and fosters more positive relationships with colleagues and family members.

· ·

## CO-AUTHORS' COMMENTS
### From the Desk of Michael Rothery

In recent years, professionals in mental health and other service settings have embraced mindfulness meditation and similar practices that appear to offer important, broadly useful techniques. Meditative/contemplative practices are believed to benefit clients suffering from depression, anxiety, and myriad other stress-related difficulties. The same practices are thought to be useful for professionals themselves, helping them become more comfortable and effective in their work. The utility of mindfulness meditation as a "coping strategy" for IPV professionals was the focus for a program described (and evaluated) in this chapter.

Consistent with reports elsewhere in the professional helping literature, the workers who took part in meditation training (and the subsequent evaluation) reported personal growth in the form of new or heightened skills: the capacity to be present, self-reflection, boundary maintenance, and self-regulation. We work with clients who need to handle stress better, especially survivors of traumas like IPV, by helping them build these same competencies. Given the stressfulness of serving such clients, it is no surprise that what helps and nurtures clients can be similarly helpful to their helpers.

The same skills of presence, reflection, boundary maintenance, and self-regulation have benefits for professionals in the IPV field, partly because much of their work is crisis intervention. The workers interviewed for the research reported in Chapter Six emphasized this, highlighting ways in which knowledge of meditation helps them respond to crises in a more balanced and effective manner. Faced with emotionally charged demands, they are better able to remain grounded (presence), to maintain awareness of their own responses (reflection), to avoid owning or taking inappropriate responsibility for problems (boundary maintenance), and to be more measured and purposeful when they do intervene (self-regulation).

One of the frequent observations by research participants seems especially important: When the skills we are discussing are used effectively, there is more flexibility or freedom to build the kind of relationship we need to cultivate to be useful; there is more room for empathy, authenticity, and compassion. When workers report gains like these, they are telling us something we will recognize as vital, regardless of where we stand on the secular-sacral continuum.

Another general "take-away" from this chapter that should be highlighted is simply the importance of self-care by helpers engaged in stressful, crisis-oriented work. Agencies responding to IPV are usually stretched, lacking time and other resources. However, it is clear that a commitment by employers to support their staff through opportunities like meditation training should be seen as an essential priority.

### From the Desk of Nancy Nason-Clark

Several years ago, I wrote a chapter entitled "From the Heart of My Laptop: Personal Passion and Research on Violence against Women" (2002) where I considered the impact on my own life of the research that I do. From how the subject matter had changed the way I do my academic work, probably forever, to the link between research and social action, this short piece reflected on the bidirectional nature of the research process. As an academic researcher, I am well positioned to speak from the heart *of my laptop*, the one place where it is safe to combine academic rigour, empirical reality, and personal passion. And what is learned has the power to change lives, challenge structures, and create synergy across distances created by professional, disciplinary, or geographical boundaries.

In the research on contemplative meditation reported in this chapter, Irene and I interviewed workers, held focus groups, participated in training venues, and *listened intently* to the struggle of those who work with traumatized clientele on a regular basis. There are risks involved—working to acknowledge and reduce these ought to be on the agenda of every service organization and each academic department that trains students who will someday staff these agencies. The importance of self-care and the risks of vicarious trauma are well recognized in the literature but practiced inconsistently in the daily lives of many first responders and agency staff.

Fostering emotional health and safety for workers as well as clients is critical for transforming lives and social structures. In this project, we were able to identify some of the features of the impact of introducing meditation—a common form of spiritual discipline observed in many religious traditions—on the intellectual and emotional experiences of those who chose to participate. Any practice that has the possibility of encouraging positive working relationships with colleagues, family members, friends, *and* those we are called by our profession to serve ought to be given serious, very serious, consideration.

### From the Desk of Robert Pynn

The introduction of centred meditation into the FaithLink program grew out of the desire to share an ancient resource of the religious communities with service providers who had been so deeply generous with sharing their own traditions and resources with FaithLink. This reciprocity demonstrated how modelling collaboration within the very structure of what we do was so important to the integrity of the program. For me, the most important motivator was the deep love and appreciation that time and common enterprise had woven.

The addition of the study was a way of giving concrete evidence of this mutual love and the impact of centring ourselves in the ultimate source of union and grace. We also hoped that the clients who were being served would experience a collateral impact.

When I first read this study's report, I was especially moved by the comments of its participants. Even under the most limiting circumstances of such a short-term experiment the results were very significant. Their comments about the wide impact of the contemplative practice were profound. Not only did the practice of Centering Prayer increase their individual capacity to manage pressures and stress along with their deepened capacity for attention and focused response but it also affected, for good, their wider relationships at home, as well as at work.

In light of meditation as an example of service providers' self-care and inner growth, I am convinced that Dr. Nancy Nason-Clark's insight about the need for self-care among service providers is spot-on. CEOs and boards of all service organizations need to set self-care as a priority and include programatic solutions in their human resources policies and manuals.

I have used modified contemplative practices at the beginning of board meetings with very positive effects on the way we worked together. With this preparation, our meetings easily move into generative discussions and develop deeper vision and commitment to our true purpose. What I am suggesting is that the contemplative way can be used wisely throughout an organization to let go of egoic agendas and deepen unified commitment to action. I hasten to say the experience of which I speak was primarily put in place as I acted as chair of a number of community-based boards of directors who were not used to anything contemplative on their action agendas. Self-care and beyond is important for everyone in an organization and thinking out of a spacious mind is critical to success.

My last observation is to say that FaithLink's meditation program and study demonstrates that while the impacts were therapeutic, Centered Prayer or meditation is not really about therapy. Therapy generally includes a focus on building up the faltering ego and helping the self cope with its many egoic needs. Contemplation practice takes its approach through the path of surrender, helping us to let go of the emotional programs of our surface self and egoic desires to which we are given to cling. This is not to suggest that the ego is the enemy and therapy an alien practice. Wisdom practitioners may also seek therapy to help them deal with heavy downloads from their unconscious released by their practice. What I am saying is that centring meditation seeks to develop an inner gesture of surrender—surrender of the surface self-synthesized by egoic feed-back loops that obscure the resilience, strength, and glory of the true self. The ancient symbol of the acorn teaches us that we can spend our lives polishing and preserving our shell or we can fall into the ground, crack open, and become a towering oak. Meditation is not about nurturing our surface shell to cope with the external forces that threaten its existence. Meditation is about transforming our narrow mind into a spacious consciousness that lifts us out of the cycles of torment and loss and helps us see who we truly are: elegantly conceived from the ray of sacred glory.

## CHAPTER RESPONDER
### Carolyn Goard, Director of Program and Member Services, Alberta Council of Women's Shelters

As a leader in the domestic violence serving community when this project was conceived, and having been part of those original conversations, it is wonderful to witness its transition from action to the printed page. Whether you are a religious leader, member of a faith community, academic researcher, or social worker/service provider reading this chapter, you will gain new insight and/or affirmation of the risks inherent in working with victims of intimate partner violence (i.e., vicarious trauma). You will also appreciate the nature of the work, its crisis focus, and the requirement for collaborative relationship development between shelters and community colleagues to ensure women's safe transition back into the community.

Results affirm that implementing a personal practice of contemplative meditation holds real promise for maintaining and enhancing personal health and well-being in the face of bearing witness to the traumatic realities for women

living in domestic violence and while working in a crisis-focused work environment. Results also suggest collaborations are strengthened by participants'
meditative practice, where focus on individual agendas broadens to include the
holistic. This collaborative work is essential to the broader work of changing
systems and structures to ensure equity of opportunity to lives free from
violence.

The challenge for those of us who are leading and funding organizations
that are providing domestic violence services is to ensure that through the allo-
cation of adequate time and resources for supervision and training, individual
workers are empowered to make choices that support their emotional well-being,
one of which may be the implementation of a meditative practice. Our success in
doing so is foundational to any individual staff member or broader organizational
system in providing and sustaining excellence to serve women who are striving to
build peaceful lives for themselves and their families.

# Faith and Belief

Belief builds walls high
separates in from out:
You become the mediator and judge of all that's true.
Maker of creeds, purveyor of laws—
a bulwark of power in the name of One
whose height your narrow mind cannot contain

Oh yes, there is some truth here but little freedom;
no open sky or perch for flight—no access to its Origin.
Sacred Presence is locked out of chambers ripe with power's abuse.

Sacred truth bears no ill, breaks through solid walls,
rides on whitened wings, renews itself in the fires of love.
No longer trapped in the systems of the mind
union and new life greet pain within the wall,
flow through dungeons of hostage minds,
open the gateways of wisdom and faith.

Love's spacious mind restores belief to its faith-full-ground,
saves it from the walls of its own certitude.
Questioning becomes its friend, transformation its true élan.

*Do you not believe it to be so???*

—ROBERT PYNN

# 7

# Reflections on the Book

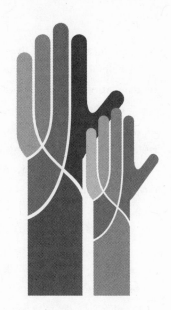

## A Panel Discussion, Part I

**INTRODUCTION**

As the preceding chapters illustrate, creating dialogue between secularly based service providers and religious/ethno-cultural communities on the issue of intimate partner violence (IPV) carries with it both philosophical and very practical components. The values upon which most secular social services are based are grounded within the Enlightenment; religious belief systems are founded on sacred, ancient texts and traditions (Chapter One). These very different perspectives influence how IPV is defined and how individuals and communities choose to respond to its occurrence. Yet, in creating a broadly based and coordinated response to IPV, religious/ethno-cultural communities must be seen as having a significant role (Chapter Three). Bringing religious/ethno-cultural and secularly based leaders into discussion for the purposes of addressing IPV brings into sharp focus these differing perspectives and practical considerations.

The practical implications of these differing perspectives are evident for both religious and ethno-cultural women who are victims of IPV (Chapter Four) and for the service professionals who seek to help them (Chapter Five). Service providers, well versed in the dynamics of IPV, have much to offer religious leaders and communities wishing to assist and support those congregant families experiencing abuse. But is there wisdom held within religious traditions that can be helpful to service providers? Our research on the effectiveness of a contemplative meditation practice suggests that there is (Chapter Six).

Given that the FaithLink program was fundamentally about collaboration, we sought to gain the responses of a cross-section of community leaders to these issues as presented in the book as outlined above. We thus convened a panel, comprising religious leaders, academics, and social service professionals. Panel members were:

- Ron Fraser, B.Ed., B.Th., M.C.S., Ed.D., director of learning services, Alberta Bible College;
- Jackie Sieppert, Ph.D., dean, Faculty of Social Work, University of Calgary;
- Jennifer Solem, mentor in Education for Ministry seminars, lay member of a Christian faith community;
- Susan Mallon, M.S.W., M.B.A., CEO, Calgary Family Services Society;
- Howard Voss-Altman, rabbi, Temple B'nai Tikvah;
- Leslie Tutty, Ph.D., professor, Faculty of Social Work, University of Calgary; and
- Carolyn Goard, M.A., psychologist, director of programs and services, Alberta Council of Women's Shelters.

Each of the co-authors was also present to moderate the discussion, to learn, and to clarify. Although our desire was to not restrict the discussion, we did pose three questions for panel members to consider:

1. Is there something that struck you as being particularly important and/or critical:
   a. To the work and model of FaithLink?
   b. To understanding and/or responding to religious/ethno-cultural women experiencing IPV?
   c. To the efficacy of a meditation practice within the context of a secular setting?

2. Taken as a whole, what insights are gained from this material regarding:

    a. How religious/ethno-cultural communities can cooperate and collaborate with secularly based agencies/services in creating a broadly based community response to IPV?

    b. What lessons emerge in fostering this collaboration?

3. The overarching theme of the book is the role religion has in responding to social issues in a secular setting. What are your thoughts?

The panel members entered into a lively and rich discussion over the course of an afternoon. Their discussion was taped and transcribed. The analysis of this wide-ranging conversation is presented in this and the following chapter. We have attempted, as much as possible, to present the conversation in the panellists' own words. Questions one and two are the focus of this chapter, while question three is the focus of Chapter Eight. Panellists also offered editorial comments, which have been incorporated.

## ABOUT FAITHLINK AND ITS WORK

The discussion began with Robert Pynn giving a brief statement of the rationale for FaithLink's creation. He described its raison d'être as helping "two solitudes"—service providers and religious communities—"dissolve the gulf between them so that the energies and resources of both could come together in addressing the issue" of intimate partner violence. He noted that the rationale was not just to help abused religious women access the positive resources of their tradition, it was also to help service providers sensitively address their beliefs in the healing process. FaithLink's founders recognized that religious communities are "significant players in addressing the issue of IPV and knew that there were untapped resources in the wisdom teachings of these spiritual communities." So the approach was "to bring together two solitudes" that could then "become... collaborators." As the vision took shape, it gained service agency support. As Howard Voss-Altman noted, FaithLink did "its best work" by bringing service providers and clergy together "and saying let's talk about what your goals are and we'll talk about our goals and we'll see where they are and how they meet up. But it's complicated...and daunting" work.

A lively discussion arose over FaithLink's qualification that its focus "was not on changing religious doctrine" (see Chapter Three). Noting the need for some Christian perspectives to embrace a theological interpretation of Scripture that is "more life-giving...and safe" for women, Jennifer Solem saw in FaithLink's work an avenue for effecting doctrinal change and wondered why the program did not espouse this role. Howard Voss-Altman took strong exception to FaithLink's position:

> We [FaithLink] are out to change doctrine and...it's fair to say that...part of this whole project...is to recognize that patriarchy as it has been promoted, developed, supported, and sanctified...needs to change....You can't just say this is what it is and you have to accept patriarchy or otherwise our doctrine is off the table.

Other panel members suggested that although doctrinal change has to come from within faith communities, the secular world "can identify problem areas."

In defence of FaithLink's position, Robert Pynn identified the program's primary purpose as that of building relationships.

> We were very careful in FaithLink to say that [changing doctrine] was not our purpose. Our purpose was again, to build a relationship with a faith community and—by engaging concerned people from that community in our process—to begin to look at what are the tentative possibilities of that community's self-understanding and their theology that would make for the breaking of violent cycles. As you get into that process, then you also begin to see what conventional thinking needs to change. Our challenge was to stimulate their awareness. True change must come from within. We tried to [create change] that way so that it could be the community's decision, as opposed to some outsider coming in to tell them how they ought to be. It's particularly true if some of us are Christians going [for example] into a Buddhist community or...a Muslim community...One walks very carefully with a high level of respect. But I think any challenges to fulfill responsibility must be grounded in an honest respect.

But how, Howard Voss-Altman wondered, do you respect theological perspectives and practices that do not conform to a liberal and modern society?

> This is a very difficult paradox that liberals find themselves in [when] confronted with [a] more conservative or more fundamentalist community that sees the world as if it were some time ago... We talk of respect, but really...when we are looking at societies... [whose]...treatment of women...is positively medieval, we look disparagingly at that without any more reservations at all....it's not the way it should be...And while I can't just walk into [a place of worship] and say, "Hey look guys—it's 2011—we're not in 1522 here—you can't do that"...at the same time...if we're accountable for the protection of people and people's safety, we also need to make very, very clear statements about those kinds of teachings. [They] are not acceptable in the realm that we're dealing with. And while we appreciate you want to learn more, part of learning more is learning about why this [patriarchal doctrine] doesn't work... It takes brave leadership on the other side as well.

This conversation ended with questions: Where is the role of dialogue when religious dogma or ethno-cultural practices are contrary to Canadian law? When laws are broken in the name of doctrine, where does dialogue begin and end? Or are we "looking out into the future, at the beginning of a journey?" Are we content to build relationships—to build a critical mass—and hope that eventually the change we think should occur will occur? What are the consequences if the tipping point does not "tip" in the direction of our liberal society? What if those cultural positions we see as abhorrent become the dominant ones—to our detriment?

## ABOUT SECULAR-SACRAL COLLABORATION

Collaboration was a central topic of discussion for the panel. Their conversation identified the foundation on which collaboration is built and some of the significant challenges faced when secularly based service providers and religious/ethno-cultural leaders attempt a collaborative approach to intimate partner violence. Carolyn Goard provided a context for this discussion by noting that the social service and justice sectors of the Calgary community experienced "an exceptional decade [approximately 1995–2005] of collaborative work and initiatives."[1] As the director of a women's shelter during this period, Goard noted that collaboration is "about relationship...[and that] in order to keep the momentum going, the relationships need to be nurtured...and ongoing." Notwithstanding the strength and creative outcomes that result from collaboration, the collaborative model is always vulnerable to change: "Relationships and people change...situations change, funding changes, lots of things change. [The hope is] that all the work, all the ground tilling and the wonderful work that has been [done]...will continue....It's an ongoing journey that we're all on."

Trust was not only defined as the broader purpose addressed by the book, and of FaithLink, but the foundation upon which collaboration between the secular and sacral communities develops and continues. But the process of creating and building trust is complicated and complex. As Ron Fraser noted, "[Trust] comes from vulnerability," and requires an appreciation and understanding of varying perspectives, which inevitably pose challenges. These include reconciling priorities, clarification of language, overcoming stereotypes, and receptivity of the "other." Giving a very practical example, Howard Voss-Altman identified the essence of this trust:

> Can a service provider know that if there's a referral to a member of the clergy, [the spiritual counsel provided by the member] is not in derogation of her [the victim's] safety? Unless those issues of trust are overcome or reconciled, you are going to have gaps.... If...some member of the clergy...puts...the sanctity of marital vows ahead of the woman's safety...[for] that service provider [it's] gonna be the end of that trust.... [S]afety, autonomy, self-determination...[are] the ultimate goal[s] here, not the preservation of a violent relationship.

Language, and the fact that the same words may carry different meanings in secular and religious contexts, and for victims of IPV themselves, highlighted for panel members the need for dialogue and understanding. Even as an appreciation for the perspective of the "other" was identified as the foundation upon which trust is built, panel members were conscious that in addition to the secular, only Christian and Jewish religious perspectives were represented around the table. Not only were other major religious traditions (e.g., Muslim, Buddhist, Hindu) not present, even for those who identified themselves as Christian or Jewish there was recognition that they only spoke for themselves and not for the whole of their respective religious communities.

Acknowledging that their discussion was framed within a limited secular–Christian–Jewish paradigm, the panel addressed some of the practical challenges in building trust across the secular–religious divide and the reality that when the issue is intimate partner violence, the safety of the victim is the primary focus and is non-negotiable. The challenge of gaining common under-standing of language, and overcoming stereotypes on both sides, was highlighted by three concepts: forgiveness, patriarchy, and violence.

Jennifer Solem opened this part of the conversation by noting that from a faith perspective, forgiveness can be "a wonderful, life-giving thing, but it [can] also be problematic in the context of...IPV." Others agreed. Michael Rothery stated,

> If...I'm a secular guy and you're a religious guy and we're talking together about some situation and you use the word "forgive-ness," as a secular guy my dukes go up. And it's not because I don't believe in forgiveness, it's because I have a lot of stereotypes about what you mean by forgiveness.

There are, Susan Mallon suggested, different levels of "intention" attached to the concept of forgiveness.

> It's a word that we have to use carefully because the understanding of what it means isn't shared at the same level. [One level, perhaps] the first level, of understanding often relates to "I forgive you, therefore it's okay."...But there can be "I forgive you" and it's not okay...[W]hen you're talking about a faith value of forgiveness, you have to take it to that most pure level. [The abusive behaviour is] not okay—absolutely not—but who are you forgiving? Are you forgiving the person or in a faith context, are you forgiving the best self of that person?...I don't know.

Robert Pynn, speaking from his Christian perspective, noted that "the process of forgiveness is tied up with repentance, an amendment of life, accountability and change...For the forgiving person [the act of letting go of the sense of violation arises] out of their own anguish...there is that sort of level [too]...But you can't leave out that accountability piece."

Patriarchy poses a very different challenge. Whereas "forgiveness" may carry different levels of meaning and misunderstandings across secular–religious lines, the concept of patriarchy is so ingrained within some ethno-cultural communities that, as Howard Voss–Altman stated, it "is simply what it is. There's often not even a word for 'patriarchy' because it's so ingrained [within the cultural fabric]. There is no 'other' thing to counter patriarchy." Using an example from his own ministry, Voss–Altman further challenged his fellow clergy to address patriarchy—in sermons, through education, and in offering support:

> We have a job to do, all of us in the clergy, which is to deconstruct patriarchy and present a new model for our people....[I]n doing so, by the way, we...gain the trust of....service providers who see that...these clergy are working on a different model so that you build trust that way....It's about [interpreting sacred text] in a modern context.

The third word that illustrated for panellists the challenge language poses in building trust across secular–religious domains is "violence." Michael Rothery wondered, "When the secular guys use words like 'violence'...[or phrases like] 'coercive abuses of power,' do our religious colleagues understand exactly what we're talking about?" He argued that what may be defined from a secular perspective as a coercive use of power may be viewed from a theological perspective as part of one's faith. "It's part of language," and depending on how words are interpreted, there may not be agreement on meaning and therefore a lack of trust: "It's so difficult [because] it's tricky."

Summing up the conversation about language, Susan Mallon articulated both the goal and the struggle: "Getting to a common language is something I think needs to happen in order to make real progress, but I'm not sure how we get there. I don't think we will make much progress [toward the goal of collaboration] until we have a common language."

A final challenge facing a collaborative model identified by panellists is the need for openness and receptivity of the "other." As Nancy Nason-Clark noted,

> Sometimes clergy do not feel welcome at the collaborative table...
> [W]hen they do make initial overture to...[for example]...visit a
> women's shelter...the reaction [from service providers is often]
> not particularly understanding. [They may not] yet understand the
> dynamics of why...[that request] may be inappropriate...So there is
> still a lot of work to be done.

The lack of receptivity also goes from clergy to secularly based service providers and is seen when religious leaders only refer to counsellors who are within their faith tradition or, worse still, attempt to handle situations of IPV themselves.

Having identified some of the challenges that make it difficult to bridge the secular-sacral divide, panellists returned to the importance of trust, trust that is grounded within relationships. Nancy Nason-Clark stated,

> It really boils down to relationship....[I]f you have strong
> relationships you can begin to ask...questions with a level
> of trust...But when you're not in a situation of mutual trust,
> [clarifying and reconciling issues] becomes impossible...[T]he
> chasm is so great there is no bridge across it. [So the questions
> become:] How does that dialogue happen? How do we build those
> relationships...in this community...in other jurisdictions?

Building on comments by Howard Voss-Altman of how stories from religious traditions can be used to teach about equality and the inappropriateness of IPV, Nancy Nason-Clark noted,

> There are all sorts of stories in the professions, too, that can be
> harnessed...I think that's what FaithLink did so extremely well...
> to bring people to the table and say there is common ground that
> we can build on...[W]hen you talk about finding the right language,
> it's a language that everybody feels comfortable with...I think

that that's where FaithLink's work was so incredibly powerful.
[It brought] individual people to the table and helped to provide
a language where they could then go back and harness their own
traditions and be...given help when they began to meet resistance,
because resistance they will meet—there's no question about that.

The value of overcoming mistrust and building cooperative working
relationships was articulated by Jennifer Solem:

Counsellors don't have to be theologians and theologians don't
have to be counsellors....[F]rom the woman's point of view, she's
coming in with a theology so she should be discussing that with
someone who's able to find the streams in tradition that are going
to be most helpful to her...because your theology is like your basic
values, your fundamental beliefs, and if spirituality is important
to you, there may be some things there that could use some
re-examining or reinterpreting or reframing into more life
affirming values.

While the FaithLink model was cited for its work in addressing this
challenge, by bringing individuals from both the secular and the religious spheres
together to discuss concerns, gain understanding, and, hopefully, decrease
mutual mistrust, for Leslie Tutty this approach raised its own challenges:

There are practical, legal, and ethical boundaries that we all have to
work with—from the service provider side, from the clergy side...
There is also a role [perhaps for FaithLink] to map out more clearly
what...these ethical...and legal issues and roles are...to map out
those boundaries in a way that helps people really practice at the
front lines.

Just as the telling by women victims of their stories allows other "women
to see themselves," perhaps, Howard Voss-Altman suggested, it may be helpful
"if clergy [could] also tell a bit about their story—for example, the first time
they encountered...IPV in their ministries, and how they've evolved over time

to handle it another way...[C]lergy also need to see themselves and put themselves in a particular context and maybe there can be some anecdotal work with clergy who have come from point 'A' to point 'B'" (another proposed project for FaithLink).

Ron Fraser identified the concept of compassion and its evident commonality within both the secularly based services sector and religious traditions as another component of mutual understanding and collaborative work. Referring to Chapter One (in particular, "Exclusion is a licence to withhold compassion..." [p. 19]), he noted that this is "really a powerful idea because you can also flop [it] around and say that inclusion then is a licence, or a call, an embodiment of compassion...[I]t might be worth exploring that in a bit more detail because... it helps define in some ways the ways in which the secular community and the sacred community can work together because compassion is at the heart of that [work]."

## MOVING BEYOND DUALISM

A short, philosophical discussion among the panellists addressed the question of the roots of violence. Chapter One speaks to the question of whether religions are to blame for violence, but for Ron Fraser, this is only part of the question. The Enlightenment, he argued,

> needs to own its own contributions to violence too...[B]ehind
> the myth of progress and behind the myth of assured results
> and autonomy...is the myth of sacrifice...that...if I have a right
> to control everything, I also have a right to sacrifice my neigh-
> bour...[V]iolence is [written] within the Enlightenment Project...
> [Perhaps, rather than seeing religion as the root cause of violence]
> maybe [religion is] part of a larger culture and an epistemology
> that is in itself violent...I see violence as a deeply human
> problem...that is state-sanctioned.

Lending his comments to this argument, Michael Rothery acknowledged that "people recognize...the 20th century as probably the...biggest bloodbath [in the] history of the cosmos and...it wasn't religious ideologies that produced all that...[In the] history of conflict [and] the human species it seems that force was always a viable option." From Ron Fraser's perspective, "we've always found ideologies of various sorts to justify violence."

But Robert Pynn gave another perspective when he suggested that taking what are essentially dualistic positions (whether rooted in religious belief systems or secular, Enlightenment thought) enhances, rather than bridges, the chasm between secular and sacral perspectives:

> I would like to suggest...the importance of overcoming solitudes, which really translates into gaining a new level of consciousness, that thinks in a unitive manner as opposed to thinking in dualism. [D]ualism is inherently violent because it gives you no alternative but for the two opposing forces to fight it out. Unitive thinking, on the other hand, takes the energies of both [opposites] and brings them together in a forward movement. The question becomes how [can] we...do that...[As Howard Voss-Altman noted earlier] there are some pathological situations to which no end of reconciliation or anything else you want to apply, can help. But we have to move away from dualism. Considering unitive possibilities helps us take our experience in relationships which [have to be unitive in order to work], into structures and programs that will lead us to a nonviolent way of dealing with each other. Unitive possibilities also offer a much more sensitive understanding of those who are caught in dualistic paradigms.

This discussion ended by taking the philosophical to the practical, with panellists making several points.

- Duality applies to both individuals and their communities.
- Violence, regardless of whether it is rooted within religious or secular systems, strips individuals [and communities] of their sense of identity and their resilience, their sense of wholeness.
- When considering the impact of violence, we have often separated the two [individuals and communities].
- Part of our work is finding a way to rebuild resilience in a way that merges both individuals and their community.

## ABOUT TRANSCENDENCE AND MEDITATION

Jackie Sieppert raised the theme of transcendence as a point of interest. He noted that for the past 200-plus years, we have relied on science "to give us meaning, to help us understand where we fit in the world, to help us understand the things that happen to us." He perceived a shift occurring in recent years, "both within the sacred community and the secular community...[with] a stronger refocusing on what the yearning is about." As he read the book, he noted phrases and terms like "yearning for transcendence," "spiritual injury," "spiritual brokenness," "spiritual wounding"—but without a corresponding focus on

> spiritual resilience or spiritual wholeness [that] are broader
> than the sacred. [It] goes back to this yearning that we all have...
> I think that the real benefit of groups like FaithLink and the real
> opportunity here for all of us is to find a way to help people achieve
> that yearning, to...understand how we work together to...change
> community norms and values...[T]hat to me is kind of at the heart
> of this. How do we...get to that yearning? How do we understand it?
> How do we work with it in a different way that combines the secular
> and the sacred? That's really the challenge that I think we have.

Howard Voss-Altman, too, was struck by the phrase "yearning for transcendence....because it's really...hard to define...[and] whether or not transcendence is how we think of it—is transcendence a question with some ultimate meaning, or [is it] a desire for affirmation in a relationship...and about belonging?" He also questioned whether meditation "lead[s] us toward ultimate meaning...[I]f meditation...leads you to a connection, then I believe it leads to ultimate meaning."

But Robert Pynn argued meditation—at least contemplative meditation—is not about finding meaning from a rational perspective. Rather, contemplative meditation is

> ultimately letting go [of] the programs of the emotional self so that
> you can...connect with your inner source, which is the core of the
> core...And finding that [at] the centre or the core or the foundation
> of life where love dwells, is a heart perception...[The process is a

letting] go of the binary systems and duality systems of the brain
so that you can move into the unitive seeing of the heart....[S]o it
is deeply about relationship and your meaning arises out of being
at home in the ultimate reality. That deep sense of belonging and
connection...[leads to creativity in] that people...can begin to work
through issues and problems of this world from a different point of
view and it's what we call unitive seeing. [It's a] struggle to do, but
it's worth the journey.

Carolyn Goard picked up on these comments by providing the context
out of which the research project on contemplative meditation, reported
in Chapter Six, emerged: "[O]ne of the discussions [by agency leaders who
participated in the project] was around...transcendence [and] going to another
level to support the whole [collaborative effort]...to be able to get above the
personal, the professional differences, and agency differences...[to broaden]
the collaborative process...to access resilience on a different [level]."

But how meditation is being used within a secular context raised concerns
for Leslie Tutty.

Cognitive behaviour therapy has now taken over meditation...It's
[become] a technique...[I]t really does raise questions about people
using a method which has the potential to be transformative but
[is disconnected from its historical religious foundation]. [T]hat's
really not a good fit.

This concern was echoed by Robert Pynn, who cautioned that a meditation
practice which is not rooted within an understanding of its cosmology...it
becomes a wellness technique...[I]t can't be used that way because that becomes
in itself an egoic application to that which is calling us beyond the egoic level of
our existence.

Other panellists expressed surprise that the research participants
identified meditation as inherently reflective—that it was an internal process—
rather than being about finding your place, about finding the relational. The
participants did not seem to connect with something broader. Others thought
that perhaps the problem was one of language, noting that there are many

different kinds of meditation and therefore different understandings. Another observation was the variation of benefits participants reported—it was very helpful for some but not so for others. One size does not fit all. However, given the positive benefits that were reported, panellists concluded that meditation should be offered to staff members as a potential self-care practice.

## ABOUT RESOURCE ACCESSIBILITY

That ethno-cultural women who are victims of violence face barriers— linguistic, religious, cultural, experiential—in accessing mainstream services was of concern for panel members. The fact is that even though mainline service agencies have, over the years, attempted to make their services more "user-friendly" for women of differing cultures, the barriers seem to remain. Carolyn Goard spoke of the efforts of women's shelter programs to imple- ment cultural competency programing, noting that it is a huge undertaking. In order to be successful, it must be embedded within the policies and culture of the agency—from the board level to the leadership level and then down to the front-line staff.

> And then you need...to do training with staff [on an] ongoing [basis]. Many smaller, not-for-profit agencies do not have the resources to implement such a broad program and therefore don't do all that well. Similarly, spiritual awareness programs require time, finances, and commitment over the long term. However difficult, shelters continue to strive to have counsellors be able to [be] more present for women in their unique realities [but] we all have such a long way to go.

Notwithstanding the efforts made to "meet clients where they are," the question remains: How can the gulf between the life stories, experiences, and world views of some clients and those of the average counsellor be bridged? Carolyn Goard articulated the challenge this way: "How in the world would I, coming from my background, begin to understand where some of the women... children [and men who] are...now in our community in terms of [what] their life and world experience has been? It's just so very different."

But Susan Mallon saw two potential avenues through which the gulf of understanding could be bridged.

> [If we had] voices within ethno-cultural communities, [we could begin to] bridge the gaps...[S]ometimes those voices might be the children—children of those immigrants who are being raised in our world, in Canada's world. [B]y the time they're eight...they have different views...[I]n terms of language, we've often use the children as interpreters with their parents.... I think kids are the ones who drive change in [immigrant] communities anyway... because kids and their parents aren't seeing the world in the same way...[So I am wondering] can the children...be our emissaries to assist with that cultural conversation?

Her second suggestion is to place attitudinal change within a longer-term view.

> We have differences in our understanding of the world based on experience and experience is, fortunately, a dynamic thing. [The traumatic experiences of those coming to Canada as refugees and immigrants] will start to mitigate as they have new experiences here. And maybe our challenge is to help influence that experience so that it starts opening possibilities for them [to ask] for help. Maybe [at first, they will ask for help only in] extreme circumstances, [but having done so] once and their experience starts to gradually broaden.

The conversation of engaging children as bridges between cultures piqued the interest of Jennifer Solem. She noted a brief comment in the book regarding the lack of spiritual supports for children who are witnesses of violence. She suggested that by getting connected with the kids, we could also offer them healing.

## SUMMARY

This chapter has offered the panel's discussion in response to the first two questions we asked them to consider in responding to this book. The work FaithLink undertook in building bridges of understanding between religious/

ethno-cultural leaders and secularly based service providers was viewed as a valuable contribution to a coordinated community response to intimate partner violence. These efforts can only benefit women who are members of religious/ethno-cultural communities and who experience intimate partner violence. The position the program took regarding religious doctrine, however, raised a fundamental question: How do organizations such as FaithLink—whose purpose it is to develop dialogue with religious communities—not directly confront doctrine or practices that place women at risk?

Developing understanding and collaborative working relationships is not without significant challenges. Panel members identified the foundations upon which collaboration is built (trust, relationship, openness to understanding different perspectives, and receptivity of the "other"), with language—and gaining a common understanding of terms—being identified as one of the barriers. The commonality of compassion and traditions held by both secular and sacral communities may hold avenues for mutuality and support. The need for legal, ethical, and professional boundaries to be clarification for transdisciplinary work to progress was identified.

Although much of the conversation focused on the practical, two topics interjected a more philosophic and metaphysical quality. The question of whether violence is rooted in religious thought was challenged: Violence emerges from religious and secular ideological structures because it is fundamentally a human problem. Dualism is inherent within both religious and secular thought and, by virtue of its paradigm of opposing forces, is inherently violent. If, however, the energies utilized by opposing forces against each other are put to forging a new alternative, the outcome becomes creative rather than destructive. This unitive thinking then holds potential for overcoming violence and building individual and community resiliency.

Yearning for transcendence—that deep human search to find meaning—was the second topic of this more abstract discussion. Panellists identified a perceived shift occurring—away from and beyond scientific-based understanding of meaning to a seeking to understand the yearning for meaning itself. This provides opportunities for programs like FaithLink to find ways to help people—both secular and sacral in orientation—to embrace this quest. Meditation may be an avenue. Meditation, however, cannot be seen or used as a wellness technique. Rather, its intent is the letting go of dualism, of finding a deep sense of belonging and connection, which gives rise to practical and different approaches to problem solving (i.e., collaboration as opposed to competition).

Although service agencies attempt to be sensitive to ethno-cultural clients, their vastly different life experiences and world views make offering meaningful assistance difficult. One possible approach to easing this distance is to utilize first-generation, Canadian-born children to assist the cultural conversation. If the first experience of seeking help is positive, the potential for additional help seeking is opened.

# The Road

The road across the field
of widening complexity
makes for unsure footing

Muscles strain for balance
in the service of forward motion.

As the day lengthens
shadows begin to cloak the
untried path beneath our feet.

In the twilight cold invades skin
sending us inward to a vow still
burning from the fire of an original vision.

—ROBERT PYNN

# 8

# Reflections on the Book

## A Panel Discussion, Part II

### INTRODUCTION

The previous chapter presents our panel's reflections on the first two of
three questions. This final chapter reports its responses to the third and last
question—and the overarching theme of the book: the panellists' thoughts
on the role religion has in responding to social issues in a secular society. In
doing so, panellists did not question that religion and religious/ethno-cultural
communities had a role—rather, they addressed themselves to the challenges
faced by secularly based professionals in incorporating an understanding of the
importance of belief into their perspective and practice. But before they entered
into this discussion, they began by commenting on the value of the book itself.

### ABOUT THE VALUE OF THE BOOK

Leslie Tutty opened this conversation by commenting on the working title
of the book ("Secular and Sacral Communities Working Together to Address
Intimate Partner Violence") and the value of the book itself: "I love the title
because...there [are] so few opportunities to actually talk about secular and
sacral communities together. I think intimate partner violence [IPV] is probably one of the first issues that really [has given us] the opportunity." She noted
that the profession of social work has its roots in religious belief and many

students have entered the profession because of their personal beliefs. Yet it has been her observation that the topic of religion is not discussed within the classroom setting and, when introduced, raises a level of unease among students. Notwithstanding the work of faculty colleagues in the area, the importance of spirituality to clients is not necessarily transferring to the workplace. So, Tutty noted, this book is "groundbreaking in that [it] talks about both of them together and [therefore gives] people permission to ask about spirituality and where [it] fits [in their work with clients.]"

Three audiences were identified for the book: women who have been victimized, service providers, and members of the clergy. Given her own research of IPV, Tutty spoke to the value of hearing directly from women:

> What's really useful about the stories and the analysis of the voices of the women is it introduces the complexities and the uniqueness of each woman. [It is] through the stories [of other women that victims begin to] see themselves and [begin to understand] the complexity of [IPV]...and the ethno-cultural...societal and religious forces [impacting their own circumstances].

In addition to gaining understanding of their own circumstances, Tutty also suggested, "It's not okay for many...women to talk about their spiritual beliefs...A book like this gives them permission to talk about the links [between their experience and their beliefs]." Again, it gives them a voice.

The panellists then turned to the second audience for the book—service providers. Not only is religion an uncomfortable topic of conversation within the educational setting, it is often avoided within the workplace. Leslie Tutty commented, "Shelter workers, police officers...there are so many service providers who probably wouldn't feel comfortable asking [clients] the question [of whether religion is of importance to them]." Jackie Sieppert echoed this observation:

> Part of the value [of the book] is in giving permission to students and future service providers to understand IPV more intimately, and then to have permission to explore spirituality...[As] social workers...we were always taught [that] we start with where the client is.

The clergy was identified as the third audience who could benefit from this book. Ron Fraser picked up on Leslie Tutty's comments about the importance for women of hearing the stories of other women by noting these stories are also "very useful to clergy." For him,

> [the stories of the women put a] face on violence...I think one of the great struggles of violence in our world is that there's no face on it...Putting a face on violence...open[s] up the possibilities for it to be very useful to clergy. What I appreciate about the work of FaithLink is [that it is] keeping the face of violence real. The more we can [recognize violence, the] more appealing it's going to be for all of us to address it as a human problem...It's a challenge that we all have to deal with whatever way we can.

But Leslie Tutty also voiced a caution for clergy to understand the complex dynamic of IPV and that impacts of abuse are unique to each woman, and to not respond out of preconceived assumptions: "[It's not as simple as saying] 'I forgive you and I will go back.' The fact of the matter is these women go back [to their abusing partners] more than they don't. [But neither do we] want clergy to...shift [their response to the other extreme of] 'You shouldn't go back.'" With increased understanding, responses can be more nuanced. She noted, "You have to leave because that's your abyss and that's not a good spot to be."

## CHALLENGES FACED IN CONSIDERING A ROLE FOR RELIGION

The challenges service providers face in responding to clients who hold religious/spiritual beliefs (see Chapter Five) was a point of special concern for the panellists from academia. In commenting on the interviews with service providers, these panellists noted that they often raised more questions than answers. Michael Rothery observed, "The ethics of [dealing with your own] theological or spiritual beliefs and the ethics of do you tell the client, do you not tell the client? How do you deal with that?...[T]here's not a lot of consensus or agreement [provided within the chapter], at least in terms of what's the right thing to do there." The lack of clarity results, Michael Rothery concluded, because "it's such thin ice. You get nervous."

Jackie Sieppert articulated the responsibility of educational institutions to address these issues. As dean of the Faculty of Social Work at the University of Calgary, he identified his commitment to

> support researchers...in building the knowledge base [to] help us understand violence and to respond effectively to [it]....[The faculty has] an obligation to graduate social workers who are professionals that understand many of the themes [addressed] in the text—everything from spirituality to self-care to collaboration....[O]ur graduates need to understand [these issues] and know how to work with them.

That there is a need to assist students and service providers in sorting out some of the issues was exemplified for her, Leslie Tutty noted, by a master's student who recently reported being "scolded for asking about spirituality [with] a client and [being] told 'You shouldn't do that—that is not okay.'" However, introducing spirituality into class discussions does raise a level of nervousness. "So there is a huge amount of work needed to even introduce [the] conversation," she said. But, "if there's anywhere that we should be able to discuss these things openly, it should be at a university," Jackie Sieppert posited. "If we get to a point where we tell our graduates that they don't have permission to ask about some areas [of a client's life], we've kind of defeated some of the basic principles of the profession."

That may be true, Michael Rothery observed, but religious clients have also been considered as "in a delusional state":

> I [am] thinking about the educator's responsibility and the difficulty of it. If you start talking about transcendental needs as sort of something that we talk about on the same level as we talk about needs for self-esteem or [other emotional states], you're really treading into new territory....[W]e are from a profession that not long ago thought that that wasn't right—neuroticism— that transcendental needs were a psychopathology problem, not a human problem....I think that educators, and the educational system, have a big role to play in this, but I don't think it's that

easy. But students are often relieved when they think they have permission to talk about this stuff.

Noting his observation that the professions tend "to suppress [religion]," Robert Pynn spoke of an interesting phenomenon experienced by FaithLink in its work with service providers. He described it as service providers with religious convictions "coming out of the closet":

We found that so many people who were in social services were originally motivated by some form of religious impulse and caring, but they consciously suppressed any of the language around that so that they would be completely fair and true to a science of profession....Unless the client brought it [religion] up...[T]here was always the caution...don't be the introducer.

That the "university environment is not always a safe place to talk about faith, spirituality, and religion" was raised by Nancy Nason-Clark—a point with which Michael Rothery agreed. She continued:

In many of the circles that we travel...it's not always a safe place necessarily to talk about some of these things. So I don't think it's surprising that many people have a kind of bifurcated way, or strategy, of living about this. They have their personal life... personal views and their values and then...there's little holes [through which it seeps into their professional life]. [When Irene and I did] the interviews [for the meditation research], we heard a lot of workers talking about some of the angst of trying to sort that out. I think it's a reflection of our training schools...and I think it's a reflection of people picking up the currents and the broader culture.

Into this serious conversation a bit of levity was interjected. Commenting on the observation of how people separate their personal from their professional selves, one panellist noted that "in education nowadays, they talk about whatever else you teach, the fundamental thing to teach is yourself." The same position is taken in seminaries, Howard Voss-Altman observed: "In seminary the professors in homiletics class would say 'the most important thing about having success as a rabbi is to be yourself...unless of course you're a schmuck, then be somebody else.'"

Others also noted the general cultural negativity toward religion. One panellist said, "There's an attitude of derision. In recent years the New Atheists have just dominated the booksellers. There's a lot of hostility out there about religion." Commenting on a blog on the *Globe and Mail*'s Faith Exchange, Howard Voss-Altman noted,

> I'm absolutely amazed by the level of vitriol that people feel about religious people or people who profess a particular faith...Just the overall tenor of "how dare people with religious points tell us about the issues of the day...[Y]ou have no right because you're the ones who are screwing the world up." So I think that it's a very uncomfortable place.

If this attitude of derision is carried into work with clients, the religious beliefs of clients are disrespected. Michael Rothery relayed the report of one student who

> had a client referred to her because the client specifically asked to see a Christian counsellor. She [asked,] "What's that about?" and the response was, "The last guy I talked to when I mentioned my belief said 'You don't believe in that junk do you?'" There was that dismissive response, so she left feeling...disrespected.... It's not just confusion and it's not just discomfort, it's also an active hostility.

Howard Voss-Altman identified trust as a significant factor: "I think for service providers it comes back to trust. If they initiate [a conversation about religion] or they hear about someone's [spiritual] needs...if they're not comfortable to refer to a clergy that they know...I think people are genuinely uncomfortable with those kinds of conversations."

Trust is also a concern for clergy, noted Ron Fraser:

> There are Christian organizations [and] good church leaders [who]
> deal with abuse issues and who are regularly referring people...
> but they will sometimes only refer to a Christian counsellor...that
> mistrust is there. But at least they're referring, which is better...
> than trying to deal with [the situation themselves] or forcing some
> sort of ideology [on the persons experiencing abuse].

The practice of the religious educational institution with which Fraser is affiliated
is to refer students who have disclosed their abuse. They have also assisted international students to lay criminal charges against abusers in other countries.

The conversation turned to practical responses by educational institutions
in addressing mistrust and bringing the secular and sacral communities closer
together in a mutual response to intimate partner violence. Robert Pynn spoke
of the original purpose of FaithLink and its work of bringing

> together service providers and clergy in a collaborative response to
> IPV. One way to begin this process was to create a consultation that
> brought together members of the two solitudes so that they could
> talk with each other and see the face of others with whom they
> could work. For many clergy it was important to know that they are
> not alone in facing an issue for which they are unprepared. There
> may be similar initiatives...that universities or colleges or theolog-
> ical schools might take based on the FaithLink model. [There may
> be a role for them to] say, "Let's invite clergy and service provides
> together so that people will find the confidence to refer and
> cooperate in healing wounds inflicted by IPV."

And Nancy Nason-Clark added, "They don't know how to refer. There are
just the very practical [issues] of: Who [do] you call? What do you say? What
will happen?"

Referring to current research she is conducting on the question of how
training in seminaries is impactful, Nason-Clark reported that

one of the things we've learned is that the training is most impactful if it's the powerful seminary professors. So in, let's say, a more conservative Protestant tradition, if the Old Testament professor, who is well loved, uses the story of Hagar[1] and talks about domestic violence, it's far more powerful in changing and enhancing the experience of the student than if a counselling professor talks about violence. So, it's not just about raising awareness generally, but it's looking for where are those positions of power within the seminary and how can you harness those in a way that will raise the whole topic to be impactful. And that, of course, becomes a much bigger challenge—[to ensure] that the issue of domestic violence isn't ghettoized as an elective course and no one takes it...There's got to be something where it's mandated in some sort of a way and diverse with those who are—let's call them—the most powerful speakers on campus.

Howard Voss-Altman picked up on the reference to Hagar, noting that

in Hebrew "Hagar" means "the stranger." Hagar means the stranger—and how women were treated, have been treated, continue to be treated as if they are strangers and therefore they can be abused or beaten or whatever....[O]ur textual traditions have a tremendous amount to teach us. Nancy, your suggestion that actually our seminaries teach those very fundamental stories is a great one. They need to be taught so that people can take those lessons out there into their ministries....They are totally within the tradition....[The] creation story [can similarly be used] to undermine patriarchy. That's why I [advocate] teaching the stories of how family dynamics can completely destroy families because that's what they're doing....[Deconstructing traditional stories as a method of teaching is not just applicable within the context of seminaries.] It's...in the social work context, too, because these are the very paradigmatic stories that actually shape the way we live.

Other panellists agreed. Nancy Nason-Clark noted, "All of the religious traditions have stories that can be harnessed in very, very positive ways...[T]here are all sorts of stories in the professions, too, that can be harnessed for hope and healing." "It's education, wherever you obtain it," said Ron Fraser. Susan Mallon added, "Somehow, we have to change our idea of education to be not just the science, but the relationships—which is what this is."

There are no easy answers to the challenges faced by service providers as they seek to meet the spiritual needs of clients who hold religious beliefs. Neither are there easy answers for educational institutions as they seek to incorporate an understanding of the importance of religious beliefs into a predominantly secularly based curriculum. Notwithstanding the very practical nature of these challenges, they also represent much broader issues. Nancy Nason-Clark summarized this portion of the discussion:

> So in a sense I think that the broader issues that we're talking about in this book [are] exactly...what many people are grap-
> pling with at different levels. When is it appropriate [to discuss religious issues]? Is it appropriate? How is it appropriate? Where are the minefields? How do you talk in a way that's respectful of other people's traditions and experiences while validating your own? And those are not easy questions. They are quite challenging questions. [From] the point of view of many of the people we had contact with, there wasn't just one answer...there's a multitude of answers. There's not just one way of understanding...your own faith tradition...[D]ifferent people have different ways that they harness [their faith] or fail to harness it with regard to responding to domestic violence.

**END COMMENTS**

As the discussion drew to a close, a number of the panellists offered general observations.

## The Impact of Economics

Ron Fraser:

> This is an interesting question not only retrospectively but at
> the present time and going forward...[A]s we see economic shifts
> happening and the relationship to social safety networks that
> we've always assumed [would be in place], the next 20, 30 years
> are going to be mighty interesting....I think religious communities,
> particularly Christian communities, may be called back into some
> of the more historic roles that they [once played]...simply because
> of the absence of public funding. I don't like that prospect because
> I like the idea of a commons in which everyone participates.

## The Challenge of a Collaborative Response to IPV

Nancy Nason-Clark:

> As I was flying into Calgary this time, I was reminded of my first
> visit...and my personal enthusiasm for bringing people together
> who have very different mindsets to tackle a common goal...
> [W]hat we've heard today...around this table is just how chal-
> lenging and difficult that is and how incredibly important it is....
> [This discussion] affirms what this book is attempting to do....
> [Bringing the secular and the sacral together to address IPV is] a
> really important task and it's a difficult task—finding the right
> language and building those relationships. [U]ltimately it's
> because there's such incredible need—that every home should be a
> safe home...And here we find ourselves where in some community
> agencies it's not safe to say you're religious and in many houses of
> worship it's not safe to say you've been violated.

## The Value of Perspective

Sue Mallon:

> [As an M.S.W. student 35 years ago,] I was part of the group
> of women who formed the first women's shelter [in Calgary]...

[W]hat always strikes me when I go back to that time is how much change has happened...[I]t's that 35 years of change which allows us today to talk about even bigger challenges of dialogue...[When I began reading the book,] I found myself...reacting a bit to the words "secular" and "sacred" as in opposition—like you're sacred and I'm secular...But by the end of [the book,] I was thinking that, for someone with a more women's lib background as mine, the theme of dialogue here is the peacemaking piece. And maybe the challenge for us today is to think of how to bring pretty disparate views [together]...It's like a whole continuum...People are somewhere along that [continuum] and the challenge is monumental actually.

## Journeying Together

Nancy Nason-Clark:

Thank you for being part of the journey, and...for being involved with FaithLink...[W]e are co-inheritors of problems on earth and we are also mandated...to go with compassion by our side...[T]he more that we model working together in the sandbox and the more that we struggle to really understand what collaboration means and to name it for when it's not collaborative, I think the closer we'll get to really making a difference in the world that we find ourselves in. [I]t's one drop of water in the bucket at a time. Thank you for walking along side and for sharing this afternoon with us.

## SUMMARY

Having identified some of the significant barriers inherent in a secular–sacral collaborative response to social issues, in particular that of intimate partner violence, the panellists turned their attention to the broader question of whether religion has a role to play in responding to social issues within the context of a secular society. That religion does have a role was not questioned by the panellists. Rather, they noted the very practical and practice challenges faced by service providers when clients hold life-shaping perspectives that are very different from their own. The responsibility falls to academic faculties, panellists asserted, to equip graduates with an understanding of a broad range of issues, including the importance of religious belief and the skills to work collaboratively with those who hold differing world views. Although much of the discussion focused on the challenges faced by secularly based faculties, there was also recognition that religious educational institutions face challenges in preparing spiritual leaders to consider addressing social issues, in concert with secularly based service providers, as within the scope of their ministry. For both the secular and the sacral, it seems, the challenge is the same: overcoming the perspective of "the other" as foreign and therefore irrelevant.

For secularly based professional faculties, incorporating a discussion of religion is breaking new ground and presents many challenges: changing perceptions of how religious beliefs are viewed within a secular framework; creating a safe and comfortable environment for both faculty and students in which religious issues can be discussed; clarifying ethical issues; providing guidance of when and how to respond to clients for whom religion holds significance. Charting this new course will not be easy, yet the panellists who raised issues of spirituality within the classroom noted that students appreciate the opportunity for the discussion.

Educational institutions—secular and religious—also have a role in addressing the mistrust that hinders collaboration between service providers and religious leaders. The panellists offered practical examples of how dialogue can be fostered and trust built by engaging each other in enhancing an understanding of differing perspectives, knowledge, and wisdom. As one panellist commented, the key is education—education that is about relationships.

Speaking to the book as a whole, the panellists identified three audiences who will find it of value: women who have been victims of abuse, service providers working with victims who hold religious beliefs, and members of the clergy. Given the discussion of the role of secularly based and religious academic faculties in including discussions of religion and social issues respective in the curricula, researchers and educators will also find benefit in this work.

# The Hours

Hours of torment
lashed across your mind,
memories of rejection
wired beneath brittle laughter:
listen to them build in dissonance
until hope is battered into a thousand wounds
that bleed inside.

All tell the deception—
the lies
glazed across the lip of love's dissemblance.

Heart retreats within a veil
woven by programs of his desire;
Dignity
falls ashen from its stolen flower.

Still, the voice of being recites an inner wisdom:

*The light shines in darkness*
*and the darkness cannot put it out.*

The shroud of lost becoming dissolves
in the flash of perceptibility—
anguish and turmoil the precondition
for a new creation.

Pass through the shining gate.
Rediscover the abundant life
where the road divides,
as the hold of the victim lets go.

*The hours of torment and loss*
*are the venom in which the antidote is found.*

Drink deep from the waters of freedom.
Weave the moments of broken brilliance
into a tapestry of life beyond the hold of his control.
Let your spirit feel the Love that seeks you,
in the light outside the wall,
where the wise see you as you truly are—
elegantly conceived from a ray of Sacred Glory.

—ROBERT PYNN

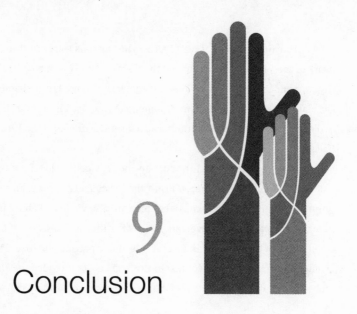

# 9

# Conclusion

## This book asked a fundamental question:

Does religion—and by extension religious communities—have a role to play in addressing social issues within the context of a secular society? It addressed this question through the issue of violence against women by their intimate partners (IPV) and the model of the FaithLink program—a unique community initiative whose purpose it was to engage religious leaders and secular service providers in creating a collaborative response to IPV. In bringing the secular and the religious spheres together, practical, ideological, and theological issues were encountered. These themes have been explored throughout the book, utilizing various presentation formats: a philosophical discussion of the question: Is religion responsible for violence in the world? (Chapter One); a summary of our current understanding of abuse against women and the religious/cultural contexts for Christian, Jewish, and Khmer Canadian women (Chapter Two); a description of the formation and work of the FaithLink program (Chapter Three); reporting the findings of three different but related research studies (Chapters Four to Six); and a discussion with community leaders (Chapters Seven and Eight). The book also reflects the contributions of four different authors through chapter authorship, poetry, and individual responses to chapters. Additionally, we sought the responses of individuals from religious and cultural communities and the service sector to respond to specific chapters.

This final chapter draws together the "lessons learned" through the work of the FaithLink program and the research projects. It also formulates recommendations for the various stakeholders who hold responsibility for a secular–sacral collaboration in responding to the social issue of intimate partner violence: religious/ethno-cultural leaders, service providers, and academic faculties.

As is clarified in the Introduction and is evident throughout this work, our focus has been on women who are victims of abuse at the hands of their intimate partners. We recognize that men are also victims of abuse initiated by their female partners. A developing body of writing and research is exploring this component of the complex issue that is intimate partner violence. The focus of women victims within the context of this book is not intended to denigrate the important exploration of the plight of male victims of intimate violence.

## LESSONS LEARNED FROM THE FAITHLINK PROGRAM

FaithLink was a pioneering enterprise, unique in its endeavour to bring religious/ ethno-cultural leaders into the broader community's and secularly based response to intimate partner violence. To this end its work included raising awareness of the issue of IPV within a number of religious/ethno-cultural communities; raising awareness with service providers of the importance of religious belief and practice to women of faith; sponsoring conferences and workshops designed to bring religious leaders and service providers together to enhance mutual understanding and develop collaborative working relationships; recognizing that assisting victims of violence is difficult work and offering supports to service providers; and conducting research. As is true with any new initiative, lessons arising from the doing form the bases on which a work moves forward. Some of the lessons learned through the work of the FaithLink program include the following.

- *Leadership is critical*: The success of a collaborative approach requires strong and committed leaders, representing religious/ethno-cultural and service-provider constituencies, who share a common vision.
- *Clarity of purpose*: The issue around which collaboration occurs (e.g., intimate partner violence) must be clearly delineated. The purpose cannot be about reinterpreting sacred texts; ecumenicalism; asking secularly

based service providers to become spiritual counsellors; or asking religious leaders to become IPV intervention specialists.

- *Vesting the work within the community*: Successful work is based on credibility within any given religious/ethno-cultural community. This requires engaging someone from within the community, preferably an established leader, who can speak the language—literally and figuratively—someone who knows the belief system, the cultural norms, and how the community "works." This person also needs an understanding of the issue of IPV, the services offered within the broader community, and how these can be accessed.

  Although the FaithLink program was independent of any given religious perspective and ethno-cultural community, for its mission to be realized, its work had to be relinquished to those religious/ethno-cultural communities with the internal resources and commitment to assume responsibility. Not only did this approach vest ownership for addressing IPV within a given community, it freed the FaithLink program to invest its energies in other communities.

- *Mistrust is a reality, but trust can be built*: Religious leaders and service providers mistrust each other. In relation to IPV, religious leaders fear service providers will not validate the importance of the spiritual, will counsel divorce, and will deny them access to congregants. Service providers fear religious leaders will not place the victim's safety as the first priority and will counsel reconciliation with the abusive partner. Although these fears may be, in many instances, misguided, they do hinder dialogue and need to be addressed. But over time trust can be built. It happens: over time; with commitment to the relationship; when both parties give up attempts to promote their own positions as the "right and only" one; and when both parties are prepared to work from within the framework of respect.

- *Religious communities can be part of the solution*: Congregations are communities that include individuals and families of differing ages, ethnicities, vulnerabilities, and strengths, which have resources and supports to offer not only their own members but also the larger society. Leaders can raise awareness of IPV within the congregation and can, with provision of appropriate tools, offer effective responses to those experiencing abuse. Religious rituals, practices, and disciplines offer sources of healing and spiritual strength.

- *It is a two-way street*: Religious/ethno-cultural communities and secularly based services each have wisdom, knowledge, and expertise to share with, and enrich the services of, the other. By mutual recognition of this reality, those in need of help can only be the benefactors.

## LESSONS LEARNED FROM RELIGIOUS/ETHNO-CULTURAL WOMEN

Although the FaithLink program worked with a variety of religious/ethno-cultural communities, its primary work was with the Christian, Jewish, and Khmer Canadian communities. As this work developed, we were increasingly aware of the influences religious beliefs and cultural norms exerted on how women viewed themselves, their relationships, and their place within their respective communities. Through a qualitative research study, we asked women from these three communities to describe how these influences affected how they and their communities defined and responded to intimate partner violence. From their discussions, we can draw a number of practical and ideological lessons.

- *Religious beliefs and culture are often inseparable*: Not only are religious beliefs nuanced through culture, the converse is also true. Additionally, both religion and culture determine how IPV is defined and addressed through the positions taken regarding gender roles and responsibilities, the primacy given to marriage and family, the importance of community and one's standing within it, and how supports are sought and accessed for family-related problems.
- *The idealism of religious beliefs collides with the reality of abuse*: The stronger a religious/cultural community holds on to utopian ideals of marriage and the family, the greater the difficulty women have in accepting the reality of abuse within their own relationships and extricating themselves from it. This often requires that they shift their perspective from a narrow and rigid interpretation of Scriptures to a more nuanced and flexible viewpoint. This can be a difficult personal journey and one that can carry significant disapproval from one's community.

- *Patriarchal structures place women at risk*: By definition, patriarchy places women in lesser and dependent positions. When patriarchal structures extend to arranged marriages, women are particularly at risk of experiencing abuse. Gender roles and responsibilities, religious and cultural expectations, and the consequences of nonconformity can act to "trap" women in intolerable situations. The risks to immigrant women entering both arranged marriages and a patriarchal religious/cultural context are increased.
- *Women have a role in finding solutions*: Women see themselves as playing significant roles in effecting change. They recognize the need to move away from sacral idealism and a categorical approach to positions that appreciate complexity and reality. They desire to work within their own communities to bring about changes and to work with service providers to increase understanding, acceptance, and accessibility to resources.
- *There is need to find common ground*: The need for religious/ethno-cultural communities to find common ground with the secular service community is evident. Issues requiring further discussion include the development of a common definition of intimate partner violence, facilitating access to secular services, education regarding IPV, and developing networks through which a broadly based—secular, religious, and ethno-cultural—community response to IPV can be implemented.

## LESSONS LEARNED FROM SERVICE PROVIDERS

The professional training received by most service providers is from a secular perspective—a world view founded on scientific inquiry, humanism, feminism, and individualism, and one in which religion has no place. Yet, as they attempt to implement a holistic approach in their work, service providers are faced with questions of how best to respond when faced with clients whose world views are shaped by religious belief. Victims of intimate partner violence who hold religious beliefs not only bring their very practical, physical and emotional needs when accessing services, they also bring spiritual needs that need to be addressed. Utilizing a qualitative methodology, we asked service providers to share their thoughts and experiences regarding how, or if, they respond to women victims of IPV who hold religious convictions. Through their responses, it became clear that not only do service providers face questions regarding the appropriateness and practicality of addressing spirituality within the context of the counselling forum, they also face significant challenges in responding to an increasingly pluralistic society. Their responses were enlightening and offer lessons for further consideration.

- *The need to find meaning*: Seeking to understand existential questions is a human need. This quest is often sought through religious beliefs. Experiencing IPV can bring the need to understand—the quest for "why"—into the forefront and initiate a spiritual journey or a re-examination of held beliefs.
- *Clarity and practice guidelines are needed*: Considering bringing the spiritual into the counselling context raises ethical concerns and practice questions—is it ethical to include any discussion of religious belief within the context of a secularly based counselling context? If one considers doing so, how is the issue introduced? How does the counsellor separate their own personal beliefs and biases from professional practice ethics? Clarifying practice principles is best addressed within the context of professional training.
- *Transdisciplinary (secular–sacral) collaboration is required*: The historical tensions between the secular and sacral are evident in the question of whether spiritual needs of IPV clients should become part of the counselling context. The needs of victims of IPV who hold religious beliefs, however, speak to the imperative for secular and religious leaders to seek common ground—to find ways of overcoming their mutual mistrust and developing open dialogue. Only when transdisciplinary connections are made will victims of IPV be free to access the professional expertise vested within secularly based services without placing in jeopardy the religious/ethno-cultural communities in which they find meaning and support.
- *Religious/cultural diversity presents challenges and offers opportunities*: The diverse ethno-cultural and religious makeup of Canadian society provides unique challenges and opportunities for seeking workable transdisciplinary collaborations. The very nature of our diverse society brings the secular–sacral fault lines into focus; provides a "living lab" for seeking solutions; and highlights the significant challenges faced by religious/ethno-cultural leaders, academics, and service agencies.

## LESSONS LEARNED FROM A MEDITATION PRACTICE

Meditation is a spiritual discipline found within the major religions of the world that hold a vision of human transformation. It has been practiced, in varying forms, for thousands of years. Contemplative meditation is intentional silence, an attitude of listening and receptivity, of being present. It is a function of consciousness—not of the intellect. Yet, in recent years, meditation has attracted the secular and scientific worlds for its potential in reducing symptoms associated with a variety of medical and psychological conditions. Our introduction of a contemplative meditation practice into a secular setting was in response to the difficult work of service providers who respond to victims of intimate partner violence, and to explore whether it had beneficial effects on the personal and relational levels. We utilized a methodology that included a period of instruction and a series of interviews spaced over a three-month period. In addition to the findings arising from this inquiry, a number of lessons also emerge.

- *Facing the risks*: Working with victims of intimate partner violence carries psychological risks to individual service providers and affects professional effectiveness and workplace environments. Responding in ways that lessen the risks becomes both an individual and an organizational responsibility. Academic faculties also carry responsibility to educate students of the risks of vicarious trauma and the importance of implementing self-care practices at both the individual and the corporate level.
- *The "knowledge" of meditation*: One of the interesting findings of the meditation study was the reporting by service providers that their work with clients was more effective. Given that these were individuals whose professional training was predominantly within the context of a secular world view, this finding suggests that knowledge other than that gained through scientific inquiry can have application within a secular setting.
- *Meditation is not a wellness technique*: It is not unusual for positive physical and psychological benefits to be realized reasonably quickly from a meditation practice. But meditation is meant to be a disciplined and consistent practice. It is only through the long term that shifts in consciousness and perspectives occur. While initial benefits can be realized with little internal struggle, the lasting benefits are often not so easily achieved.

- *Meditation facilitates collaboration*: Meditation, in its varying forms, is a common component of most religious traditions that hold an ideology of transformation. As such, meditation is a quest for spiritual awareness. It is through the transformative process of moving from a dualistic, intellectual, doing-focused perspective to one that is unitive in nature— marked by connectedness, relationship, being, reflection, cooperation, and flexibility. It is these latter qualities that facilitate collaboration. As such, meditation may hold a key for successful secular-sacral working relationships to develop.

· ·

We have explored, through example, research, and discussion, the question of whether religion has a role in responding to social issues within the context of a secular society. Lessons have emerged that speak clearly to the position that religion does have a role to play, particularly as it relates to the social issue of intimate partner violence. It is also evident that this role is best fulfilled through collaboration between religious/ethno-cultural leaders, service providers, and the academic community. Each has a part to play. The following recommendations are intended to further the discussion and facilitate collaborative responses to intimate partner violence.

## RECOMMENDATIONS FOR RELIGIOUS/ETHNO-CULTURAL LEADERS

Intimate partner violence is as prevalent within religious/ethno-cultural communities as it is within the general population. Spiritual and community leaders hold positions of influence that can be utilized to raise awareness, offer counsel and support, and educate. They can assist those affected by intimate partner violence by considering the following recommendations.

- Learn about IPV—the complexity of the relationship, the forms it takes, the defence mechanisms often utilized by the abusing partner, and its effects.
- Always work from the priority of safety for the victim.
- Commit to raising awareness of IPV within your congregation/community, and put protocols in place that guide leaders in responding appropriately to incidents of IPV when they occur within your congregation/community.

- Examine your theology and cultural norms to ensure that they are not placing women at increased risk of becoming victims and remaining in abusive relationships. Commit to affecting changes as required.
- Learn about the resources available within the broader community for those affected by IPV—victims, child witnesses, those who act abusively—and how to access them.
- Connect with service providers, take advantage of opportunities for discussion, and develop collaborative working relationships.
- Commit to respecting differing perspectives while recognizing that those affected by IPV need the expertise held by secular professionals and the spiritual guidance you offer.

## RECOMMENDATIONS FOR SERVICE PROVIDERS

An array of services is involved in responding to instances of intimate partner violence: shelters, counselling agencies, and police, legal, and justice services. In many communities these services have banded together to form a coordinated response. Given the influence religious beliefs and cultural norms have, it is important that spiritual and ethno-cultural leaders also be part of a collective, broadly based community response to IPV. The following recommendations may prove helpful to social services leaders as they consider engaging with religious/ethno-cultural leaders in creating a broad-based and collaborative community response to IPV.

- Commit to reaching out to religious/ethno-cultural leaders. Remember your "world" appears just as forbidding to them as theirs does to you.
- Work with colleagues (e.g., create a working committee to explore the potential of engaging religious/ethno-cultural leaders).
  - Begin with available connections you may already have. There may be staff members within your organizations who are members of religious/ethno-cultural communities. They can facilitate introductions and open discussions.
- Become a resource to religious/cultural leaders who are interested in learning about IPV. This may take the form of providing information, establishing connections to facilitate referrals, and/or organizing events where leaders and service providers can discuss mutual concerns and build relationships.

- As relationships with religious leaders develop, identify those leaders who understand the dynamics and who are open to being a resource to clients seeking spiritual counsel.
- Commit to respecting different perspectives. Clarify purposes and work to that end.

## RECOMMENDATIONS FOR ACADEMIC FACULTIES

Academic faculties that train religious leaders and those that train service providers function as very separate entities. Religious schools and seminaries are, by definition, focused on theology, its practice and application. Faculties engaged in preparing social service professionals are based within universities and are grounded within a secular, humanistic perspective. Yet these schools—religious and secular professional—hold unique opportunities for facilitating collaborative work between their respective graduates. With recognition by secularly based faculties of the significant role religious beliefs play in the perspective of women of faith, and with recognition by religious schools and seminaries of the prevalence of intimate partner violence within religious communities, each faculty has something to offer the other. The following recommendations speak to avenues through which collaboration between the secular and the sacral can be enhanced.

### For Religious Schools and Seminaries

- Include information about intimate partner violence within the curricula for ministerial students.
  - Ensure that it is given the importance it deserves (e.g., vest it within a required course taught by a professor with status within the faculty).
  - Invite a faculty member from the local school of social work to present on the subject.
  - Engage students in discussions on the relationship between the secular and the religious in addressing social issues. Have someone from a university faculty take part.
  - Arrange for students to visit social service agencies and programs that offer help to those affected by IPV.
- Connect with university faculties and offer to collaborate with them on the issue of the importance of religious beliefs being recognized by

secular professionals when working with clients for whom spirituality is important.

- Connect with initiatives within the broader community that may be attempting to build collaborative working relationships.

**FOR PROFESSIONAL FACULTIES**
- Include information about religion, its influence, and the importance it hold for adherents into the curricula for students preparing for social service work. Discussions should include:
  - guidance in how religious issues can be addressed from an ethical perspective;
  - the importance for counsellors to explore with clients whether religious beliefs hold significance for them;
  - opportunities for students to become aware of their own spiritual perspectives, biases, and hesitations when venturing into what may be a conflicted or uncomfortable subject;
  - the concept of collaboration between secularly training professionals and religious/ethno-cultural leaders (e.g., is it possible, how can it be achieved?);
  - invitations to faculty members from a local seminary or religious leaders to participate in these discussions.
- Take a leadership role within the community to facilitate discussion between service providers and religious/ethno-cultural leaders (e.g., sponsor events, share relevant research).
- Conduct research: A culturally diverse and multireligious society presents many challenges and questions worthy of further exploration:
  - How do service providers respond sensitively and effectively to clients who bring with them unique religious/cultural requirements and perspectives?
  - How can members of ethno-cultural communities be assisted in accessing available resources when doing so is foreign to their culture and experience?
  - Some communities hold to centuries-old religious beliefs and cultural norms grounded within patriarchal perspectives. How can women in these communities who experience intimate partner violence be assisted and supported?

- How do we respect differing perspectives and advocate for the safety of women?

We have argued that secular–sacral collaboration is not only desirable but possible. Further research and practical experience is required.

## CONCLUDING COMMENTS

Intimate partner violence is ubiquitous within all of society—regardless of economics, education, profession, or religion or ethno-cultural community. It requires a response that includes all segments of society, a response that calls for secular-based service providers and religious/ethno-cultural communities to work collaboratively together. The challenges in achieving this level of collaboration are significant, but they can be met. The beginning point is in the recognition—by both religious and secular leaders—that religion does have a role to play in responding to social issues. It is only as the secular and the sacral develop collaborative working relationships that those who are members of religious/ethno-cultural communities and who experience intimate partner violence—direct victims, child witnesses, abusive partners—receive the help they need and deserve.

# Acknowledgements

This book is not only a collaborative effort by its authors. Others have graciously contributed their reflections and wisdom, thereby adding richness to the themes discussed. Some offered their thoughts on individual chapters; others met for an afternoon of discussion of the work itself. Their names follow.

We would also like to recognize The Calgary Foundation and Brian Felesky for their support of the publication of this book. The Foundation works in collaborative philanthropy to strengthen charities and engage citizens. Brian Felesky, of Felesky Flynn LLP, is well respected for his support of social initiatives and was a special friend of the FaithLink project.

## CHAPTER RESPONDERS

**Christine Berry** has extensive experience as a Registered Psychologist, working with couples, individuals, families and groups. She has worked as a therapist, educator, supervisor, researcher and program director for those affected by intimate partner violence.

The late **Reverend Jake Kroeker** was the senior pastor of First Baptist Church in Calgary, prior to retiring in 2009. He was actively involved with the community, having served on committees and boards of directors for both social service- and religious-based organizations.

**Pol Ngeth** is a survivor of the Khmer Rouge genocide, an immigrant to Canada, a social worker and a very active member of the Khmer Canadian community in Calgary. Pol has worked extensively with immigrants, initiated research, made presentations and produced documents on refugee trauma and domestic violence.

Miriam Mollering is passionate about assisting victims of sexual and domestic violence. As Pastor of Life Care Ministries, she brings her counselling skills to the congregation of Centre Street Church in Calgary. Miriam has been recognized for her work by the American Association of Christian Counselors and the Evangelical Order of Certified Pastoral Counselors of America.

Before she retired, Bev Sheckter was the Executive Director of Jewish Family Services Calgary. A professional social worker, Bev focused her career on serving many disadvantaged populations, including the disabled, the unemployed, and abused women. She also led many boards of voluntary organizations and has been honoured for her dedication to the Jewish community in Calgary.

Cynthia Wild has applied her professional social work training to addressing the issue of intimate partner violence. She currently directs client service programming for victims of violence at the YWCA in Calgary, and has been the animator of the Fire in the Rose program—a grassroots, faith-based violence prevention program.

**PANELLISTS**
Dr. Ron Fraser served as President of the Alberta Bible College for 27 years. He has a long-held interest in abuse issues, particularly those involving power, gender and theological teaching. He served on the Mayor's Task Force on Family Violence in Calgary, and for many years was a trained mediator, serving families and Christian communities.

Prior to assuming management responsibilities at the Alberta Council of Women's Shelters, Carolyn Goard offered clinical counselling to children and families. She has served as an executive and board member for many non-profit organizations, including Calgary Family Services, YWCA Calgary, and RESOLVE Alberta.

Susan Mallon has worked in the Calgary social services sector for over 30 years as a municipal administrator with Homefront Calgary, The Alliance to End Violence, and as CEO of Calgary Family Services. She has served as a board member to various non-profit organizations and sustains an interest in developing innovative ways to bring social justice to all citizens.

**Jackie Sieppert** currently serves as Dean of the Faculty of Social Work at the University of Calgary. His primary research interests and activities focus on evaluation and accountability mechanisms in social policy, administration of human services, and the use of technology in social work practice.

As a mentor with the Education for Ministry program, **Jennifer Solem** works with laypersons interested in understanding Christian beliefs, with an emphasis on connecting faith with practical living. She recognizes the value of initiatives such as the FaithLink project—which consider the whole person, including deeply held spiritual beliefs—for individuals striving for healing.

Before retiring, **Dr. Leslie Tutty** was a full professor with the Faculty of Social Work at the University of Calgary. Her research focused on prevention programs and services for victims of family violence. For a number of years Leslie served as the Academic Research Coordinator of RESOLVE Alberta.

**Rabbi Howard Voss-Altman** has been the spiritual leader of Temple B'nai Tikvah, Calgary's Reform Jewish congregation, since 2002. Besides his rabbinic training, Rabbi Howard has clinical pastoral experience and emergency chaplain experience, having completed his training in Ohio. He is also educated as a lawyer.

# Notes

## 1 | Secular–Religious Conversations about Violence

1. See Spiegel (2013) for a useful discussion of hypnotism's current status.

2. EMDR stands for eye movement desensitization and reprocessing.

3. It is beyond the scope of this chapter to be comprehensive respecting what is, as noted, a very active, developing field (supported by well-endowed organizations such as the American John Templeton Foundation that funds work by high-profile scholars from a range of disciplines on ultimately spiritual questions). Readers who would like to pursue this issue in more depth may find some examples of recent work helpful. Ward (2008) and Clayton (2008) offer a general overview. Respecting physics and religion, see Davies (2007), Polkinghorne (2005, 2007), or Clayton & Davies (2006). Respecting neurology and religion, see Murphy and Brown (2007). Respecting evolution and religion, see Conway Morris (2004), Haught (2006), or Van Huyssteen (2006).

4. Wiinikka-Lydon (2010) offers a disturbing case study demonstrating how rapid and thoroughgoing such distortions can be in the context of civil war, but the same dynamics can affect religious women under more normal circumstances. As examples, beliefs about patriarchy, submission, forgiveness, and the sanctity of marriage are easily and often used to thwart women's efforts to make safer lives for themselves.

5. Chapters 17 and 18 of Taylor (2007) are recommended for more depth and detail respecting these matters than is possible here.

6. Gray makes this case very nicely, though he does not distinguish religion and ideology. Instead, he writes as if any ideological movement is essentially a religion.

7. We note that there are some writers who object to a feminist analysis of IPV, a recent example being Dutton (2006). See Rothery (2009) for a review of Dutton.

8. This move is endorsed by others writing about transcendence: "'Transcendence' is a relative term, referring to the human capacity to overcome some existing state or level of consciousness, including knowledge. In such basic terms, transcendence is everywhere and for everyone" (Archer, Collier, & Porpora, 2004, p. 27).

9. In the Hebrew Bible account, of course, Noah celebrates the dawning of the new age by getting drunk and a serious family rift ensues. Disillusionment is a utopian's frequent lot.

10. This is not always going to be an *easy* way forward, of course. Consider patriarchy as a case in which the *substance* of beliefs and practices is problematic regardless how they are expressed. On the other hand, especially with cultural diversity becoming a prevalent fact of life, most people working in the field will acknowledge that concessions to cultural realities are often required. Given that, we can acknowledge that patriarchal families may

always be ideologically problematic to a degree but that it is still true that they are of greater concern when patriarchal ideals are expressed in a fundamentalist style.

11. Theologian Paul Tillich (2001) has written convincingly about doubt as an essential companion to faith in our modern age.

12. Readers interested in this argument are invited to consult Margaret Archer (2000), who devotes the early chapters of *Being human: The problem of agency* to a thorough, forceful discussion of the dehumanizing potential in postmodernism.

## 2 | Intimate Partner Violence

1. This unpublished definition, developed by the Calgary Domestic Violence Committee, is accepted by domestic violence service agencies working in the Calgary, Alberta, community.

2. This term was coined by Dr. Nancy Nason-Clark.

## 3 | FaithLink

1. Religious beliefs and cultural mores are often intertwined and cannot be easily or arbitrarily separated. Additionally, some communities define themselves ethnically. The term "religious/ethno-cultural" is meant to capture these complex connections.

2. The survey was sponsored by ACAV, the United Way of Calgary and Area, and the Calgary Injury Prevention Coalition.

3. RESOLVE (Research and Evaluation for Solutions to Violence and Abuse) is a regional research network involving the three Canadian Prairie provinces supporting projects that have in common the active participation of community- and university-based researchers and a commitment to provide results that are useful in policy and practice development, as well as useful in academic settings.

4. Funding sources included Alberta Children's Services; the National Crime Prevention Strategy, Community Mobilization Program; the Ecumenical Task Force for the Prevention of Family Violence; Status of Women Canada; the Canadian Women's Foundation; the Roman Catholic Diocese; the Calgary Anglican Diocese; and private donors.

5. This comment was shared at the FaithLink presentation in rural Alberta in the spring of 2007.

6. The term "wounded healer" was coined by Nouwen (1994).

7. Comments made on workshop evaluations.

8. Comments also made at various FaithLink-sponsored conferences and workshops by religious leaders.

9. A response on a March 2007 FaithLink conference evaluation form.

10. Although the meditation practice Dr. Bourgeault presented at these events is based within the Christian faith, she was careful to not present it as an exclusive discipline. Rather, she was careful to note that each of the great religions have similar meditative traditions.

11. This sample is unlikely to be representative of all of Calgary's Christian religious leaders. It was assumed that respondents were those who had an interest in IPV issues and may have been weighted toward those with whom Faithlink had already established a connection.

## 4 | Finding Their Voices

1. The contents of this chapter are taken from a larger research report: Sevcik, I., Rothery, M., & Nason-Clark, N. (2010). *Finding their voices: Women from religious/ethno-cultural communities speak out about family violence.* Available at http://www.ucalgary.ca/resolve/. The authors wish to thank RESOLVE Alberta for making this report available through its website.

## 5 | Incorporating Spirituality into Practice

1. As noted in the Introduction, we prefer to use the term "religion" rather than "spirituality." However, because of the predominant use of the term "spirituality" in the references cited in this chapter, and the almost exclusive use of the term "spirituality" when service providers refer to either their own experience or their work with clients, we have chosen to use the construct of spirituality throughout this chapter.

## 7 | Reflections on the Book, Part I

1. Both the Specialized Domestic Conflict Court and FaithLink were initiatives that emerged during this decade.

## 8 | Reflections on the Book, Part II

1. Genesis 21:9–21: Abraham and Sarah were unable to have children. Sarah suggests that Abraham sleep with Hagar, a servant, in order to have a baby. Abraham and Hagar have Ishmael, but jealousy arises and Abraham, with Sarah's encouragement, asks Hagar to leave and expels her into the desert, with Ishmael.

# References

Allender, D. (2008). Raping Eve: Facing the unrelenting theory of Adam. In C.C. Kroeger, N. Nason-Clark, & B. Fisher-Townsend (Eds.), *Beyond abuse in the Christian home: Raising voices for change* (pp. 24–34). Eugene, OR: Wipf and Stock Publishers.

Altfeld, S. (2005). Family violence in the Jewish community: Existing knowledge and emerging issues. *Journal of Religion & Abuse, 7*(3), 57–62.

Anderson, D.K., & Saunders, D.G. (2003). Leaving an abusive partner: An empirical review of predictors, the process of leaving and psychological well-being. *Trauma, Violence and Abuse, 4*(2), 163–191.

Archer, M.S. (2000). *Being human: The problem of agency.* Cambridge, United Kingdom: Cambridge University Press.

Archer, M.S., Collier, A., & Porpora, D.V. (2004). *Transcendence: Critical realism and God.* New York, NY: Routledge.

Armstrong, K. (1993). *A history of God: The 4,000-year quest of Judaism, Christianity and Islam.* New York, NY: Ballantine.

Armstrong, K. (2006). *The battle for God.* New York, NY: Knopf.

Augustine. (1961). *Confessions* (R.S. Pine-Coffin, Trans.). London, United Kingdom: Penguin.

Barrett, M.J. (1999). Healing from trauma: The quest for spirituality. In F. Walsh (Ed.), *Spiritual resources in family therapy* (pp. 267–285). New York, NY: The Guilford Press.

Baskin, C. (2002). Circles of resistance: Spirituality in social work practice: Education and transformative change. *Currents: New Scholarship in the Human Services, 1*(1). Retrieved from http://fsw.ucalgary.ca/currents_prod_v1/articles/baskin_v1_n1.html

Beaman-Hall, L., & Nason-Clark, N. (1997). Partners or protagonists: Exploring the relationship between the transition house movement and conservative churches. *Affilia: Journal of Women and Social Work, 12*(2), 176–196.

Beaulaurier, R.L., Seff, L.R., Newman, F.L., & Dunlop, B. (2005). Internal barriers to help seeking for middle-aged and older women who experience intimate partner violence. *Journal of Elder Abuse & Neglect, 17*(3), 53–74.

Beaulaurier, R.L., Seff, L.R., Newman, F.L., & Dunlop, B. (2007). External barriers to help seeking for older women who experience intimate partner violence. *Journal of Family Violence, 22,* 747–755.

Becvar, D. (1997). *Soul healing.* New York, NY: Basic Books.

Beres, L. (2004). A reflective journey: Spirituality and postmodern practice. *Currents: New Scholarship in the Human Services, 3*(1). Retrieved from http://fsw.ucalgary.ca/currents_prod_v1/articles/beres_v3_n1.html

Berthold, S.M. (2000). War traumas and community violence: Psychological, behavioral, and academic outcomes among Khmer refugee adolescents. *Journal of Multicultural Social Work (The Hawarth Press), 8*(1/2), 15–46.

Besthorn, F.H. (2002). Expanding spiritual diversity in social work: Perspectives on the greening of spirituality. *Currents: New Scholarship in the Human Services, 1*(1). Retrieved from http://fsw.ucalgary.ca/currents_prod_v1/articles/besthorn_v1_n1.html

Bhuyan, R., Mell, M., Senturia, K., Sulivan, M., & Shiv-Thoraton, S. (2005). "Women must endure according to their karma:" Cambodian immigrant women talk about domestic violence. *Journal of Interpersonal Violence, 20*(8), 902–921.

Biestek, F. (1957). *The casework relationship*. Chicago, IL: Loyola University Press.

Blair, R.G. (2000). Risk factors associated with PTSD and major depression among Cambodian refugees in Utah. *Health & Social Work, 25*(1), 23–30.

Bonadonna, R. (2003). Meditation's impact on chronic illness. *Holistic Nursing Practice, 17*(6), 309–319.

Bourgeault, C. (2003). *The Wisdom way of knowing: Reclaiming an ancient tradition to awaken the heart*. San Franciso, CA: Jossey-Bass.

Bourgeault, C. (2004). *Centering prayer and inner awakening*. Cambridge, MA: Cowley Publications.

Calhoun, C., Light, D., & Keller, S. (1997). *Sociology* (7th ed.). New York, NY: The McGraw-Hill Companies Inc.

Canda, E.R. (2002). A world wide view on spirituality in social work: Reflections from the US experience and suggestions for internationalization. *Currents: New Scholarship in the Human Services, 1*(1). Retrieved from http://fsw.ucalgary.ca/currents_prod_v1/articles/canda_v1_n1.html

Carlson, T.D., Kirkpatrick, D., Hecker, L., & Killmer, M. (2002). Religion, spirituality, and marriage and family therapy: A study of family therapists' beliefs about the appropriateness of addressing religious and spiritual issues in therapy. *The American Journal of Family Therapy, 30*, 157–171.

Catani, C., Schaver, E., & Neuner, F. (2008). Beyond individual war trauma: Domestic violence against children in Afghanistan and Sri Lanka. *Journal of Marital and Family Therapy, 34*(2), 165–176.

Chung, R.C-Y. (2001). Psychosocial adjustment of Cambodian refugee women: Implications for mental health counselling. *Journal of Mental Health Counselling, 23*(2), 115–126.

Clayton, P. (2008). *Adventures in the spirit: God, world, divine action*. Minneapolis, MN: Fortress.

Clayton, P., & Davies, P. (Eds.). (2006). *The re-emergence of emergence: The emergentist hypothesis from science to religion*. New York, NY: Oxford University Press.

Clemans, S.E. (2004). Life changing: The experience of rape-crisis work. *Affliia, 19*(2), 146–159.

Clemens, N.A., Corrida, R.B., & Wasman, M. (1978). The parish clergy as a mental health resource. *Journal of Religion and Health, 17*, 227–232.

Clews, R. (2004). Spirituality in an undergraduate social work curriculum: Reflective assignments at the beginning and the end of a programme. *Currents: New Scholarship in the Human Services, 3*(1). Retrieved from http://fsw.ucalgary.ca/currents_prod_v1/articles/Clews_v3_n1.htm

Clifford, W.K. (1947). *The ethics of belief and other essays*. London, United Kingdom: Watts.

Cohen, E., Dekel, R., & Solomon, Z. (2002). Long-term adjustment and the role of attachment among Holocaust child survivors. *Personality and Individual Differences, 33*, 299–310.

Cohen, E., Dekel, R., Solomon, Z., & Lavie, T. (2003). Posttraumatic stress symptoms and fear of intimacy among treated and non-treated survivors who were children during the Holocaust. *Social Psychiatry Psychiatric Epidemiology, 38*, 611–617.

Coholic, D. (2002). Practice principles for social work and spirituality—A focus on practice models and relationships. *Currents: New Scholarship in the Human Services, 1*(1). Retrieved from http://fsw.ucalgary.ca/currents_prod_v1/articles/coholic_v1_n1.html

Coholic, D. (2003). Student and educator viewpoints on incorporating spirituality in social work pedagogy—An overview and discussion of research findings. *Currents: New Scholarship in the Human Services, 2*(2). Retrieved from http://fsw.ucalgary.ca/currents_prod_v1/articles/coholic_v2_n2.html

Conway Morris, S. (2004). *Life's solution: Inevitable humans in a lonely universe*. Cambridge, United Kingdom: Cambridge University Press.

Cook, W.R. (2007). *The lives of great Christians: Part 1*. Chantilly, VA: The Teaching Company.

Costa, D.M. (2005, November 7). Compassion fatigue: Self-care skills for practitioners. *OT Practice*.

Davies, J., Lyon, E., & Monti-Catania, D. (1998). *Safety planning with battered women: Complex lives/difficult choices*. Thousand Oaks, CA: Sage Publications.

Davies, P. (2007). *Cosmic jackpot: Why our universe is just right for life*. New York, NY: Orion.

Dawkins, R. (2006). *The God delusion*. New York, NY: Houghton Mifflin.

DeVoe, E.R., Borges, G., & Conroy, K. (2001). Domestic violence and the Jewish woman: An exploratory study. *Journal of Religion & Abuse, 3*(1/2), 21–45.

Dutton, D.G. (2006). *Rethinking domestic violence*. Vancouver, BC: UBC Press.

Dyson, F. (2002). Science & religion: No ends in sight. [Book Review of *The God of hope and the end of the world*, by John Polkinghorne]. *The New York Review of Books, 49*(5), 18–21.

Easteal, P. (1994). Violence against women in the home: How far have we come? How far to go? *Family Matters, 37*, 86–93.

Ellenberger, H.F. (1970). *The discovery of the unconscious: The history and evolution of dynamic psychiatry*. New York, NY: Basic Books.

Figley, C.R. (Ed.). (1995). *Compassion fatigue: Coping with secondary traumatic stress disorder in those who treat the traumatized*. New York, NY: Brunner Mazel Publishers.

Figley, C.R. (Ed.). (2002). *Treating compassion fatigue*. New York, NY: Brunner-Rutledge.

Finley, J. (2005). *Christian meditation: Experiencing the presence of God*. New York, NY: HarperCollins Publishers.

Fisher-Townsend, B. (2008). Searching for the missing puzzle piece: The potential of faith in changing violent behavior. In C.C. Kroeger, N. Nason-Clark, & B. Fisher-Townsend (Eds.), *Beyond abuse in the Christian home: Raising voices for change* (pp. 100–120). Eugene, OR: Wipf and Stock Publishers.

Funderburk, J.R., & Fukuyama, M.A. (2001). Feminism, multiculturalism, and spirituality: Convergent and divergent forces in psychotherapy. *Women & Therapy, 24*(3/4), 1–18.

Gall, T.L., Basque, V., Damasceno-Scott, M., & Vardy, G. (2007). Spirituality and the current adjustment of adult survivors of childhood sexual abuse. *Journal for the Scientific Study of Religion, 46*(1), 101–117.

Giesbrecht, N., & Sevcik, I. The process of recovery and rebuilding among abused women in conservative evangelical subcultures. *Journal of Family Violence, 15*(3), 229–248.

Girard, R. (2001). *I see Satan fall like lightning.* (J.G. Williams, Trans.). Maryknoll, NY: Orbis.

Girard, R. (2004). *Oedipus unbound: Selected writings on rivalry and desire.* Stanford, CA: Stanford University Press.

Goldman, M. (1999). The Violence against Women Act: Meeting its goals in protecting battered immigrant women. *Family and Conciliation Courts Review, 37,* 375–392.

Goldner, J., Penn, P., Sheinberg, M., & Walker, G. (1990). Love and violence: Gender paradoxes in volatile attachments. *Family Process, 29,* 343–364.

Grams, W.A., Stone Carlson, T., & McGeorge, C.R. (2007). Integrating spirituality into family therapy training: An exploration of faculty members' beliefs. *Contemporary Family Therapy, 29,* 147–161.

Gray, J. (2007). *Black mass: Apocalyptic religion and the death of utopia.* Toronto, ON: Doubleday Canada.

Grodner, E., & Sweifach, J. (2004). Domestic violence in the Orthodox Jewish home: A value-sensitive approach to recovery. *Affilia, 19*(3), 305–316.

Haley, J. (1977). *Uncommon therapy: The psychiatric techniques of Milton H. Erickson, M.D.* New York, NY: Norton.

Hardacre, H. (1993). The impact of fundamentalisms on women, the family, and interpersonal relations. In M.E. Marty & R.S. Appleby (Eds.), *Fundamentalisms and society: Reclaiming the sciences, the family, and education* (pp. 129–150). Chicago, IL: University of Chicago Press.

Hathaway, J.E., Willis, G., & Zimmer, B. (2006). Listening to survivors' voices. *Violence against women, 8*(6), 687–719.

Haught, J.F. (2006). *Is nature enough? Meaning and truth in the age of science.* Cambridge, United Kingdom: Cambridge University Press.

Hedges, C. (2002). *War is a force that gives us meaning.* New York, NY: Anchor.

Heggen, C.H. (1993). *Sexual abuse in Christian homes and churches.* Scottdale, PA: Herald Press

Helminski, K.E. (1992). *Living presence: A Sufi way to mindfulness & the essential self.* New York, NY: G.P. Putnam's Sons.

Hinton, D.E., Chhean, D., Pich, V., Pollack, M.H., Orr, S.P., & Pitman, R.K. (2006). Assessment of post traumatic stress disorder in Cambodian refugees using the clinician-administered PTSD scale: Psychometric properties and symptom severity. *Journal of Trauma and Stress, 19*(3), 405–409.

Hinton, D.E., Chhean, D., Pich, V., Safren, S.A., Hoffman, S.G., & Pollock, M.H. (2005). A randomized controlled trial of cognitive-behavior therapy for Cambodian refugees with treatment-resistant PTSD and panic attacks: A cross-over design. *Journal of Trauma and Stress, 18*(6), 617–629.

Hitchens, C. (2009). *God is not great: How religion poisons everything.* New York, NY: Grand Central.

Hodge, D. (2005). Spiritual lifemaps: A client-centered pictorial instrument for spiritual assessment, planning, and intervention. *Social Work, 50*(1), 77–87.

Hodge, D. (2008). Constructing spiritually modified interventions: Cognitive therapy with diverse populations. *International Social Work, 51*(2), 178–192.

Hodge, D., & Nadir, A. (2008). Moving toward culturally competent practice with Muslims: Modifying cognitive therapy with Islamic tenets. *Social Work, 53*(3), 31–41.

Hyman, I., Forte, T., DuMont, J., Romans, S., & Cohen, M.M. (2006). The association between length of stay in Canada and intimate partner violence among immigrant women. *American Journal of Public Health, 96*(4), 654–659.

Iliffe, G., & Steed, L.G. (2000). Exploring the counselor's experience of working with perpetrators and survivors of domestic violence. *Journal of International Violence, 15*(4), 393–412.

Ipsos-Reid. (2003). *God and other mysteries: A look into the religious and spiritual beliefs of Canadians.* Retrieved from www.ipsos-na.com/news/results.cfm?geo=1

Javed, N., & Gerrard, N. (2006). Bound, bonded and battered: Immigrant and visible minority women's struggle to cope with violence. In M.R. Hampton & N. Gerard (Eds.), *Intimate partner violence: Reflections on experience, theory, and policy* (pp. 33–45). Toronto, ON: Cormorant Books.

Jenkins, P. (2002). *The next Christendom: The coming of global Christianity.* Oxford, United Kingdom: Oxford University Press.

Jerryson, M.K., & Juergensmeyer, M. (Eds.). (2010). *Buddhist warfare.* New York, NY: Oxford University Press.

Jones, J.W. (2010). Conclusion: A fundamentalist mindset? In C.B. Strozier, D.M. Terman, & J.W. Jones (Eds.), *The fundamentalist mindset* (pp. 216–220). New York, NY: Oxford University Press.

Joseph, N. (2008). *HBI: Untying the knots.* Unpublished document, Hadassah-Brandeis Institute, Brandeis University, Waltham, Massachusetts. Retrieved from http://www.brandeis.edu/hbi/gcrl/images/NormaWP.pdf

Joyce, K. (2009). Biblical battered wife syndrome: Christian women and domestic violence. Retrieved from http://www.alternet.org/module/printversion/124174

Kabat-Zinn, J., Massion, A.O., Kristeller, J., Peterson, L.G., Fletcher, K.E., Pbert, L, Lenderking, W.R., Santorelli, S.F. (1992). Effectiveness of meditation-based stress reduction program in the treatment of anxiety disorders. *American Journal of Psychiatry, 149*(7), 936–943.

Keating, T. (2002). *Intimacy with God: An introduction to centering prayer.* New York, NY: The Crossroad Publishing Company.

Kellerman, N.P.P. (2001). The long-term psychological effects and treatment of Holocaust trauma. *Journal of Loss and Trauma, 6,* 197–218.

Kennedy, P. (2007). On radical orthodoxy [MP3], *Ideas.* Canada: Canadian Broadcasting Corporation.

Kinzie, J.D., Cheng, K., Tsai, J., & Riley, C. (2006). Traumatized refugee children: The case for individualized diagnosis and treatment. *The Journal of Nervous and Mental Disease, 194*(7), 534–537.

Kirkwood, C. (1993). *Leaving abusive relationships: From the scars of survival to the wisdom of change.* London, United Kingdom: Sage Publications.

Kivel, P. (2002). Jewish men and Jewish male violence. *Journal of Religion & Abuse, 4*(3), 5–13.

Kiyoshk, R. (2003). Integrating spirituality and domestic violence treatment: Treatment of Aboriginal men. *Journal of Aggression, Maltreatment & Trauma, 7*(1 & 2), 237–256.

Kroeger, C.C., & Nason-Clark, N. (2001). *No place for abuse: Biblical & practical resources to counteract domestic violence*. Downer's Grove, IL: InterVarsity Press.

Kroeger, C.C., & Nason-Clark, N. (2010). *No place for abuse: Biblical & practical resources to counteract domestic violence* (2nd. ed). Downer's Grove, IL: InterVarsity Press.

Kroeger, C.C, Nason-Clark, N., & Fisher-Townsend, B. (Eds.). (2008). *Beyond abuse in the Christian home: Raising voices for change*. Eugene, OR: Wipf and Stock Publishers.

Küng, H. (1990). *Freud and the problem of God* (C. Murphy, Trans., Enlarged ed.). New Haven, CT: Yale University Press.

Lewin, K. (1951). *Field theory in social science*. New York, NY: Harper & Brothers.

Lifton, R.J. (1989). *Thought reform and the psychology of totalism: A study of "brainwashing" in China* (2nd ed.). Chapel Hill, NC: University of North Carolina Press.

Lifton, R.J. (1993). *The protean self: Human resilience in an age of fragmentation*. New York, NY: Basic Books.

Lifton, R.J. (2003). *Superpower syndrome: America's apocalyptic confrontation with the world*. New York, NY: Nation.

Livingston, D.J. (2002). *Healing violent men: A model for Christian communities*. Minneapolis, MN: Fortress Press.

MacLeod, I., & Pauson, M. (Eds.) (1989). *Webster's new dictionary and thesaurus*. New York: Windsor Court.

Majonis, J. (2004). T. Chalmers, C.S. Loch and M.E. Richmond's development of increasingly secular, interpersonal, and purposeful helping methods. *Currents: New Scholarship in the Human Services, 3*(1). Retrieved from http://www.ucalgary.ca/ currents/files/currents/v3n1_majonis.pdf

Majumdar, M., Grossman, P., Dietz-Waschkowski, B., Kersig, S., & Walach, H. (2002). Does mindfulness meditation contribute to health? Outcome evaluation of a German sample. *Journal of Alternative Complementary Medicine, 8*(6), 719–730.

Marshall, G.N., Berthold, S.M., Schnell, T.L., Elliot, M.N., Chun, C-A., & Hambarsoomians, K. (2006). Rates and correlates of seeking health services among Cambodian refugees. *American Journal of Public Health, 96*(10), 1829–1835.

Marty, M.E. (2005). *When faiths collide*. Malden, MA: Blackwell.

Marty, M.E., & Appleby, R.S. (1991a). The fundamentalism project: A user's guide. In M.E. Marty & R.S. Appleby (Eds.), *Fundamentalisms observed* (pp. vii–xiii). Chicago, IL: University of Chicago Press.

Marty, M.E., & Appleby, R.S. (Eds.). (1991b). *Fundamentalisms observed*. Chicago, IL: University of Chicago Press.

Marty, M.E., & Appleby, R.S. (Eds.). (1993). *Fundamentalisms and society: Reclaiming the sciences, the family, and education*. Chicago, IL: University of Chicago Press.

Mason, O., & Hargreaves, I. (2001). A qualitative study of mindfulness-based cognitive therapy for depression. *British Journal of Medical Psychology, 74*(2), 197–212.

McGrath, A.E. (2004). *The twilight of atheism: The rise and fall of disbelief in the modern world*. New York, NY: Doubleday.

McKernan, M.S. (2004). *Radical relatedness: Exploring the spiritual dimensions of family service work*. Edmonton, AB: The Muttart Foundation.

McLaughlin, A.M., Rothery, M., Babins-Wagner, R.R., & Schleifer, B. (2010). Decision-making and evidence in direct practice. *Clinical Social Work Journal, 38*, 155–163.

Medscape Psychiatry & Mental Health. (2005). Compassion fatigue: An expert interview with Charles R. Figley, MS, PHD. Retrieved from http://medscape.com/viewarticle/513615

Menjivar, C., & Salcido, O. (2002). Immigrant women and domestic violence: Common experiences in different countries. *Gender & Society, 16*(6), 898–920.

Miles, A. (2000). *Domestic violence: What every pastor needs to know*. Minneapolis, MN: Augsburg Press.

Miles, A. (2008). Calling the pastor. In C.C. Kroeger, N. Nason-Clark, & B. Fisher Townsend (Eds.), *Beyond abuse in the Christian home: Raising voices for change* (pp. 35–46). Eugene, OR: Wipf and Stock Publishers.

Miller, M.A. (1994). *Family violence: The compassionate church responds*. Waterloo, ON: Herald Press.

Moon, R. (2008). Bruker v. Marcovitz: Divorce and the marriage of law and religion. *Supreme Court Law Review, 42*(2d), 36–62.

Muesse, M.W. (2007). *Religions of the axial age: An approach to the world's religions*. Chantilly, VA: The Teaching Company.

Murphy, N., & Brown, W.S. (2007). *Did my neurons make me do it? Philosophical and neurobiological perspectives on moral responsibility and free will*. New York, NY: Oxford University Press.

Nash, M., & Stewart, S. (2005). Spirituality and hope in social work for social justice. *Currents: New Scholarship in the Human Services, 4*(1). Retrieved from http://fsw.ucalgary.ca/currents_prod_v1/articles/nash_v4_n1.html

Nason-Clark, N. (1997). *The battered wife: How Christians confront family violence*. Louisville, KY: Westminster John Knox Press.

Nason-Clark, N. (2002). From the heart of my laptop: Personal passion and research on violence against women. In J. Spickard, M. McGuire, & S. Landres (Eds.), *Personal knowledge and beyond: Reshaping the ethnography of religion* (pp. 27–32). New York, NY: New York University Press.

Nason-Clark, N. (2004). When terror strikes at home: The interface between religion and domestic violence. *Journal for the Scientific Study of Religion, 43*(3), 303–310.

Nason-Clark, N. (2006, October). When terror strikes at home: The role of religious professionals. Faith-based forum on family violence for justice professionals and clergy, West Palm Beach, FL.

Nason-Clark, N. (2008). When terror strikes the Christian home. In C.C. Kroeger, N. Nason-Clark, & B. Fisher-Townsend (Eds.), *Beyond abuse in the Christian home: Raising voices for change* (171–183). Eugene, OR: Wipf and Stock Publishers.

Nason-Clark, N. (2009). Christianity and the experience of domestic violence: What does faith have to do with it? *Social Work & Christianity, 36*(4), 379–393.

Nason-Clark, N., Kroeger, C.C., & Fisher-Townsend, B. (2011). *Responding to abuse in Christian homes: A challenge to churches and their leaders*. Eugene, OR: Wipf and Stock Publishers.

Nason-Clark, N., McMullin, S., Fahlberg, V., & Schaefer, D. (2010). Referrals between clergy and community-based resources: Challenges and opportunities, *Journal of Family and Community Ministries, 23*(4), 50–60. Retrieved from http://www.baylor.edu/fcm_journal/index.php?id=59472

Newberg, A., & Waldman, M.R. (2009). *How God changes your brain*. New York, NY: Ballantine Books.

Nouwen, H.J.M. (1994). *The wounded healer: Ministry in contemporary society*. London, United Kingdom: Darton, Longman & Todd.

Nussbaum, M. (2001). *Upheavals of thought: The intelligence of emotions*. Cambridge, United Kingdom: Cambridge University Press.

O'Hanlon, B. (2006). *Pathways to spirituality: Connection, wholeness and possibility for therapist and client*. New York, NY: W.W. Norton & Company.

Paden, R. (2000). Popper's anti-utopianism and the concept of an open society. *The Journal of Value Inquiry, 34*(4), 409–426.

Pesner, J. (2006). Not the Garden of Eden: Some truths about domestic violence in the Jewish community. *Journal of Religion & Abuse, 8*(1), 89–94.

Pietrzak, J., Ramler, M., Renner, T., Ford, L., & Gilbert, N. (1990). *Practical program evaluation: Examples from child abuse prevention*. Newbury Park, CA: Sage Publications.

Plato. (1993). *The republic* (D. Lindsay, Trans.). New York, NY: Everyman's Library.

Polkinghorne, J. (2005). *Faith of a physicist*. Minneapolis, MN: Augsburg Fortress.

Polkinghorne, J. (2007). *Quantum physics and theology: An unexpected kinship*. London, United Kingdom: Yale Universiy Press.

Popper, K.R. (1971a). *The open society and its enemies: The high tide of prophecy* (5th ed., vol. 2). Princeton, NJ: Princeton University Press.

Popper, K.R. (1971b). *The open society and its enemies: The spell of Plato* (5th ed., vol. 1). Princeton, NJ: Princeton University Press.

Popper, K.R. (1986). Utopia and violence. *World Affairs, 149*(1), 3–10.

Porpora, D.V. (2004). The human project. In M.S. Archer, A. Collier, & D.V. Porpora (Eds.), *Transcendence: critical realism and God* (pp. 155–167). New York, NY: Routledge.

Raj, A., & Silverman, J.G. (2007). Domestic violence help-seeking behaviors of South Asian battered women residing in the United States. *International Review of Victimology, 14*, 143–170.

Reibel, D.K., Greeson, J.M., Brainard, G.C., & Rosenzweig, S. (2001). Mindfulness-based stress reduction and health-related quality of life in a heterogeneous patient population. *General Hospital Psychiatry, 23*(4), 183–192.

Richardson, J.I. (2001). *Guidebook on vicarious trauma: Recommended solutions for anti-violence workers*. Centre for Research on Violence Against Women and Children in London, Ontario, for the Family Violence Prevention Unit, Health Canada. Ottawa, ON: National Clearing House on Family Violence.

Robinson, W.F. (1998). The quest for the heart of the work: An ontological approach to spirituality and psychotherapy/counselling. *Psychodynamic Counselling, 4*(3), 335–348.

Rosenzweig, S., Reibel, D.K., Greeson, J.M., Brainard, G.C., & Hojat, M. (2003). Mindfulness-based stress reduction lowers psychological distress in medical students. *Teaching and Learning in Medicine, 15*(2), 88–92.

Rothery, M. (2009). Review of *Rethinking domestic violence* by D. Dutton. *Canadian Review of Social Policy, 59*, 130.

Rothery, M., Nason-Clark, N., Sevcik, I., Barlow, A., Pynn, R., Silverstone, A., & Walroth, K. (2005). *FaithLink evaluation interim report*. Calgary, AB: RESOLVE Alberta and FaithLink. Unpublished.

Rothery, M., Tutty, L., & Weaver, G. (1999). Tough choices: Women, abusive partners, and the ecology of decision-making. *Canadian Journal of Community Mental Health, 18*(1), 5–18.

Saakvitne, K.W., & Pearlman, L.A. (1996). *Transforming the pain: A workbook on vicarious traumatization*. New York, NY: W.W. Norton & Company.

Sack, W., Clark, G.N., & Seeley, J. (1996). Multiple forms of stress in Cambodian adolescent refugees. *Child Development, 67*: 107–116.

Schmotkin, D., & Blumstein, T. (2003). Tracing long-term effects of early trauma: A broad-scope view of Holocaust survivors in late life. *Journal of Consulting and Clinical Psychology, 71*(2), 223–234.

Sevcik, I., & Reed, M. (2008). It's everybody's business. In C.C Kroeger, N. Nason-Clark, & B. Fisher-Townsend (Eds.), *Beyond abuse in the Christian home: Raising voices for change* (pp. 146–166). Eugene, OR: Wipf and Stock Publishers.

Sevcik, I., Reed, M., Pynn, R., & Silverstone, A. (2006). *Building bridges of collaboration: How religious/spiritual communities and service providers came together to address issues of family and sexual abuse*. Calgary, AB: FaithLink. Unpublished.

Sevcik, I., & Rothery, M. (2007). *Actions and achievements: Program evaluation 2006*. Prepared for FaithLink Executive Committee and Alliance to End Violence Board of Directors. Calgary, AB. Unpublished.

Shapiro, F. (2001). *Eye movement desensitization and reprocessing: Basic principles, protocols and procedures* (2nd ed.). New York, NY: Guilford.

Shapiro, F. (2002). *EMDR as an integrative psychotherapy approach: Experts of diverse orientations explore the paradigm prism*. Washington, DC: American Psychological Association.

Shapiro, F. (2003). EMDR and information processing in psychotherapy treatment: Personal development and global implications. In M.F. Solomon & D.J. Siegel (Eds.), *Healing trauma: Attachment, mind, body, and brain* (pp. 196–220). New York, NY: W.W. Norton.

Simpson, J. (Ed.). (2009). *Oxford English dictionary* (2nd on CD-ROM (v. 4.0) ed.). Oxford: United Kingdom: Oxford University Press.

Smith, E. (2004). *Nowhere to turn: Responding to partner violence against immigrant and visible minority women: Voices from frontline workers*. Ottawa, ON: Canadian Council on Social Development.

Spiegel, D. (2013). Tranceformations: Hypnosis in brain and body. *Depression and Anxiety, 30*, 342–352.

Statistics Canada. (1993, November 18). The violence against women survey. *The Daily*.

Statistics Canada. (2008). *Family violence in Canada: A statistical profile 2008*. Ottawa, ON: Canadian Center for Justice Statistics.

Strozier, C.B., Terman, D.M., Jones, J.W., & Boyd, K.A. (Eds.). (2010). *The fundamentalist mindset*. New York, NY: Oxford University Press.

Suchocki, M.H. (1999). *The fall to violence: Original sin in relational theology*. New York, NY: Continuum.

Taylor, C. (1989). *Sources of the self: The making of the modern identity*. Cambridge, MA: Harvard University Press.

Taylor, C. (2002). *Varieties of religion today*. Cambridge, MA: Harvard University Press.

Taylor, C. (2007). *A secular age*. Cambridge, MA: Belknap.

Thorson, M. (2008). Forgiveness and the Christian community. In C.C. Kroeger, N. Nason-Clark, & B. Fisher-Townsend (Eds.), *Beyond abuse in the Christian home: Raising voices for change* (71–77). Eugene, OR: Wipf and Stock Publishers.

Tillich, P. (2001). *Dynamics of faith* (2nd ed.). New York, NY: Perennial Classics.

Todd, S. (2004). Feminist community organization: The spectre of the sacred and the secular. *Currents: New Scholarship in the Human Services, 3*(1). Retrieved from http://fsw.ucalgary.ca/currents_prod_v1/articles/todd_v3_n1.html

Tolle, E. (2004). *The power of now: A guide to spiritual enlightenment.* Vancouver, BC: Namaste Publishing.

Tutty, L. (2006). There but for fortune: How women experience abuse by intimate partners. In M.R. Hampton & N. Gerrard (Eds.), *Intimate partner violence: Reflections on experiences, theory, and policy* (pp. 9–30). Toronto, ON: Cormorant Books.

Tutty, L.M., Rothery, M.A., & Grinnel, Jr., R.M. (1996). *Qualitative research for social workers.* Needham Heights, MA: Allyn and Bacon.

UCLA (University of California, Los Angeles) Semel Institute. (2011). Mindfulness research at UCLA Psychoneuroimmunology Center (PNI). Retrieved from http://marc.ucla.edu/body.cfm?id=18

UNFPA (United Nations Population Fund). (2005). *The promise of equality: Gender equity, reproductive health and the millenium development goals.* New York: Author.

Unger, K. (2005). Web extra: Mindfulness for the masses. Retrieved from http://www.npr.org/templates/story/story.php?storyId=4770779

Van Huyssteen, J.W. (2006). *Alone in the world? Human uniqueness in science and theology.* Grand Rapids, MI: William B. Eerdmans.

Ward, K. (2008). *The big questions in science and religion.* Conshohocken, PA: Templeton Foundation.

Ware, K.N., Levitt, H., & Bayer, G. (2003). May God help you: Faith leaders' perspectives of intimate partner violence within their communities. *Journal of Religion & Abuse, 5*(2), 55–81.

Way, I., VanDeusen, K.M., Martin, G., Applegate, B., & Jandle, D. (2004). Vicarious trauma: A comparison of clinicians who treat survivors of sexual abuse and sexual offenders. *Journal of International Violence, 19*(1), 49–71.

Wiinikka-Lydon, J. (2010). The ambivalence of Medjugorje: The dynamics of violence, peace, and nationalism at a Catholic pilgrimage site during the Bosnian war (1992–1995). *Journal of Religion and Society, 12*, 1–18. Retrieved from http://moses.creighton.edu/JRS/2010/2010-3.html

Williams, M.B., & Poijula, S. (2002). *The PTSD workbook.* Oakland, CA: New Harbinger Publications Inc.

Yick, A.G., & Berthold, S.M. (2005). Conducting research on violence in Asian American communities: Methodological issues. *Violence and Victims, 20*(6), 661–677.

Yoshihama, M. (2001). Immigrants-in-context framework: Understanding the interactive influence of socio-cultural contexts. *Evaluation and Program Planning, 24*(3), 307–318.

# Index

Aboriginal spirituality, 127
ACT (acceptance and commitment therapy), 13
apocalypticism, 13–15

Beaman, Lori, 61
being present, 151, 156, 157, 158
Biestek, Felix, 139–40
Bourgeault, Cynthia, 72–73, 149, 169, 170, 172

calming effect, 155, 156, 157, 158–59, 160, 164
Centering Prayer, 152, 168, 170–71
children, 47–48, 66, 78, 91, 97, 98, 128, 196
Christian community
    barriers to disclosing IPV, 33, 88, 95–96
    ideas for improving IPV resources, 97, 98, 99
    prevalence of IPV within, 29
    reaction to FaithLink, 81–82
    redemption/accountability conflict within, 89–90
    reliance on religious community for help with IPV, 50–51, 93–94
    research into its familiarity with IPV, 74–75
    response of church to IPV, 37–41
    views on what religious leaders need to do about IPV, 111–12
compassion, 17–20, 21, 191
connectedness, 165
contemplative meditation, 151–52.
    See also meditation
cultural competency programming, 195

danger, feelings of, 153–54
desensitization, 153
divorce, 89, 92, 95, 100–01
domestic abuse. See intimate partner violence (IPV)
doubt, 17
dualism, 192, 197

education, 204–06, 207–09, 212, 225–26
Erickson, Milton, 5

FaithLink
    best practices of, 63–64
    community reaction to, 75–76
    efforts in secular/religious collaboration, 60–63, 68, 69, 70–71, 189–90
    evaluation of, 76–77
    formation and early growth of, 60–63
    helping religious communities with IPV, 60–67
    lessons learned from, 216–18
    mission of, 6, 27, 183
    professionals' view of, 78–80
    religious community reaction to, 80–82
    research by, 73–75
    resources produced by, 66–67, 75, 76
    study on addressing spirituality in IPV cases, 116–36
    study on meditation, 147–72
    study on religious women's views of IPV, 85–110
    and value of Overcoming Conflicting Loyalties, 201–03
    and vicarious trauma, 72–73

view on changing religious doctrine,
184–85
fear, 32, 50, 96
forgiveness, 38–41, 89–90, 187–88
Franklin, Benjamin, 4
fundamentalism, 15–17

Gassner, Johann, 4
gender, 10–11
genocide, 47–49, 96
groundedness, 164

Holocaust, 47, 48
*Hope and Healing: Domestic Violence Resources for the Church* (2004–2007), 66
hypnotism, 4–5

intimate partner violence (IPV)
barriers to disclosing, 32–35, 43, 94–96
defined, 28, 53–54, 96–97, 105, 111–12
denial of, 30, 31, 44–45, 50, 54, 87,
92–93, 97, 103
dynamics that complicate, 36–37
effects of, 32, 35, 67–68
and FaithLink research into Christian
church familiarity of, 74–75
importance of *Overcoming Conflicting Loyalties* to, 203–05
prevalency of, 28–31
religious communities' response to,
37–47
religious communties' ideas for
improving resources for, 96–101
study on addressing spirituality in cases
of, 116–36
study on religious women's views of,
85–110.
*See also* FaithLink; religious beliefs and
practices; religious communities/
leaders; religious women as IPV
victims; resources for help with IPV;
secular/religious collaboration; social
service agencies

Jewish community
barriers to disclosing IPV, 33–34, 95–96
and FaithLink, 66, 80–81
and Holocaust, 47, 48, 93
ideas for improving IPV resources,
97–98, 99
Judaic response to IPV, 41–45
prevalence of IPV within, 29–31
reflections on IPV, 87, 88, 91–93
reliance on religious community for
help with IPV, 50–51

Khmer Canadian community
access to IPV resources, 94
barriers to disclosing IPV, 34, 50, 94, 96
Buddhist response to IPV, 46–47
cultural background of, 45–49, 96
FaithLink's work with, 66–67
ideas for improving IPV resources, 98,
100, 111
Pol Ngeth's view of his community's
dealing with IPV, 106–08
prevalence of IPV within, 31
reflections on IPV, 87, 88, 90–91

language fluency, 96

meditation
as help for vicarious trauma, 72–73
lessons learned from, 221–22
panel discussion on, 193–95
professional perspectives on, 13, 172–77
study on its effect on IPV counsellors,
147–72
summary of panel's findings on, 197–98
men as victims of IPV, 100, 216
Mesmer, Franz, 4
mindfulness–based stress reduction
(MBSR), 147

Nason–Clark, Nancy, 60, 61
nihilism, 20

*Overcoming Conflicting Loyalties* (Rothery,
    Nason-Clark and Pynn), 201–03

patriarchy, 10–11, 184–85, 188, 208, 219
Pol Ngeth, 106–08
Popper, Karl, 14, 15
positive self-image, 163–64
post-traumatic stress disorder (PTSD), 32,
    48–49
Pynn, Robert, 60, 62, 72, 149

religious beliefs and practices
    as counterweight to secular values,
        20–21
    defined, 118
    effected by IPV, 67–68, 103
    and FaithLink's attitude towards
        changing, 184–85
    importance to IPV victims, 51–52, 131–32
    including within social work programs,
        204–06, 212, 225–26
    and meditation, 159, 166, 169–72
    negative attitude towards, 203–09
    professional perspectives on incorpor-
        ating in IPV cases, 115, 136–41
    pros and cons of implementing in IPV
        cases, 132–35
    redemption/accountability conflict,
        89–90
    of service providers, 205
    study on addressing in IPV cases,
        116–36.
    *See also* religious women as IPV victims;
        science v. religion; secular/religious
        collaboration
religious communities/leaders
    access to IPV resources, 93–96, 104–05
    as choice of help by religious victims,
        50–51, 101–02
    conflict with secular help, 3–5
    and FaithLink, 60–67
    ideas on how to improve IPV resources,
        96–101, 105–06

lessons learned from involvement in
    IPV cases, 217–18
questions regarding effectiveness in
    IPV response, 59–60
recommendations for, 222–23, 224–25
response protocol for, 67
response to IPV, 37–47
service providers' view of in IPV cases,
    59–60, 126–29
suggestions of how they can help
    prevent IPV, 54–56, 129.
*See also* Christian community; Jewish
    community; Khmer Canadian
    community
religious women as IPV victims
    barriers to disclosing, 33–35, 94–96
    beliefs as challenge for, 35, 88–89, 92,
        95, 104
    caught between secular and religious
        help, 3–4, 70
    choice of religious community for help,
        50–51, 206
    as helpers, 51
    lessons learned from, 218–19
    study of their views on IPV, 85–110.
    See also religious beliefs and practices;
        religious communities/leaders
repentence, 38–41
RESOLVE Alberta, 76, 232n3
resources for help with IPV
    and cultural factors in, 49
    increasing accessibility to, 195–96
    and increasing collaboration between
        secular and religious help, 129–30
    produced by FaithLink, 66–67, 75, 76
    religious communities access to, 93–96,
        104–05
    religious communities' ideas on how to
        improve, 96–101, 105–06

safety, 153–54
science v. religion
    call for transdisciplinary dialogue
        between, 6–7

and compassion, 17–20
history of conflict between, 4–5
and responsibility for world violence,
    7–10
on utopianism, 13–15
view of fundamentalism, 16–17
view of transcendence, 11–13
and views on patriarchy, 10–11
secular/religious collaboration
    calls for, 21–24, 53–54, 101
    and FaithLink, 60–63, 68, 69, 70–71,
        189–90
    ideas for how to increase, 129–31
    importance of, 210–11
    lessons learned from, 216–18, 220
    and meditation, 222
    panel discussion on, 185–91
    professional perspectives on, 136–41
    reasons for mistrust over, 69–70
    recommendations for building, 222–26
    service provider view of, 127–28, 135
    summary of panel's findings on, 197
self-awareness, 164–65
self-care, 151, 154–55, 157–58, 163
service providers. See social service agencies
slowing down, 164, 165
social service agencies
    conflict with religious help, 3–5
    connecting with immigrant cultures,
        195–96
    economics of, 210
    help with vicarious trauma, 72–73
    IPV victims reluctance to approach,
        49–51, 94–96, 100
    lessons learned from, 219–20

recommendations for, 223–24
and religious beliefs of service providers,
    205
skepticism of religion, 115
study on addressing spiritual needs of
    clients, 116–36
study on effect of meditation on IPV
    counsellors, 147–72
work with FaithLink, 68
spiritual awareness, 152
St. Augustine, 7, 12
stress, 151, 155–58
surrender/surrendering, 120, 152, 159,
    160–61, 162–63, 169, 176

telephone line, 99
transcendance, 11–13, 193–95, 197–98
translation, 66–67

utopianism, 13–15

vicarious trauma, 72–73, 150–51, 152–55,
    167–68
violence
    differences in understanding of, 188
    ideologies and, 12–21
    roots of, 191–92
    science/religion debate on responsibility
        for, 7–10.
    See also intimate partner violence (IPV)
vulnerability, 22, 154, 166

Walroth, Karen, 60
wisdom, 23–24